Vices and Virtues

PART I

EARLY ENGLISH TEXT SOCIETY

Original Series, No. 89

1888 (reprinted 1967)

PRICE 30s.

Vices and Virtues

BEING

A Soul's Confession of its Sins

with

Reason's Description of the Virtues

A MIDDLE-ENGLISH DIALOGUE
OF ABOUT 1200 A.D.

EDITED BY

F. HOLTHAUSEN

PART I
TEXT AND TRANSLATION

Published for
THE EARLY ENGLISH TEXT SOCIETY
by the
OXFORD UNIVERSITY PRESS
LONDON   NEW YORK   TORONTO

UNIVERSITY PRESS

Great Clarendon Street, Oxford OX2 6DP
United Kingdom

Oxford University Press is a department of the University of Oxford.
It furthers the University's objective of excellence in research, scholarship,
and education by publishing worldwide. Oxford is a registered trade mark of
Oxford University Press in the UK and in certain other countries

© The Early English Text Society 1888

The moral rights of the authors have been asserted

Database right Oxford University Press (maker)

First Edition published in 1888
Reprinted 1967

All rights reserved. No part of this publication may be reproduced,
stored in a retrieval system, or transmitted, in any form or by any means,
without the prior permission in writing of Oxford University Press,
or as expressly permitted by law, or under terms agreed with the appropriate
reprographics rights organization. Enquiries concerning reproduction
outside the scope of the above should be sent to the Rights Department,
Oxford University Press, at the address above

You must not circulate this book in any other form
and you must impose this same condition on any acquirer

Published in the United States of America by Oxford University Press
198 Madison Avenue, New York, NY 10016, United States of America

British Library Cataloguing in Publication Data
Data available

Library of Congress Cataloging in Publication Data
Data available

Original Series, 89

ISBN 978-0-19-722260-7

VICES AND VIRTUES.

A SOUL'S CONFESSION OF ITS SINS,

WITH

REASON'S DESCRIPTION OF THE VIRTUES,

A MIDDLE ENGLISH DIALOGUE OF ABOUT 1200 A.D., FROM THE
STOWE MS. 240 IN THE BRITISH MUSEUM.

[*Translation.*]

... any man may do. They all are refused by God's own mouth, which says thus: *Vade prius reconciliari fratri tuo*, 'Go first and be reconciled with thy brother. No offer is so dear to Me as the love of God and of all men.'

Of sorrow.

Again, there is another secret sin that has deceived me and many other souls. It is called *tristitia*, that is, sorrow. This is one of the cardinal sins, although it be secret. It is called sorrow—*tristitia mortem operante*, 'sorrow working death'—because all good which is begun to be done for God's love displeases it. This cursed spirit makes the religious man, who has renounced all worldly things for God's love, sorrowful and dreary and heavy in God's works, and often causes [him] to regret that he ever has done so. So he does the men who have promised to forsake sins, and so he does also the men who have promised God to do good, or to seek saints, or to fast, or to do some other good thing. In every wise he tries how he may hinder good works, or cause them to be done with displeasure, and with sorrow, and unblithely.

Of sloth, listlessness.

Again, this deceptive sin has a sister, who is called *accidia*, that is, sloth, who has deceived me many times through my negligence. It has made me heavy and slow in God's works through idleness; it has often caused me to consume other people's sore toil quite unearned. Often it has made me sleep where I ought to have been awake in God's service by day and by night. Such [as I], no other might be. This cursed sin is one of the cardinal sins,

[*The beginning of the MS. is lost.*]

æni mann mai don. Alle hie bieð forsakene on godes awene muðe, ðe ðus seið: Vade prius reconciliari *fra*tri tuo[2], 'Ga arst *and* seihtle wið ðine broðer. Nis me nan ofrende swa lief swa godes luue *and* alre mannes.'

Of sorinesse.

GIET is an oðer derne senne ðe me *and* mani3e oðre saule hafð beswiken. Hie hatte tristicia, þat is, sarinesse. Þes is an of ðe heued-sennes, ðeih hie dierne bie. Hie is icleped sarinesse, tristicia mortem[3] operante, 'sarinesse deað wurchende,' for ðan hire ofþingþ of alle gode ðe a3unnen bieð for godes luue te donne. Ðes awer3ede gast, hie makeð ðane religiuse man, ðe alle world-þing for godes luue hafð forlaten, sari *and* drieri *and* heui on godes workes, *and* ofte doð ofþenchen þat he æure swo haueð[4] idon. Al swo he deð þo men ðe sennen habbeð forhaten te laten, *and* swa h(i)e[5] doð iec ðo menn ðe habbeð gode behaten god te donne, oðer hal3e to sechen, oðer to fasten, oðer sum oðer god te donne. On alle wise he fandeð hu he mu3e gode weorkes letten, oððe mid ofðanche *and* mid sarinesse and unbleðeliche[6] hes don [don].

Of a-solknesse. Vnlust.

ÐIES swikele senne haueð 3iet ane suster, ðe is icleped accidia, ðat[7] is, asolkenesse, ðe me haueð ðurh mire 3emeleaste mani3e siðes beswiken. Hie me haueð imaked heuy *and* slaw on godes weorkes ðurh idelnesse; hie me haueð ofte idon eten oðermannes sare swink all un-of-earned. Ofte hie me haueð idon slæpen ðar ic scolde wakien on godes seruise be dai3e *and* be nihte. Swilch hit non oðer bien ne mihte. Ðies awer3ede senne is on of ðe heued-sennes, *and* hie beswikð mucheles ðe mare ðe me of hire

---

[1] *page* 1.   [2] *Evangelista. red at side.*
[3] Sanctus Paulus. *red at side.*   [4] haued *MS.*
[5] *The* ( ) *mean that the letter they enclose is a correction over the line or in the margin.*   [6] *and* unbleðeliche *on erasure by another hand.*
[7] ðat *corrected from* ðad, *the d being crossed red and a red* t *added.*

and it deceives much the more as one takes little heed of it. That is the end of this sin, that it would that one should take no heed of oneself, but that he should lead his life in sloth and in idleness even up to his last day, and that he should therefore be condemned to the pain of hell. This is sooth, take heed who will!

Of pride.

After this comes another, which is called *superbia*, that is, pride. It was the beginning of all sins, and it brought the brightest angel from the height of Heaven down into the depth of hell. Concerning it is written: *Deus superbis resistit,* 'God withstands all proud men.' Because all those who will exalt themselves are adversaries of God. God Himself says that they shall be lowered. Therefore I am low and powerless, because I have been proud and haughty, and have thought much of myself. Neither ever hated I this cursed cardinal sin, nor shunned [it] as I should, but I often did on account of it what God would not. Woe to me for that! This same pride, though it has lot and part among all other sins, nevertheless has one, that is very near to it and very compliant, which has very often deceived me, that is, *vana gloria*, vain glory or vain boasting. This makes the man who is deceived by it, double his sin; just as the man who has slain a man against God's prohibition, boasts then that he is well avenged on his enemy; or if he has deceived a maiden, or a rich lady who is wedded, thereby he thinks all the better of himself, and so becomes deceived. Because he never wept over this, but still adds more thereto, that is, if he for his sins goes out of the country to seek saints, or if he fasts much, or gives alms, then he often boasts, or does them in such wise, that he has praise thereof and so loses [the merits of] them. Thereof says the Gospel: *Receperunt mercedem suam,* 'They have received their reward.' These are all who do any good, and like-praise thereof. Think hereof ye that do your good [deeds] before men! Some others leave the world and take the clothes of a religious order, and soon esteem themselves holy, and think unworthily of others. They nevertheless

litel ȝeme nimþ. Þat is þe ænde of ðessere senne, ðat hie wolde
ðat man none ȝieme ne name of him seluen, ac ðat he on slauþhe
and on ydelnesse his lif ladde anon to his ande-daiȝe, and ðat he
herfore wurðe fordemd into helle pine. Ðis is soð, neme ȝeme se
ðe wile!

¹ Of modinesse. pride.

HIERAFTER cumþ an oðer, ðe is i-cleped superbia, þat is,
mcdinesse. Hie was anȝinn of alle sennes, and hie brohte
ðane brihteste angel fram ðare heuene heinesse niþer into helle
depnesse. Of hire is ȝewriten: Deus superbis resistit, 'Godd
wiðstant alle modi mannen.' Forðan hie bieð godes wiðerwinen,
alle ðo ðe willen hem seluen heiȝin. Godd seið him self ðat hie
sculen bien ineðerede. Hierfore ic am neðer and unmihti, forðan
ic habbe (ȝeben) prud and modi, and michel ilaten of me seluen.
Ne ðese wereȝede heaued-senne ic næure ne hatede ne ne scunede
swa swa ic scolde, ac ofte ich dede ðurh hire ðat ðe godd nolde.
Wa me ðas! Dies.ilche modinesse, ðeih hie habbe hlot ² and dale
mang alle oðre sennes, naðelæs hie haueð ane, ðe is hire swiðe
neih and swiðe hersum, ðe me haueð swiðe ofte beswiken, þat is,
Vana Gloria, idel wulder ³ oðer idel ȝelp. Ðies dieð ðe manne
ðe ðurh hire is beswiken ðat he twifealdeð his senne; alswo ðe
man ðe haueð islaȝe anne mann aȝeanes godes forbode, ðanne ȝelpð
he ðat he is wel iwreken of his unwine; oðer ȝif he hafð beswiken
an maiden, oðer an riche lafdi ðe is bewedded ⁴, ðar ⁵ of he lat ðe
bett of him seluen, and swa he wurð beswiken. For ðan he næure ⁶
ðis ne beweop ⁷, ac ȝet ðar to more he ecð, ðat is, ȝif ⁸ he for his
sennes farð ut of lande halȝen te seken, oðer he michel fast, oðer
almesse doð, ðat he ofte biȝelpð, oðer on swilche wise hes dieð, ðat
he herienge ðar of hafð and swa hes forliest. Ðarof seið ðat godspell: Receperunt mercedem suam, 'Hie habbeð inumen here
lean.' Ðat bieð alle ðe ani god doð, and ðar of herienge luuieð.
Ðencheð herof ȝe ðe doð ȝewer god teforen mannen! Sume oðre
forlæteþ ðe world and nimeð ðe cloðes of religiun, and sone hem
seluen healdeð for hali, and unwurð healdeþ of oðre ⁹, ðe neure ȝiete

---

¹ page 2. ² loth MS. ³ wu on erasure. ⁴ dd corrected from ðd.
⁵ r on erasure. ⁶ e on erasure.
⁷ a small red ð inserted above between p and a. ⁸ Gif MS. ⁹ odre MS.

[do not repent] their own sins with humility nor with true repentance. Some think well of themselves, if they are of high family, or if they are of a high office, or if they have some high command [authority], or if men of the world esteem them holy men; they forget too much themselves within, and hearken to the idle works without. Hereof I am conscious myself that this cursed spirit has made me [such], that I have greatly sinned against my Lord God Almighty.

(*Here ought to be put ill-will, which this soul seems to forget in its confession.* Envy should not be forgotten, *because death entered the earth through the devil's cunning and ill-will.*)

Of disobedience.

Again, I have much misdone through another sin which is called *inobedientia*, that is, disobedience. As the angel was driven out of the kingdom of Heaven for pride, so was Adam, our forefather, out of Paradise for this disobedience. For that, he suffered death—and afterwards, all mankind—and the pain of hell more than five thousand winters [years], until Christ released him by obedience. All who see, and read, or hear this, I beg and warn, for the love of God and for your dear soul, that you hate and shun, above all things, this cursed sin. For it we shall all suffer death, as those have done who were before us. It is the key of all the other sins; no sin can be done but through disobedience. So deeply has God forbidden us all the cardinal sins, as he did Adam the tree of Paradise, both by the old law and also by the new one. What shall I do, wretched soul, that am guilty through disobedience, because I never have been obedient, neither to God, nor to my spiritual fathers, nor to my baptism, nor ever yet kept obedience well? But pray we all our Lord Christ, who was obedient to His Father even [bieteð] here aȝene seunen mid eadmodnesse ne mid soðre berewsinge. Sume læteð¹ wel² of hem seluen, ȝif hie bieð of heiȝe kenne, oðer³ ȝif he bie of heiȝe menstre, oðer ȝif he hafð sum hei obedience, oðer ȝif menn of ðe world hes healdeð for hali menn; hie⁴ forȝiteð to swiðe hem seluen wið-innen, *and* harkieð to ðe idele werkes wið -uten. Her-of ic am becnawe me self ðat ðie[s] iwerȝede gast me hafð idon, ðat ic am swiðe forȝelt aȝeanes mine laferde god almihtin.

[*The following comment is written at the top of the page.*]

(Hic deberet poni inuidia, q*uam* ui*detur* obliuisci hec anima in sua confess*i*one. **Nith nere nohutt te forȝeten,** q*ui*a sapi*entia et* inuidia diaboli, mors intrauit in or*b*em terre, et c*etera*.)

Of vnbuhsumnesse⁵.

ȜIET ic habbe muchel misdon ðurh ane oðre senne þe is ȝecleped in*o*bediencia, þ*at* is, unhersumnesse. Al swa ðe angel was ȝedriuen ut of heuene riche for modinesse, swa was Adam, ure forme fader, ut of *p*aradise for ðessere unhersumnesse. For hire he ðolede deað, *and* seððen all mankenn, *and* ðe pine of helle ma ðanne fif ðusend wintre, al hwat Crist him liesde wið hersumnesse. Alle ðe ðis isieð, and radeð, oðer ȝehiereð, i bidde *and* warni, for ðe luue of gode⁶ *and* for ȝuer lieue saule, þat ȝie hatien *and* scunien, ouer alle þing, ðes awerȝhede senne. For hire we sculen alle deað þolien, al swo habben idon ðe te-foren us wæren. Hie is kœie of alle oðre sennes; no*n* senne ne mai bien idon bute ðurh unhersumnesse. Al swo diepliche hafð godd us forboden alle heaued-sennes, swo he dede Adame ðe treu of paradise, aiðer ðurh ðare ealde laȝwe *and* iec ðurh ðare n(i)ewe. Hwat do ic, wrecche saule, ðe am forgilt ðurh unhersumnesse, for ði ðat ic⁷ naure hersum ne habbe ibien, ne gode, ne mine gastliche faderes, ne min cristendom, ne obedience nauerȝiete wel ne h(i)eld? Ac bidde we alle ure lauerd Crist, ðe was hersum his fader anon to ðe deaðe⁸,

---

¹ læted *MS*.   ² *page 3*.   ³ ð *on erasure*.   ⁴ h *on erasure*.
⁵ *Originally* vnhersumnesse, h *altered to* b; uh *written above* er, er *underlined by a different hand*.   ⁶ g *corr. from* d.
⁷ ic wrecche saule *MS.*, *the last two words underlined*.   ⁸ d *corr. from* ð.

unto death, that, as we lose this short life by disobedience, He will give us might that we may be obedient to Him in all good works even until death, and so may go forth into the eternal life which He has promised us through His mercy.

Of swearing oaths.

Again, here is more of the evil kind of seed, that has often made me forswear God's own name and also His saints, and in many ways to curse myself, or one of my friends whom I helped to swear, and in such wise fancied to help both of us, and brought both of us into much harm. This I did against God's commandment, which says: *Nolite jurare, neque per coelum neque per terram*, 'Do not swear, neither by Heaven nor by earth, nor by any other thing, but yea, yea, nay, nay.' All that we swear more, is evil and sin. Some fancy to be guiltless of this sin, because they are compelled to the oath. Though one compel me to the oath, one does not compel me to forswear, but to say the truth concerning what I am accused of. If I were a true Christian, I would rather suffer the death of the body, than kill the wretched soul so piteously.

Of lying.

Often I have committed another sin, since I could speak, up to this day, that is *mendatium* by name, that is, lying, which has polluted all the offspring of Adam, who could or might speak, save Christ alone, who is rightly called Truth, and Saint Mary, His mother. The same devil is rightly called father of lying, when he said: *Ero similis altissimo*, 'I shall be like the Highest.' This was the first lie that ever was found. There thou liedst, thou false devil! and so thou doest still, concerning all that thou ever promisest. Thou thinkest well to accuse me before God for this sin; but I accuse myself now before God and before all His saints, and forsake thee and all thy leasings. There is nothing more contrary to Christ, who is called Truth, than lying is. Beware who will!

þat, al swo we forlieseð ðis scorte lif ðurh unhersumnesse, ðat he us ȝiue mihte ðat we moten him bien hersum on alle gode ¹ woerkes anaon to ðe deaðe, *and* swa cumeð forð *in* to ðe eche liue ðe he hafð us behoten ðurh his mil(d)ce.

Of oðe(s) ² sueriingge.

GIET hier is mare of ðe eueles kennes sade, ðe me hafð ofte idon godes aȝwene name forsweren ³ *and* ec his halȝen, and a manies kennes me seluen to weriȝen, oðer sume of mine friende ðe ic halp to sweriȝen, *and* on swilche wise wende helpen unc baðe, *and* brohte unc baðe *in* to muchele harme. Þis ic dede aȝean godes ⁴ bebode, ðe seið : Nolite iurare, neq*ue* per celu*m* neq*ue* per ter*r*am, 'Ne sweriȝeð, naiðer ne be heuene ne be ierðe, ne bie nan oðer ðing, bute ia, ia, næi, nai.' Al þat we more sweriȝeð, swo it is euel *and* senne. Sume weneð bien sacleas of ðessere senne, for ðan ðe me nett hem to ðan aðe. Þeih me niede me to ðan aðe, me ne net me noht te forsweriȝen, ac soð te seggen of ðan ðe ic am bicleped. Ȝif ic ware riht cristeneman, ic wolde bliðelicor þoliȝen ðas lichames deað, ðanne ic wolde ðe wrecchede saule sa rewliche acwellan.

Of lesinge.

OFT ic habbe beuclen an oðer ⁵ senne, fram ðat ic cuðe speken, ȝiet to ðese daiȝe, ðat is mendatium be name, ðat is, leasinge, ðe all Adames ofspring hafð be-smiten, ðe speken cuðen oðer mihten, wið-uten Crist ane, ðe is mid rihte icleped soðh, *and* sæinte Marie, his moder. De selue dieuel is icleped mid rihte fader of leasinge, ða ða he sade : Ero simil*is* altissimo, ⁶ 'Ic scal bien ȝelich ðan heisten.' Ðis was ðe forme leasinge ðe æure was ȝefunde. Dar ðu luȝe, ðu lease dieuel, *and* swa ðu diest ȝiet, of al ðat tu aure behatst. Du me þen(c)st wel to wreiȝen tó-fore gode for ðessere senne ; ac ic wreiȝe me nu te-fore gode *and* teforen alle his halȝen, *and* te forsake *and* alle ðine leasinges. Nis nan ðing mare aȝeanes Criste, ðe is icleped soð, ðanne is leasinge. Bie war se ðe wile !

---

¹ *page* 4.   ² o *corr. above* a.   ³ *another* s *inserted over the first* r.
⁴ ȝodes *MS.*   ⁵ oder *MS.*   ⁶ *page* 5.

Of evil backbiting.

Another sin is called *detractio*, which reaves God's love from man's heart, that is, evil backbiting. It has often made me guilty against God's prohibition, that forbids me all evil speeches, and reproves me thus: *Sedens adversus fratrem tuum loquebaris*, 'Thou satst,' He said, ' over against thy brother, and both of you each day cry to Me, who am your Father, and say : *pater noster*. Before him thou spokest good, behind him evil, so that he did not hear it. Thus thou didst, and I was still; and therefore thou thoughtst that I was like thee, that it pleased Me as it did thee. But thou shalt stand before Me on Doomsday, and before all mankind, where I shall reprove thee with the same words which thou often hast heard in order to warn thee, and thus say: *Dilexisti malitiam super benignitatem*. That is : 'Thou lovedst evil more than good, to speak unrighteousness more than righteousness ; therefore God Almighty shall destroy thee, both body and souL Go away from Me, thou cursed, forth with the devil !' Who is there that is not adread of this great thunderclap that comes out of God's own mouth ? Take heed who will ! How great danger it is to break God's prohibition !

Of deceit.

Again, I have committed more bad practices. I have deceived my fellow-Christian with fair words which I have spoken unto him, and have shown him otherwise by my works, and have often promised him upon my word of honour, what I never afterwards accomplished for him. If I bought from him or sold him anything, it was always more preferable to me, that I should gain and he lose, than that our bargain should be given up. God forbids us to have twofold weights or twofold measures, but [bids us] give and lend joyfully, without earthly meed, to all that have need and beseech us, for His love, for the same goods that He has lent us. Sooth to say, I do not know whether I ever yet did anything that I would not have some kind of reward thereof, either

Of heuele[1] bafte(s)pache.

DETRACTIO hatte an oðer senne, ðe reaueð godes luue of mannes hierte, ðat is, euel bafte-spache. Hie me haueð ofte ȝemaked forȝielt aȝeanes godes forbode, ðe me forbett alle euele spaches, *and* ðus me undernemð: Sede*n*s aduersus fratre*m* tuum loq*u*ebaris, 'Ðu sate,' (he seið), 'aȝeanes ðine broðer, ðe ælche dai baðe clepieð to me, ðe am ȝure fader, *and* seggeð: pater noste*r*. Aȝeanes him ðu spake (god), bafte him euele, þat he it ne herde. Ðus ðu dedest, *and* ic was stille; *and* for ði ðu wendest þat ic ðe ware ilich, þ*at* hit likede me swa swa hit dede ðe. Ac ðu scalt stonden tefore me a domesdaiȝe, *and* teforen all manke*n*ne, ðar ic ðe scal underneme*n* mid ða ilche wordes ðe ðu ofte hafst ȝeherd for ðe te warnien, *and* ðus cweðen: Dilexisti maliciam sup*er* benignitate*m*. Ðat is: 'Ðu luuedest euelnesse mare ða*n*ne godnesse, unrihtwisnesse more to spekene ða*n*ne rihtwisnesse; for ði ðe scal god almihti[2] forliesen, baðe lichame *and* saule. Ga awei fram me, ðu ȝewereȝede, forð mid te dieule!' Hwa is ðat nis ofdradd of ðese mu-[3]chele ðpunresleiȝ[4] ðe cumþ ut of godes auȝene muðe? Nime ȝieme se ðe wile! Hu michel haht hit is godes forbod te brekene!

Of swicedome.

GIET ich habbe ma vnðeawes beuolen. Ic habbe beswiken min emcriste*n* mid faire wordes ðe ic to him habbe ȝespeken, *and* oðerlicor mid weorkes him ȝekydd, *and* uppe mine lahfulnesse ofte him behet, þ*at* ic næure eft him neȝelæste. Gif ich at him ani þing bouhte oðer him sealde, æure me was leuere þ*at* ic biȝate and he forlure, ða*n*ne unker chepinge bileafde. Godd us forbett ðat we ne sculen habbe twifeald wæiȝe ne twifeald imett, ac ðat we sculen bliðeliche ȝiuen *and* leanen, wið-uten eröliche mede, alle ðe niede habbeð *and* us for his luue besecheð of ðan ilche gode ðe he us hafð ilænd. Soþ to seggen, ic not ȝif ich[5] auerȝete ani ðing dede ðat ic nolde habbe sumes kennes (lean), oðer[6] of ðouhtes

---

[1] *The first* e *corrected above* u. [2] almihti*n* MS. [3] *page* 6.
[4] *a* ç *above* re. [5] ich *corrected over* hit.
[6] *Before* oðer *is* ðer *of* underdotted, *behind it one word erased.*

of thoughts or of words or of works; and if I had not, methought that it was not well bestowed, when I had done it.

Of cursing.

Again, we find that the apostle says: *Maledici regnum Dei non possidebunt*, that is, 'The cursing men, who so blithely will curse, they never may dwell in the kingdom of Heaven,' because they curse God's handiwork, that He has blessed. Hereof I am guilty, and acknowledge that I have cursed, both clerics and laymen, relations and strangers, and many things which I should not curse.

Of impatience.

Another sin is named *impatientia*, that is, unbearingness [impatience]. It seizes the man whom it overpowers, that he may not control himself neither in thoughts, nor in words, nor in works. So it has done me always too oft. Through it I am guilty against God, who gave me example, first of Himself, and afterwards with holy words instructed me: *Qui te percusserit in maxillam, praebe ei et aliam*, 'Who smites thee under the ear, turn to him the other,' He said, 'and do good for evil. If he cursed thee, do thou bless him.' This I never did; but if my Lord God would chastise me with any rod, as a father does his son, I was impatient at it, and both thought and said: 'Why should such mishaps come to me? Many another was there who had misdone more, and no mishap came, but he had all bliss and rest enough.' Therefore said God Almighty of me and my like: *Et dimisi eos secundum desideria cordis eorum*, 'I let them [go],' He says, 'after their own will; after what their heart lusted, I followed them.'

Of self-will.

Through this sin I, unhappy soul, fell into another sin, which is called *propria voluntas*, that is, self-will. Certainly, God has rejected that same man who omits to do God's and his spiritual fathers' oðer of wordes oðer of weorkes; *and* ȝif ic nadde, me ðuhte *þat* hit nas naht[1] wel betowen, ðar ic hit idon hadde.

Of werȝhinde.

EFT we findeð ðat ðe apostel seið : Maledici[2] rengnum dei non possidebunt, ðat bieð : ' Ða werȝinde menn, ðe swa bleðeliche willeð werȝien, *þat* hie naure on heuenriche wuniȝen ne muȝen,' for ði ðat hie werȝieð godes handiwerc, ðe he hafð iblesced. Herof ic am sceldi, *and* wel am becnawe ðat ic ȝewerȝed habbe aiðer ȝe hodede ȝe leawede, sibbe *and* framde, *and* mani þing ðe ic werȝi ne scolde.

Of vnðolemodnesse.

INPACIENCIA hatte an oðer senne[3], *þat* is, unþolemodnesse. Hie benemð ðe manne [4] ðe hie ouermai, ðat he ne mai wealden him seluen ne a þouhtes, ne on wordes, ne on weorkes. Swa hie haueð me idon aure to ofte. Þurh hire ic am forȝelt aȝeanes gode, ðe me forbisne ȝaf, arst of him seluen, *and* seððen mid haliȝe wordes me wissede : Qui te percusserit in maxillam, (prebe[5]) ei et aliam, ' Se ðe smit under ða eare, want to ðat oðer,' he sade, ' *and* do god aȝean euel. Gif he ðe wereȝede[6], ðu hine blesci.' Ðis ne dede ic næure ; ac ȝif min lauerd godd me wolde swingen mid ani swinge[7], al swa fader doð[8] his sune, ic was ðar aȝean unþolemod, *and* aiðer ðohte *and* ec sæide : ' Hwi me scolde cumen swilche unȝelimpes ? Mani oðer was ðe more hafde misdon, *and* non unȝelimp ne cam, ac hadde alle blisse *and* reste inowh.' For ði saide god almihti[9] be me *and* be mine i-liche[10] : Et dimisi eos secundum desideria[11] cordis eorum, 'Ich hem let,' he seið, ' after here awene wille ; after ðan ðe here herte leste, ic hem folȝede.'

Of aȝen-wille.

DURH ðessere senne ic, unȝesali saule, fel in to an oðer senne, ðe is icleped propria voluntas, *þat* is, auȝen-wille. Ȝewiss hafð godd forworpen ðan ilche mann ðe lat godes (wille) *and* his

---

[1] *Corrected from* naltt.   [2] ditci *or* dicci *MS.*   [3] sennne *MS.*   [4] *page* 7.
[5] *Added over the line and twice at side.*   [6] d *barred red ; and* ðu *MS.*
[7] swinke *MS.*   [8] *Corrected from* deð.   [9] almihtin *MS.*
[10] *an erasure between* i *and* l.   [11] s *on erasure.*

will, unless He again through His great mercy take it [this sin] away from him, before he goes out of this life. No creature that is rational, as are angels and men, ought to have their self-will, because they are not, nor ever can be, righteous nor good, save they follow God's will in all ways. Therefore we find in the holy Writ : 'The man that will follow his self-will, he is hostile to God, as is the man who is hostile to the king and wishes to deprive him of his crown.' Christ Himself says in His Gospel : *Non veni facere voluntatem meam,* 'I came not to give you an example of doing My own will, but I came in order to do My Father's will.' When Christ was born, the angels of Heaven came and sang that precious song, *Gloria in excelsis Deo,* and proclaimed peace to all those men who have good will, that is, to none but those who love and follow God's will. Alas and well-a-day, that I have followed my own self-will, so that I have to suffer for my obstinacy evermore, except God's holy mercy deliver me !

Of unrighteousness.

Another sin is called unrighteousness, which has ever too long deceived me with its treacherous vices. It is always against righteousness, because no man can be saved, except he be righteous and not twofold [double-faced], neither in speeches nor in deeds. Other have I been than I have shown myself. Men see me outside. I and my like, we are on the outside like the dead man's tomb, that without is whited, and within is stinking and full of worms. So have I been full of evil thoughts. Woe to me for this! *Mea culpa!* Because I have not had right belief, nor fast hope, nor true love to our Lord God as I should, therefore I have been unmighty and unstrong against all these foresaid sins. I cannot number nor tell all the sins, nor all the vices, nor all the wonders that I, wretched sinful one, have done and committed, since I first could sin. But of Him who alone knows them, the Almighty God, I beg mercy and forgiveness.

gastliche faderes (wille¹) to donne, bute he eft ðurh his muchele mildce hes him benime, ær ðane he of ðese liue fare. Non scafte ðe is scadwis, al swo bieð angles *and* menn, ne aȝeð te hauen here aȝen -will, forðan hie ne bieð, ne ne muȝen bien, næure riht-wise ne gode, bute hie folȝin godes wille on alle² wisen. Forðan we findeð on hali write: 'Se mann ðe wile folȝin his aȝen wille, he is aȝeanes gode, alswa is ðe mann ðe is aȝeanes ðe kinge *and* wile his curune him benemen.' Crist self seið on his godspelle: N o n *ueni facere uoluntatem meam,* 'Ne cam ic noht te ȝiuen ȝew for-³bisne of mire aȝene wille to donne, ac i cam for to donne mines fader wille.' Ða ðe Crist was ȝeboren, ða comen ða aingles of heuene *and* sunge ðane derewurðe sang, Gloria in exselsis deo, and bodeden sibsumnesse to⁴ alle ðo mannen ðe god wille habbeð, ðat nis non bute ðo ðe godes wille luuieð *and* folȝið. Weilawei *and* walawa, ðat ic min aȝen iwill swa habbe ifolȝed, ðat im min unȝewill awh aure ma te þoliȝen, bute godes hali mildse me aliese⁵!

Of hunrihtwisnesse.

UNRIHTWISNESSE hatte an oðer senne, ðe me haueð æure to longe ȝedweld mid hire swikele unðeawes. Hie is æure aȝean rihtwisnesse, forðan no man ne mai bien ȝeborȝwen, bute he bie rihtwis and naht twifeald, ne on speches ne on dades. Oðer ic habbe ibien ðanne ic habbe me i-sceawed. Menn me isieð wiðuten. Ic *and* mine iliche, we beoð wiðuten al swa ðe deade man[n]es þruh, þe is wiðuten ihwited, *and* wið-inne stinkende⁶ *and* full of wermes. Swa ic habbe ibien full of euele þohtes. Wa me þas! Mea culpa!

Forði ðat ich nabbe ihafd rihte ileaue, ne faste hope, ne soðe luue to ure lauerde gode swa swa ic scolde, forði ic haue bien unmihti and unstrong onȝeanes alle þese forenammde sennes. Ic ne mai rimen ne tellen alle ðo sennes, ne alle ðo unðeawes, ne alle ðo wundren ðe ich, wrecche senfulle, habbe idon *and* beuolen, seððen ic arst mihte seneȝin. Ac him ðe hes one wat, almihti god, ic bidde are *and* forȝiu[en]esse.

---

¹ *Added over the line and at side.*   ² *Corrected from* allt.   ³ *page* 8.
⁴ *Corrected from* do.   ⁵ es *corr. from* ss.   ⁶ de *corr. from* dr.

Of the five senses.

Again, my heart accuses me of the five senses that God assigned me to look after my wretched body, that is, *visus, auditus, gustus, odoratus, et tactus;* that is, sight, hearing, taste, and smell, and touch. These five senses, betoken the five golden Bezants [talents] which the Lord entrusted to his thrall in order to gain therewith. So did the good servant that gained five others. Therefore his Lord said to him : ' Well then, good servant ! Over little things thou wast true ; over great things I shall set thee. Go into thy Lord's bliss ! ' This I have not earned, that have done no good with the same Bezants of the five senses, but through them and through my carelessness I have lost my Lord's property. Each day messengers come into my thoughts that I shall soon come before Him, and give Him answer, what I have done with His property. He will have it well coined, and by right weight well weighed, and of well refined gold ; and except I have this, in those days when He sends after me, I shall hear rueful tidings. 'Answer Me now, thou unhappy soul,' He will say, ' what hast thou so long done in the world ? A long respite I gave thee well to do if thou wouldst, and little good thou hast gotten with the five Bezants of the five senses I entrusted to thee. More than five thousand Bezants of good thoughts, and of good words, and of good works, thou mightst have gained if thou wouldst, in the long space I gave thee ; but thou, poor soul, wouldst not think of thy departure, when thou shouldst separate thyself from thy body, and come before Me, and answer Me for all thy deeds.' Then He calls His tormentors, and bids them take me, and bind me, both hands and feet, and throw me into the uttermost darkness. The inmost darkness is in the heart which will not foreshow whither he shall go when he goes hence. The uttermost is the darkness of hell, where never yet light came, save those nights when Christ's soul came therein after His chosen ones. But always there is weeping and wailing through the great heat

Of ðá fíf wittes.

GIET me wreið min herte of ða fíf wittes ðe god me (be)tahte to lokin of mine wrecche¹ lichame, þat is², visus, auditus, gustus, odoratus, et tactus, þat is, ʒesihthe, ʒeherhþe, smac, and smell, and tactþe. Ðas fíf wittes, hie tacniþ ða fíf gildenene besantes ðe ðe hlauerd betahte his þralle (for)³ to biʒeten ðar mide. Swa dede ðe gode þrall ðe biʒatt oðer fíf. For ði his hlauerd him sede: 'Wel ðe, gode ðrall! Ouer litel þing ðu ware trewe; ouer michel þing ic ðe scal setten. Ga in to ðine lauerdes blisse!' Þis ne habbe ic nauht⁴ ofearned, ðe no god ne habbe idon mid ðo ilke besantes of ðe fíf wittes, ac ðurh hem and þurh mine ʒemeleaste ic habbe mines lauerdes eihte forloren. Ælche dai me cumeð sonden on mine þohtes þat ic scall neuliche cumen te-foren him, and ʒiuen him and-sware, hwat ic habbe mid his eihte ʒedon. He wile hes habben wel imotet⁵, and bi rihte wæiʒe wel i-wæiʒen, and wel imered gold; and bute ich þis habbe, ðas daiʒes ðe he after me sant, ic scal iheren reuliche tidinge. 'Andswere me nu, þu un-ʒesælie saule,' he wile seggen, 'hwat hafst ðu swa lange idon on ðare worelð? La[n]gne first ic ðe ʒaf wel to donne ʒif ðu woldest, and litel god ðu hafst biʒeten mid ða fíf besantes of ðe fíf gewittes ðe ic þe betahte. Mo ðanne fíf ðusende besantes of gode þohtes, and of gode wordes, and of⁶ gode woerkes, ðu mihtest habben biʒeten, ʒif ðu woldest, on ða lange firste ðe ic ðe ʒaf; ac ðu, earme saule, noldest þenchen of ðine for(ð)siðe, þat tu fram ðine lichame.⁷ scoldest skelien, and tefore me cumen, and me andswerien of⁶ alle ðine dades.' Ðanne clepeð he his pineres, and hat hem me nemen, and binden me, baðe han⁸-den and fiet, and werpen me in ðe uttreste þiesternesse. Þe inreste⁹ þesternesse¹⁰ (is) in¹¹ ðare hierte ðe ne wile forsceawin h(w)ider¹² he scal ðanne he henen farð. Þe uttreste (i)s¹³ se þiesternesse of helle, ðar næure ʒiete liht ne cam, bute ðas nihtes ðe Cristes saule ðar inne cam after his ʒekorene. Ac æure ðar is wop and woninge for ðare michele hæte and unʒe-

---

¹ The underdotted letters are scarcely legible. ² page 9. ³ On the margin.
⁴ nauth MS. ⁵ So has the MS. ⁶ os MS., the f not being crossed.
⁷ Only li ... me still legible. ⁸ page 10.
⁹ The final e on erasure and an s erased behind it. ¹⁰ On erasure.
¹¹ i corrected into ñ. ¹² w red above the line. ¹³ s corr. from i.

and immeasurable burning, and there is gnashing of teeth through the immeasurable chill ; and there is sorrow and pain through the great despair that comes at the thought that they never more shall see God nor one of His saints, nor relation or strangers who will be saved, but evermore shall dwell with the awful devils, who are so loathsome and so grisly to look at, that if a man now saw one just as he is in his proper shape, he would soon be out of his wit, and endure this [madness] evermore without end. I cannot think, nor say with mouth, nor write in a book, all the pains of hell. Woe to them that they ever were created, who deserve these pains! Understand, all who read or hear this, and have wit to understand, God's great forbearance towards us in this life, how He admonishes us each day, and says to us: *Convertimini ad me, et agite poenitentiam,* 'Turn to Me,' He says, 'ye that are turned away from Me, through the devil's lore, take and do penance, each after what his sin is; and speed, because your end-day is near, and comes unawares as a thief by night. Fast, and keep vigil, and turn from evil, and do good, weep and wail, sigh and yearningly beg mercy and forgiveness, the little while we dwell here. Because, unless ye earn it here, mercy will never betide you elsewhere.' Those who will not listen to nor observe these, God's holy words, listen to what the Holy Ghost says through the prophet David : *Maledicti qui declinant a mandatis tuis, Domine,* ' Cursed be all they, Lord, who will not hold Thy commandments!' Those who are not adread of this awful cursing, that all ordained each day curse the while they sing God's praise at prime, listen to another cursing that comes out of God's own mouth, because this curse is nothing but an earnest of the last [curse], when God shall say Himself with much awe : *Discedite a me, maledicti, in ignem æternum,* 'Go away from Me, ye cursed by all ordained heads, into everlasting fire, ye that would not listen to My counsel, nor love My commandments, nor hold them. Be gone away from Me, forth with the devils, where ye never more again shall see Me !' All ye that have Christ's charity, that is, God's

mæte brene ¹, *and* ðar is chiueringe of toðen for ðe unmate chele ;
and ðar is sorwȝe *and* sarinesse for ðare muchele ortrewnesse ðe
cumþ of ðan ȝeþanke ðe hie næure mo godd² ne sculen isien ne nan
of his halȝen, ne sibbe ne fra*m*de ðe iborȝe*n* sculen bie*n*, ac aure 4
ma wunien mid ða eifulle dieulen, ðe bieð swa laðliche *and* swo
grislich³ an to lokin, ðat ȝif a ma*n*n iseiȝe nu anne⁴ al swilch al
se he is on his ȝekynde, he scold*e* sone bie*n* ut of his iwitte, *and*
ðis poliȝen æure ma wið-uten ande. Ne mai ic þenchen, ne mid 8
muðe segge*n*, ne on boke write, alle ðo pine*n* of helle. Wa he*m*
ðatt h(i)e æure iscapene waren, ðe ðo pine*n* of-earniþ ! Vnder-
standeþ, alle ðe ðis radeþ oðer ihereð, *and* witt habbeð to understonden, þe muchele ðolemodnesse of us on ðese liue, hv godd us 12
meneȝeð alche dai, *and* to us seið : Conuertimini ad me, *et*
agite penite*n*ciam, ' Wandeð to me,' he seið, ' ȝie ðe berð iwant
fram me, ðurh dieules lare, *and* nemeð *and* doð scrift⁵, [æll]ch after
ðat his senne is ; *and* spedeð ȝeu, forðan ȝure ænde-dai neihȝeð, *and* 16
cumð unȝewares al swa þief be nihte. Fasteð *and* wakieð *and*
buȝeð fram euele *and* doð god, we[p]eð⁶ *and* wanið, sihteþ *and*
ȝeorne biddeð are *and* forȝiuenesse, ða litle hwile ðe we her
wuniȝið. For-ðun, bute ȝif ȝe⁷ hier (hit) ne of-earniȝeð, ne 20
wurþ ȝeu næure milce elleshwar.' Da ðe nelleð ðese godes hali
(wordes) hlesten ne healden, harkið hwat se haligast seið ðurh ðe
profiete Dauið : Maledicti qui declinant a ma*n*datis tuis,
dom*i*ne, ' ȝewerwed bien hie, lauerd⁸, alle ðe ðine behode healden 24
nelleð.' Da ðe ne bieð ofdrad of ðessere eisliche werȝinge, ðe
alle hadede⁹ ællche dai werȝið ðar hwile ðe h(i)e singeð godes
lofsang at prime, harkieð an oðer wariȝing ðe cumþ ut of godes
awene muþe, forðan ðes werȝinge nis bute erres of ðare laczste, 28
ðanne god seið hi*m* self mid muchele eiȝe : Discedite a me, maledicti, i*n* igne*m* eternu*m*, ' Gað aweiȝ fra*m* me, ȝie iwerȝede of
alle hadede hafde, in to ðan eche fiere, ȝie ðe nolde*n* mine rad
hleste*n*, ne mine bebode luuien ne healde*n*. Witeð awei fra*m* me, 32
forð mid ða dieule*n*, ðar ȝie naure ma eft me ne ȝesien !' Alle
ðe habbeð Cristes kariteð, ðat is, godes luue *and* ma*n*nes, wepeð

---

¹ n *written over a blotted-out letter.* ² gode *MS.* ³ e *erased after* h.
⁴ añne *MS.* ⁵ *The following three or four letters are totally destroyed.*
⁶ w *half,* p *totally destroyed.* ⁷ *page* 11. ⁸ l *corrected from* h.
⁹ i *scratched out before* h.

and man's love, weep and wail ever with me, and let us try to cool God's wrath with tears, which are very agreeable to Him with other sacrifices of bitter sorrow! He who knows all things knows that they sorely pain me. To you I cry also who are dwelling in fellowship with the Lord God, and to our Lady St. Mary. Mother of mercy, I beg thee, through thy great mercy, that thou beseech for me forgiveness of my sins of Jesus Christ, thy dear son, that has might to forgive all sins, through the same love He has to my kind which He had from thee without a .... thereof has given as lot and part His flesh and His blood, through which I believe firmly that I should have mercy and pity, if I received it as worthily, as it was worthy. To all the saints who here were born in this life, and now are dwelling with our Lord God, I cry and beg through the great charity that is in you, that ye think of us who are here in this wretched life, where the way is slippery, and we are easy to fell, and where many foes are, before and behind and on each side. We thank God and praise Him after our might, who has brought you out of this great wretchedness. Pray ye that we may come to you, not through our deserving, but through God's great mercy and through your [merits]. So truly as He had mercy and pity on you, and sent you the gift of the Holy Ghost without merits, as truly may He have mercy and pity on us, who are His handiwork as well as you, and may grant us that we may, with your help and with His holy grace, so lead here this short life, that we may ever abide with you in bliss, and evermore love Him and praise Him in eternity. Amen.

Now, dear friend, thou that raisedst me, sinful soul, from death, [and] through God's grace instructedst and warnedst [me] to do well, —may God requite thee!—and taughtst me to be conscious of my sins, now thou hast heard [by] my bemoaning that I am so very guilty: for the love of God I beseech thee that thou teachest me still, in what wise I might best be reconciled to my Saviour Christ,

OF THE FIVE SENSES.

and wanieð forð mid me, *and* fondie we te kelien gode(s) wraðða mid teares, ðe him bieð swiðe icueme mid oðre loke [1] of sare birewnesse! He hit wat ðe wat alle þing, ðat sare hie me reweð. To ȝeu ic clepiȝe iec ðe bieð wuniȝende mid ȝemaneliche hlauerde *gode*, 4 [*and*] to ure lafdi sainte Marie. Moder of mildce [2], ðe ic bidde, for ðine muchele mildze, ðat tu me besieke [3] forȝiuenesse of mine sennes to Iesu Criste, þine lieue sune, ðe hafð [4] mihte te forgiuene alle sennes, for ðare ilke luue ðe he hafð [5] to mine ikynde ðe he nam of 8 ðe wið-uten a [6] .... ðarof iȝiuen hafð lott *and* dale, his flesc *and* his blod, ðurh hwan ich [7] ilieue fastliche are *and* mildze to habben, ȝif ic hit swa wurðliche underfenge, swa hit wurðe wære. To alle ðo halȝen ðe hier on liue waren iboren, *and* nu mid ure 12 lauerde gode wuniȝende bieð, ic clepie *and* bidde for ðo muchele kariteð ðe is an ȝeu, ðat ȝie ðenchen an us ðe bieð hier on ðese arme [8] liue, ðar ðe wei is slider *and* we lihtliche to fællen, and fele unwines, teforen *and* baften *and* on alche side. We ðankieð 16 gode *and* herieð after ure mihte, ðe ȝew haueð of ðessere (michele) wrecchade ibroht [9]. Biddeþ ðat we moten to ȝew cumen, naht for ure earninge, ac for godes muchele mildce *and* for ȝewer! Al swa soðliche swa he hadde are *and* mildze of ȝeu [10], *and* ða giue of ðe 20 hali gaste ȝew sænte wiðuten earninge, sa soðliche habbe he are *and* mildce of us, ðe bieð his handeweorc al swa ȝie, *and* us unne ðat we moten, mid ȝeure helpe *and* mid his hali grace, swa ðis scorte lif her laden, ðat we moten forð mid ȝew on blisse wuniȝen, 24 *and* him eure ma luuien *and* herien on ecnesse. Amen.

NV, lieue friend, ðu ðe me, senfulle saule, aweihtest of deaðe, ðurh godes grace wissedest *and* warnedest wel te donne, —ȝielde þe godd!—and lardest ðat ic scolde bien icnawe of mine 28 sennes, nu ðu hafst iherd mine bemone þat ich am swa swiðe forȝelt [11]: for ðe luue of gode ic ðe besieche ðat [tu] [12] me wissi ȝiet, an hwælche wise ic mihte betst sahtlin wið mine halend Criste, ðe

---

[1] ðe—bieð and icueme—loke *repeated, but this time is written* icweme *and* lake.   [2] *cp. page* 17, *note* [1].   [3] b *and* k *not distinct*.
[4] lieue : : : : : h : fð (*scarcely visible*).
[5] *Only* ilke...he h...ð *clear*.   [6] *Half a line illegible*   [7] *page* 12.
[8] *A letter before* a *scratched out*.   [9] *Corrected from* ibroltt.
[10] *Corrected from* ȝeli.   [11] *Corrected from* fortelt.   [12] *Erased*.

whom I chose as Lord through His own mercy, if I sinful might have mercy in this short time. And I will blithely listen to thy counsel, and all the more blithely, if thou wouldst show me thy unknown name.

How Reason answers and says to the soul.

Almighty God be thanked that thou so well understandest thyself! *Haec mutatio dextrae excelsi,* 'This turning is truly through God's right hand.' Now as thou wilt so eagerly know my name, I will tell thee forsooth. I am a gleam of God's face that was shaped in thee, dear, dear soul, *Ratio* by name, that is, Discernment. I left thee, because thou followedst more thy self-will than thou didst my counsel. When I went from thee, then went forth with me the same good will and that good mind which God had shaped in thee, all three of us after His own likeness to help thee. Then thou couldst do no good nor any of the holy virtues that God had shaped to help thee. They all went away from thee, because thou followedst thy self-will and leftst God's own likeness. Thus the devil betrays many other souls that prefer to follow their bodies' will, than to learn God's lore or follow it. When the cursed spirits saw that thou wast naked and helpless, they spoke between themselves and said: 'Let us go to this idle and empty soul, since it has let discernment go from it, and follows the will of its flesh. It desires all that we desire. Let us keep together with it against all the holy virtues that ever strive against us!' Afterwards came to thee the cursed spirits of greed, of drunkenness, of lechery, of covetousness, and many others, all too many, and have ruled thee after their own will in their thraldom ever too long. Now as thou hast forsaken them through God's grace, now is great need to thee that thou understandest with sharp wit what these virtues are, which can shield thee from these cursed spirits, and with God's help and with theirs may bring thee ihc cheas to lauerde ðurh his awene mildce, ӡif¹ ic senfulle are mihte habben on ðese scorte time. And iç bliðeliche ðine rad wile hlesten, and micheles ðe bliðe ²-liker, ӡif ðu me ðin uncuðe name³ woldest kyðen.   4

Hu andsweveð Ratio *and* syeð to þare saule.

ALLMIHTI godd bie ӡeþanked ðat tu swa wel understan(c)st ðe seluen! Hec mutacio dextere excelsi, 'Dies wændinge is iwi(s) ðurh godes swiðere hand.' Nu ðu⁴ wilt mine name swa 8 ӡiernliche witen, soð ic ðe wile seggen. Ic am an leme of godes anlicnesse ðe was iscapen on ðe, lieue, lieue⁵ saule, Racio be name, þat is, scadwisnesse. Ic ðe forliet, for(ðan⁶) ðu folӡedest mare ðin aӡen iwill ðanne ðu dedest mine rad. Da ðe ic wænte fram ðe, 12 ða⁷ wente forð mid me ðe ilche gode wille *and* ðat gode imiend ðe godd hafde iscapen on ðe, us alle ðrie after his aӡen anlicnesse ðe to helpe. Da ne mihtest ðu nan god don ne nan of ðe hali mihtes ðe godd hadde iscapen ðe to helpen. Alle hie wanten awei 16 fram ðe, for ðan ðe ðu folӡedest ðin aӡen(e) wille *and* forliete godes au(ӡ)ene anlicnesse. Þus beswikð ðe deuel maniӡe oðre saules ðe willeð folӡin bleðelicher here lichames wille, ðanne hie willen godes lare liernin oðer folӡin. Da ðe werewede gastes 20 iseiӡen ðat ðu naked ware *and* helpleas, ða spaken hie hem betwienen *and* seiden: 'Wuten we fare te ðessere idele saule *and* amti, seððen hie hafð forlaten scadwisnesse fram hire, *and* folӡeð hire flesches wille. All hie wile ðat we willeð. Healde we forð 24 mid hire aӡeanes alle ðe hali mihtes ðe æure winneð aӡeanes us!' Seððen comen⁸ to ðe ða werӡede gastes of giuernesse, of drunkenesse, of galnesse, of ӡitsinge, *and* manie oðre, alles to fele, *and* þe habbeð iwelt after here aӡene wille on here þewdome æure to longe. Nu 28 ðurh godes grace þu hes hafst forsaken, nu is þe michel nied þat ðu understande mid scarpe witte hwat hie bien, þese mihtes, ðe ðie muӡen scilden fram ðese ӡewerӡede gaste(s), *and* mid godes fultume *and* mid here ðe muӡen bringen ham to ðin earde, ðar ðu 32

¹ Gif *MS.*   ² *page* 13.   ³ name me *MS.*   ⁴ ð *corrected from* w.
⁵ li *looks like* k.   ⁶ *On the margin.*   ⁷ ð *corr. from* o.   ⁸ *page* 14.

home to thy land, whereto thou wast shaped. And know that forsooth, without them thou wilt never come there! This too few souls ever understand, and therefore they often are bereft of many good things, and in the end often deceived.

Of right belief.

One holy virtue is called *fides recta*, that is, right belief. It is the beginning of all Christianity, it can earn much happiness from our Lord God, because it believes what it never saw. Therefore said Christ: 'Blessed are the men who believe in Me and never saw Me!' This holy virtue makes thee believe that Father and Son and Holy Ghost are called one true Almighty God in three persons, and in oneness ever honoured with the Holy Trinity. Thou shalt believe that the Father is unbegotten, the Son begotten by the Father, as His Wisdom, in Heaven without mother, and on earth without father. The Holy Ghost comes from both of them, as the Love of both of them. These three are even in age and in wisdom, and in goodness and in strength, and in every wise after their godhead. This I believe. This one true God, He is without beginning in Himself, even although He is the beginning of all things which are shaped. So much He loved mankind, that He sent His own Son, who took our kind in soul and in body without sin, and is both true God and true man. He took this manhood as He who was God's Wisdom, very wonderfully from St. Mary the holy virgin, through the Holy Ghost. Through His manhood He suffered death, and through His godhead He arose from death, and ascended into Heaven, and sitteth on His Father's right hand, whence He shall come on Doomsday to judge all mankind. *Qui bona egerunt ibunt in vitam aeternam, qui vero mala in ignem aeternum.* 'Then shall they all who have done good go into eternal life, and they that have done evil and not atoned, they shall go into eternal fire.' If thou wilt be sure of right faith, confess with St. Peter: 'Thou art the Christ, the Son of the living God,' and hearken what He to gescapen were¹. And ðat wite ðu to soþe, wið-uten hem ne cumst ðu ðar naure! Þis understandeþ auer to feawe saules, and for ði hie bieð ofte bireaued of maniȝe gode, and at ten ænde ofte beswiken.

4

Of rihte ȝeleaue.

AN hali mihte is icleped fides recta, þat is, rihte ȝeleaue. Hie is anginn of alle cristendome, hie mai michele eadinesse of-earnin at ure lauerde gode, for ðan ðe hie iliefð ðat hie næure niseih. For ði sade Crist: 'Eadi bieð ða menn ðe on me belieuen and næure me ne seiȝen!' Þis hali mihte ðe dieð ilieuen ðat fader and sune and hali gast is an soþ almihti godd on þrie hades inammned, and an annesse ȝewurðed forð mid ðare hali ðrinnesse. Ðu scalt ilieuen þat þe fader is un-akenned, ðe sune of ðe fader akenned, al swa hiswisedom, on heuene wið-uten moder, and on ierðe wið-uten fader. Þe hali gast, he cumþ forþ of hem bam, al swa here beire luue. Ðese ðrie bieþ emliche on ielde² and on wisdome, and on godnesse and on strengþe, and on alles kennes wisen after here godd-³cundnesse. Ðis ic ilieue. Ðies an soð godd, he is wiðuten anginne on him seluen, and þeih he is anginn of alle ðing ðe iscapene bieð. Swa muchel he luuede mannkynn, þat he his awene sune sænte, ðe nam ure ȝekynde on saule and on lichame wið-uten sennen, and is baðe soð godd and soð mann. Ðese manniscnesse he nam alswo he ðe was godes wisdom, swiðe selcuð-liche of sainte Marie ðe hali maiden, ðurh ðe hali gaste. Ðurh his mannisnesse he þolede deað, and ðurh his goddcundnesse he aras of deaðe, and steih in to heuene, and sitt on his fader swiðre, ðanen he cumþ a domesdai al mann-kenn to demen. (Qui bona egerunt ibunt in uitam eternam, qui uero mala in ignem eternum⁴). 'Ðanne sculen hi alle ðe god habbeð idon to ðan⁵ eche liue, and þo ðe euele habbeð idon and naht ibett, he sculen in to ðan eche fiere.' Gif ðu wilt bien siker of ⁶ rihte ileaue, ðane sei ðu forð mid seinte Petre: Tu es Christus⁷, filius (dei uiui)⁴, and harke hwat he him andswarede: Beatus es, Simon Bariona, 'Eadi art þu,

8

12

16

20

24

28

32

---

¹ were corr. from wore.   ² ielelde MS.   ³ page 15.   ⁴ On the margin.
⁵ dan MS.   ⁶ eche li blotted out.   ⁷ xp̄c MS.

answered him: *Beatus es, Simon Barjona,* 'Blessed art thou, because no earthly man taught thee this, that I am Christ, the Son of the living God; but My Father in Heaven revealed it unto thy heart. And upon this stone that thou here hast named, Christ, God's Son, I will rear My Church, in order that all they who ever believe this which thou believest, shall be My limbs, and I their head. And so we shall be one body and one Church, *et portae inferi non praevalebunt adversus eam,* 'The gates of hell may not have any strength against this faith.' The gates of hell are the cardinal sins assuredly, for through them one goes into hell. But no sin nor any devil may have strength against this good faith, that Christ, God's Son, can and will forgive all sins to them who believe in Him and work thereafter. In this little lesson I cannot say all that were good to hear of this holy virtue. But what our holy Fathers wrote before us, and taught in the *Credo in Deum* and in *Quicunque vult,* all that believe thou firmly, else neither thou nor any man may be saved except we believe all that. But nevertheless I will, on God's behalf, that thou be warned, so that thou follow not any heretics, who misbelieve much. Of all such whom he had turned to Christ with much labour said the apostle: *Timeo ne frustra laboraverim,* 'I am afraid,' he said, 'that all my trouble on you has been lost, who take heed of days, what one day can be better than another to begin something, or a new moon better than an old moon to go into a new house or to lead home a wife.' Except the doctor who watches the new or old [moon], after man's nature, and the carpenter who carves his timber according to the moon, which is a natural thing; all else is error, which has been retained from heathendom, or except it be of sowing seed on account of the nature of these seeds of the earth. But do as the apostle teaches thee, who says: *Quaecunque vultis facere, in nomine Domini facile,* 'All that ye have to do, do it in God's name, with good belief, and it shall go well with you.' Again, know forsooth, and believe it well, that nothing may happen nor betide thee, neither evil nor good, nor in right nor

OF RIGHT BELIEF.

forðan ðe ðis ne tahte ðe non eor(ð)lic[1] mann, þat ic am Crist, godes liuiendes sune; ac min fader on heuene hit openede in to (þine) herte. And uppe þese stane ðe ðu hier hafst ȝenamd, Crist, godes sune, ich wille araren mine cherche, (ðat alle) ðe aure ðis (be)lieueð[2] þat tu ȝeliefst, hie sculen bien mine lemen, and ich here heaued[3]. And swa we sculen bien an lichame (and) an cherche, *et* porte inferi non preualebunt aduersus eam, 'Do ȝaten of helle ne muȝen hauen none strengþe aȝean ðessere ileaue.' Da ȝaten of helle, ðat bieð ðo heuedsennes fulliwis, (for) ðurh hem me farð in to helle. Ac ne mai non senne ne non dieuel habben strengþe aȝean ðessere gode[4] ileaue, þat Crist, godes sune[5], mai and wille alle sennes forȝiuen hem ðe on him belieueð and ðar after wercheð. On ðessere litle radinge ic ne mai al seggen þat god ware to iheren of ðessere hali mihte. Ac ðat ðe ure hali faderes teforen us writen, and tahte on ðe credo in deum and on quicunque uult, all ȝelief ðu fastliche, elles ðu ne namann ne mai bien ȝeboreȝen bute we all ðat ilieuen. Ac naðelas ic wille, a godes half, ðat tu bie ȝewarned, ðat tu ne folȝhi none dwelmenn, ðe muchel misleueð. Of al swi(che)[6] sade ðe apostel, þe he mid muchele iswinke hadde iwant to Criste: Timeo ne frustra laborauerim, 'Ic am ofdrad,' he sæde, 'ðat[7] ich habbe al forloren min ȝeswink on ȝeu, ðe nemeð ȝeme of daȝas, hwilch an dai bie betere ðan an oðer to anginnen sumþing, oðer newe mone betere ðan æld-mone in to newe huse te wænden oðer wif ham to leden.' Wið-uten ðe læche ðe loceð (after)[8] mannes ikynde[9] þe newe oðer elde, and ðe wrihte his timber to keruen after ðare mone, ðe is ikyndelich þing; elles hit is al ȝedwoll and of haðenesse ȝiet wið-healden, bute hit bie eft of sade te sawen for ðas sades ȝekinde of ðare eorða. Ac do al swo ðe apostel ðe tachþ and seið: Quecunque uultis facere, in nomine domini facite, 'All ðat ȝe habbeð to donne, an godes name doþ hit, mit gode ȝeleaue, and ȝew scal wel ȝelimpen.' Eft wite ðu to soðe, and wel hit ilief, ðat na þing ne mai ðe ȝelimpen ne to-cumen, neiðer ne euel ne god, ne on

---

[1] eor(d)lic *MS.*
[2] be *put above an underdotted* i.
[3] u *put above an underdotted* f, *the second* e *corrected from* o.
[4] *page* 16.   [5] sune ne *MS.*   [6] che *over erasure.*   [7] ð *corr. from* o.
[8] *On side, a word in the text scratched out.*   [9] y *written over* r.

in wrong, nor in health nor in sickness, nor through fire nor through water, nor through man nor through devil, nor through any of the things which both of them may do, except as God will allow it to them. When good comes to thee, and it well befalls thee, thank thy Lord God for it, and believe that it is through His great goodness, and not through thy merit. Again, when some evil or some mishap betides thee, in whatsoever wise it comes, believe not as some, who never well believed, say that they met evil foot, priest or monk; or some other error they entertain, and say that he had not good handsel who sold him that. Whatsoever harm or mishap befalls thee, think that thou art well deserving of the evil, because thou hast well earned it, that and much more; and thank thereof God very willingly, and so thou mayst make that all this evil may turn out to be of much good to thee.

Christ Himself says a remarkable thing of this blessed virtue: *Omnia possibilia sunt credenti,* 'All the things which ever the well-believing man wishes have done, they are granted him by God's own mouth through this holy virtue.' Again, He said of it a parable, that it is like the mustard-corn, which is little in sight and great in strength. The more one beats and stamps it, the stronger and better is it. Just so is it concerning the man who has with him this blessed virtue: the more he is troubled with griefs, temptations of the devil or of man, the stronger and better is he in good works. Again, it is written about it: *Fides sine operibus mortua est,* 'Faith without works is dead.' 'Many believe with words,' said the apostle, 'with works they forsake.' So does the devil, he believes, but he nevertheless does no good. And so there are all too many men that believe, and do not work accordingly. Beware who will!

Of firm hope.

After this comes another holy virtue that is called *firma spes,* that is, firm hope in God Almighty. All that her sister, the right faith, says to her, she trusts in it all firmly. This same holy virtue, where it comes and is with man, makes worthless to him all the fair things which in the deceptive world seem fair; he does wele ne on wauȝhe, ne on hale¹ ne on unhale, ne ðurh fier ne ðurh water, (ne ðurh manne ne ðurh dieule), ne ðurh nan ðare þinge ðe hie baðe muȝen don, bute al swo godd hit wile hem poliȝen. Þanne ðe cumþ god, and þe wel ilimpþ, þanke ðar of ðine lauerde gode, and ilief ðat hit is for his muchele godnesse, and noht for ðin earninge. Ðanne ðe cumþ eft sum euel oðer sum unȝelimp, an hwilche(s) kennes wise ðe hit æure cumþ, ne ȝelief ðu naht al swa sume, ðe naure wel ne ȝeliefden, seggeð þat hie imetten euel fot, priest oðer munec; oðer sum oðer dwel hie driueð, and seggeð þat he nafde naht gode han(d)sselle ðe him þat sealde. Hwilch harm oðer hwilc unȝelimp ðe ðe to-cumþ, þench ðat ðu art wel wurðe ðes eueles, for ðan ðe ðu hit hauest wel ofearned, þat and michele more; and ðanke ðerof gode swiðe ȝierne, and swa ðu miht don ðat all ðat euel ðe mai wanden te michele gode.

Crist self seið an selcuð þing of ðessere eadi mihte: Omnia possibilia sunt credenti, 'Alle ðo þing ðe æure ðe wel beliefde (mann)² wile habben ȝedon, hie bieð him iteiþed of godes auȝene muðe ðurh ðessere hali mihte.' Giet he sade of hire ane forbisne, ðat hie is ȝelich ðe seneueies corne, ðe is litel an sei(ht)þe and michel on strengþe. Æure ðe mann ðe hit more bat and stampeþ, ðe hit strengere and betre is. Also is of ðe manne ðe ðese eadi mihte mid him haueð: ðe he more is swaint mid deules, fondinges of dieule oðer of manne, ðe he strengere and betere is on gode werkes. Eft is iwriten bie hire: Fide(s) sine operibus mortua, 'Ileaue wið-uten werkes, hie is dead.' 'Maniȝe ilieueð mid wordes,' sæde ðe apostel, 'mid werkes he forsakeð.' Swo deð deuel, iliefð, ac he ðar after no god ne deð. And swa bieð alle(s) to fele menn ðe ȝelie³-ueð, and noht ðar after ne werchep. Bie ȝewar se ðe wile!

Of feste hope.

HIER after cumþ an oðer hali mihte ðe is icleped firma spes, þat is, fast hope to godalmihti. All ðat hire suster, ðe rihte ȝeleaue, hire seiȝeð, all hie hit fastliche hopeð. Dies ilke haliȝe mihte, ðar ðe hie cumeð and bieð mid ðe manne, hie makeð him unwurð alle ðo faire þinges ðe on ðare swikele woreld⁴ faire þen-

---

¹ page 17.   ² On side.   ³ page 18.   ⁴ r corrected from l.

not account it more than filth, compared with the great mirth he hopes to have in the kingdom of Heaven. That is the same that St. Paul teaches us in his Epistles, who says thus: *Apparuit gratia Dei omnibus hominibus erudiens nos*, 'God's grace,' he says, (which he called it), 'God's Son showed Himself to all men, and He taught us that we should forsake the frail belief of heathendom, and all worldly evil lusts, and live moderately, and rightly, and piously, awaiting the blessed hope and the coming of the great bliss of Christ, God's Son, when He comes again to show Himself, and to repay all the promises He promised us, that is, that He will turn the body of our humility into great brightness, so that it shall shine as bright as the sun, like the angels with God evermore in mirth and in bliss.' Nobody may have this blessed hope, unless he well believe it and love it truly. Therefore, said David, the prophet: *Multi dicunt: quis ostendit nobis bona?* 'Many say,' he said, 'who do not believe well: Who is he, that can show us the good things that ye promise us? Here we may see all the world's weal and have it, but it is a mere assumption whether we may have what ye promise.' What doest thou say, David? Hast thou any certainty hereof? Teach us, instruct us, it is need! *Signatum est super nos lumen vultus tui, Domine*; *dedisti laetitiam in corde meo*. 'Yes,' he says, 'we are all sure of God's promise, because the light of His face is marked right upon us. I know Him, and believe well by a token He has given me.' *Dedisti laetitiam in corde meo*, 'Thou, O Lord, gavest bliss into my heart, so that to me there is naught of all the world's bliss. And Thou hast given me this as an earnest of that eternal bliss.' Dear soul, if thou hast this bliss in thy heart, which does not come from any world's bliss, then thou mayst be sure of God's grace; and if thou hast not, do not cease neither night nor day ere thou have it. But listen to what this same prophet says of him who had got it: *Dilexisti justitiam et odisti iniquitatem, propterea unxit te Deus Deus tuus oleo laetitiae*; 'Because,' he

cheð; ne telþ hie namore ðarof ðanne of horewe, aȝeanes ðare
michele¹ merhþe ðe hie hopeð te habbene on heuene riche. Þat is
se ilke ðe san[c]tus Paulus us takð on his pisteles, *and* þus
seið: Aparuit gratia dei omnibus hominibus erudiens 4
nos, 'Godes grace,' he seið, *þat* he clepede her, 'godes sune hine
sceawede alle mannen, *and* he us tahte ðat we scolden forsaken ða un-
wraste ileaue of hæðen-dome, *and* alle woreldliches euele lustes, *and*
maðliche libben, *and* rihtliche, *and* arfastliche, anbidende ða eadi 8
hope *and* ðane to-cyme of ðare² michele blisse of Criste(s), gode(s)
sune, þanne he cumþ eftsones to sceawien him seluen, *and* to ȝielden
alle ðo behotes ðe he us behiet, þat is, þat he wile þane lichame of
ure e(a)dmodnesse *in* to michele brihtnesse³ wanden, ðat he scal 12
scinen swa *briht* swa sunne, emlich ðo aingles mid gode æure mo
on merhþe *and* on blisse.' Ne mai no man ðese eadi hope habben,
bute he hit wel ilieue and soðliche luuie. For ði sade Dauið, ðe
profiete: Multi dicunt: quis ostendit nobis bona? 'Maniȝe 16
seggeð,' (he) sade, 'ðe noht wel ne belieueð: Hwo is, þat us muȝe⁴
sceawin ða gode ðe ȝe us behoteð⁵? Hier we muȝen isien al ða
werdles wele *and* habben; of ðan ðe ȝie behoteþ is a wene hweðer
we it habben muȝen.' Hwat seist þu, Dauið? Hafst þu aniȝe 20
sikernesse herof? Tach vs,⁶ wisse us, hit is nied! Signatum
est super nos lumen uultus tui, domine; dedisti leticiam
in corde meo. 'Ȝise,' (he) seið, 'we bieð all siker of godes
behate, forðan ðat liht of his ansiene is (ȝe)marked riht uppen 24
us. Ich hine icnawe, *and* wel ilieue be are tacne ðe he hafð iȝiuen
me.' Dedisti leticiam in corde meo, 'Ðu, hlauerd, ȝaue blisse
on mire herte, ðat me nis naht of alles woreldes blisse; and þese ðu
hauest iȝiuen me to earres of ðare eche blisse.' Lieue saule, ȝif ðu 28
ðese blisse hauest on ðine hierte, ðe ne cumþ of nanes woreldes
blisse, ðane miht þu bien siker mid⁷ godes grace; *and* ȝif ðu ne
hafdst, ne swic ðu naure niht ne dai ær ðu hes habbe. Ac hærce
hwat tes ilke profiete seið be him ðe hes hadde biȝeten: Dilex- 32
isti iusticiam et odisti iniquitatem, propterea vnxit te

---

¹ hope *blotted out.*   ² r *corr. from* s.   ³ *Before* h *an* s *blotted out.*
⁴ muȝen *MS.*   ⁵ teð *on erasure.*   ⁶ *page* 19.
⁷ mid *corrected over of.*

said, 'thou lovedst righteousness and hatedst unrighteousness, therefore thy Lord hath anointed thee with the oil of bliss.' Oil has three qualities in it: it will float over all liquids (so will God's love be over all other loves); it will burn in the lamp brightly (so will this virtue give good example to all them that dwell in God's house); it softens all hardness (so does this holy bliss all sorrow for sins). Well [is] him that may get it! All the men who labour in this toilsome world, they all labour for some hope they have, which often deceives them in the end. David: *In illa die peribunt omnes cogitationes eorum,* 'At their end-day all their thoughts they had thought to carry out will perish.' But those who labour for this blessed hope, they are not deceived. Have thou no trust in gold nor in silver, nor in any possessions of the world, nor even in man. It is written: *Maledictus homo qui confidit in homine,* 'Cursed be the man who hath his trust in man, who turneth his heart and his thoughts more to man's service than to God's.' Let all thy trust be upon our Saviour Christ, who will raise thee and thy body from death as truly as He Himself arose from death, and will bring thee unto eternal life! If thou shouldst live as long as this world lasteth, and always sufferdst pain, thou couldst not earn so much happiness as is promised to thee. But thy Lord earned it on the holy cross; therefore thou hast to bear thy cross after His instruction, who said: *Qui vult venire post me, tollat crucem suam et sequatur me,* 'Who will come after Me into Heaven, let him bear his cross on earth as I did, and so he may follow Me and come where I am.' The cross betokens pain. Pain thyself for His love who suffered pain for thee unto death, in fasting, and in watching, and in patience, and in restraining thy self-will. If thou thus doest, then thou bearest thy cross. Never let it seem to thee so bitter, that this hope does not sweeten it. So it did all the holy martyrs. All the kinds of pains men might do to them men did to them; this holy virtue made them all sweet to them. So it did [make sweet] to all deus deus[1] tuus oleo leticie, 'Forðan,' he sade, 'ðat tu luuedest rihtwisnesse *and* hatedest unri(h)twisnesse, for ði haueð ðin lauerd ismered þe mid ða ele of blisse.' Ele hafð þrie ȝekynden on him: hit wile flotten ouer[2] alle wætes, swa wile godes luue bien ouer alle oðre luuen; hit wile on lampe bernen brihte[3], swa wile ðes mihte gode forbisne ȝiuen alle hem ðe on godes huse wunien; hie liþegað (alle [h]ardnesse), swa dieð ðies haliȝe blisse alle sarinesses of sennes. Wel him ðe hes biȝeten mai! Alle ðo menn ðe swinkeð on ðessere swinkfulle[4] world, alle hie swinkeð for sumere hope ðe hie habbeð, ðe hem ofte aten ande beswikð. Dauið: In illa die peribunt[5] omnes cogitaciones eorum, 'On here ænde-daiȝe forwurðeð alle here þohtes ðe hie hadden iþoht to donne.' Ac ðo ðe swinkeð for ðessere eadi hope, hie ne bieð naht becaht. Ne haue ðu hope te golde ne to seluer, ne to none[6] wor(d)lles eihte, ne forðen te manne. Hit is iwriten: Maledictus homo qui confidit in homine, 'ȝewerȝed bie ðe mann þe haueð his hope te manne, þe[7] want his herte *and* his (ȝeþanc[8]) more to mannes seruise ðanne te godes.' All bie ðin hope uppen ure halende Criste, þe wile araren þe *and* þine[9] lichame of deaðe swa soðliche swa he him self aros of deaðe, *and* bringe þe to ðan eche lif! Gif ðu liuedest swa lange swa ðes woreld ilast, *and* æure þoledest pine, ne mihtest ðu of-earnin swa michel eadinesse swa ðe is behaten. Ac ðin lauerd hes ofearnede on ðare hali rode; for ði ðu aust te berene ðine rode after his wissinge, ðe sade: Qui uult uenire post me, tollat crucem suam et sequatur me, 'Se ðe wile cumen after me in to heuene, bere his rode on ierðe swa ic dede, *and* swo he mai me folȝin *and* cumen ðar ic am.' Rode tacnieð pine. Pine ðe seluen for his luue ðe ðolede pine for ðe anon to ðe deaðe, on fasten *and* on wacchen *and* on þolemodnesse, *and* on ðine awene wille to laten. ȝif[10] ðu ðus dost, ðanne berest þu þin rode. Ne þinche hit te næure swa bitter, ðat þies hope hit ne sw(i)eteð. Swa hie dede alle ðo halie martirs. Alle ðas kennes pines ðe me hem mihte don me hem dede; all ðis halie mihte hes makede hem swiete. Swa hie dede alle ðe hali

---

[1] *deus deus on erasure.* [2] *Corrected from* osier. [3] *Five or six words erased.*
[4] fullle *MS.* [5] b *corrected over* d. [6] nones *MS.* [7] *page* 20.
[8] *Written above* seruise. [9] þ *corr. from* b. [10] 3 *corrected from* G.

the holy confessors and the holy virgins all that they suffered through it. So it does still in this time to monks, canons, anchorites, and hermits. For this blessed hope they forsake father and mother, wife and children, house and home, and all the world's weal and bliss. So do pilgrims who forsake their own country, and go into other lands. So ought to do all who ever do any good. They all shall do it in order to have reward from God Almighty in the other world and not here; that be their hope! The holy apostle calls these three holy virtues together, *fidem, spem, caritatem*, and says that this which is called *caritas*, is the highest and best of these three, and so it is above all the others. Therefore it shall last evermore, as well in this world as in the other. Of it, we will tell something by God's grace.

Of charity.

Caritas is very holy, because God Himself is called *caritas*, that is, love of God and man. God dwells within all who have this holy love, and they within God. Understand now well, how God dwells in the man who has this blessed virtue, and so thou mayst know, whether God dwells in thee and whether thou hast this virtue. God dwells in the man who loves Him in such a wise that He kindles his heart and his thoughts with the fire which Christ brought on earth. At first He gives him light in his heart, in order to see the good which he ought to do. Of this blessed light said St. John the Evangelist: *Erat lux vera quae illuminat omnem hominem venientem in hunc mundum.* He said of Christ, God's Son, that 'He was the true light which lighteth every man that cometh into this life.' He is called God's Wisdom. He instructs the man's thoughts to whom He comes, either through holy writings or through holy sermons, which He sends him through some wise man in whom He is dwelling. Then comes the Holy Ghost who is an all burning fire, as He came upon the apostles, and inflames the heart, and reminds it often by day and by night and brings it into good will. If confessores and ðe hali uirgines all ðat hie ðoleden ðurh hire. Swa hie doð ȝiet on ðese time munekes, kanunekes, ancres, and eremites. For ðessere eadi hope hie forlateð fader and moder, wif and children, hus and ham, and alle worldes wele and blisse. Swa doð pilegrimes ðe lateþ her awen eard, and fareð in to oðre lande. Swo aweð to donne alle ðe æure ani god doð. Alle hie hit don for to habben lean of godalmihtin on ðare oðre worled and naht hier; þat bie here hope! Đe hali apostel namneð ðese þrie haliȝe mihtes to-gedere, fidem, spem, karitatem[1], and seggeð þat þies ðe hatte karitas, is heiȝest and betst of ðese þrie, and swo hie is ouer alle oðre. For ðan hie scal æure mo ȝelasten, aiðer on ðessere worled and ec on ðare oðre. Of hire we willeð sumdæl keðen be godes grace.

Of charite.

CARITAS is swiðe hali, forðan ðe godd self is icleped karitas, þat is, godes luue and mannes. Alle ðe habbeð ðese halie luue, godd wuneð inne hem, and hie inne gode. Vnderstond nu wel, hu godd wuneð on ða manne ðe ðese eadi mihte haueð, and swa ðu miht ȝecnawen, ȝif godd wuneð on ðe and ȝif ðu ðese mihte hafst. Godd wuneð on ða manne ðe him luueð. On ðelliche wise þat is, þat he his herte (and) his ȝeþanc on-alð mid ða fiere ðe Crist brohte on ierðe. Arst he ȝifð (him) liht on ðare hierte, to ȝesiene ðat god ðat he aw te donne. Of ðesen eadiȝen lihte[2] sade sanctus Iohannes ðe godspellere: Erat lux uera que illuminat omnem hominem uenientem[3] in hunc mundum. He sade be Criste, godes sune, þat 'he was ðat soðe liht þe lihteþ alche manne ðe cumþ on ðese liue.' He is icleped godes wisdom. He wisseð ðes mannes iðang[c] ðe he to-cumð, oðer ðurh haliȝe writes oðer ðurh hali sermuns, þe he him ðurh sume wise manne ðe he is inne wuniende[4], sant. Þanne cumþ ðe hali gast ðe is all fier barnende, swa he com up ðe apostles, and analð[5] ðe hierte, and meneȝeð hie ofte be daiȝe and be nihte, and bringþ hie on gode wille. Gif ðe herte bliðeliche underfoð godes hali wordes ðe

---

[1] page 21.   [2] Corr. from ðese eadiȝe mihte.   [3] u on erasure.
[4] wudiende him MS.   [5] anald MS.

the heart blithely receives God's holy words which come from His Son, who is Wisdom, and receives them with much love as the Holy Ghost, who is the Love of both of them: then comes thereafter Almighty God the Father and gives the power to do all this, and [they] make their abode in this blessed soul. Thus Christ promised that He and His Father would love the man and be abiding with him who would love Him and keep His words. Thus says the Gospel: *Si quis diligit me, sermonem meum servabit; et pater meus diliget eum, et mansionem apud eum faciemus.*

Now, thou hast heard, how God abides in the man who loves Him; hear now, how the man may abide within God, as St. John says: *Qui manet in caritate, in Deo manet, et Deus in eo,* 'He that dwelleth in love, dwelleth in God, and God in him.' Some misunderstand here the holy Writ, [and many a one] assumes, if he gives blithely to eat and to drink, and of his other property gives for God's love blithely, and himself lies in some cardinal sin, which he will not give up, but hopes to be saved through his doing so much for God's love. Against this says God Himself: *Si recte offers, et non recte dividis, peccasti,* 'If thou rightly offerest and doest not rightly divide, thou sinnest more than thou doest good.' Thou givest thy own to God, and thyself to the devil. That is not rightly divided; for better is a good soul, than all the world with all its possessions. If thou lovest the same thing that God firmly forbids thee, how canst thou then abide in charity, that is, love of God and of men? How canst thou love thy neighbour as thyself, when thou lovest not thyself? The holy Writ says: *Qui diligit iniquitatem, odit animam suam,* 'The man who loves unrighteousness, hates his own soul.' For when he breaks God's forbidding, then he is unrighteous; and through his unrighteousness he brings his soul into the pain of hell. Nevertheless let the man never cease to give alms, because, whatsoever becomes of him, he remains not unrewarded. If thou wilt surely abide in charity and in God, then do thou as we find it

OF CHARITY.

cumþ fram[1] his sune, ðe is wisedom, *and* hes mid michele luue underfoð al swa ðane hali gast, ðe is here beire luue : ðanne ðar after cumþ almihti godd ðe fader *and* ȝifð ðe mihte al[2] ðis te donne, *and* makieð here wunienge on ðessere eadi saule. Þus behet Crist ðat þe mann ðe him wolde luuiȝen *and* his wordes healden : þat he *and* his fader hine scolden luuiȝen *and* mid him wuniende b(i)en. Þus seieð ðat goddspell: Si quis diligit me, sermonem meum seruabit; et pater meus diliget eum, et mansionem apud[3] eum faciemus. Nu ðu hafst ȝeherd, hu godd wuneð on ðe manne ðe him luueð; harke nu, hu ðe man mai wuniȝen inne gode, al swo sanctus Iohannes seið: Qui manet in karitate, in deo manet, et deus[4] in eo, ' Se ðe wuneð on karite, he wuneð on gode, *and* godd on him.' Sume mis-understondet[5] (hier) ðis hali writt, weneð, ȝif he ȝifð bleðeliche to eten *and* to drinken, *and* of his oðer eihte doþ for godes luue bleðeliche, and him self lið on sume heaued-senne, ne ðo ne wile læten, ac hopeð te bien iboreȝen ðurh ðat he dieð swa michel for godes luue[6]. Hier aȝean seið god him self: Si recte offers, et non recte diuidis, peccasti, ' Gif ðu riht offrest *and* noht riht ne sciftst, ðu senegest mare ðan ðu god do.' Du ȝifst[7] ðine eihte gode, *and* ðe seluen ðe dieule[8]. Þat nis naht riht iscift ; for ðan betere is an god saule, ðan all ðe woreld mid all hire eihte. Gif ðu luuest ðat ilke þing ðe godd fastliche ðe forbett[9], hu miht ðu ðanne wuniȝen on karite, þat is, luue of gode *and* of mannen ? Hu miht ðu luuiȝen ðine nexte al swa ðe seluen, (ðane þu ne luuest noht þe seluen ?) Ðat hali writ seið : Qui diligit iniquitatem, odit animam suam, ' Þe man ðe luueð unriht-wisnesse, he hateð his awene saule.' Forðan ðanne he brecþ godes forbod, þanne is he un-rihtwis; *and* ðurh his unrihtwisnesse he bri[n]gþ his saule in to helle pine. Naðelas ne læte ðe mann neure almesse te donne[10], for ðan[11], hwat swo æure of him betide, ne wurþ hie naht un-forȝolden. Ȝif ðu wilt sikerliche wuniȝen on karite *and* on gode, þanne do ðu alswa we hit a boke finden

---

[1] f *corr. from* a.   [2] *page* 22.   [3] apuð *MS.*   [4] ðs *MS.*
[5] t *on erasure.*   [6] luuen *MS.*   [7] ȝ *corr. from* G.
[8] ð. d. *on erasure.*   [9] forbettt *MS.*   [10] *page* 23.
[11] for ðan *twice in MS., the first crossed red.*

written in the book, that is, that thou shouldst work, with right belief and with firm hope and with true love the good things which thou believest. All thou knowest that God forbids, avoid doing it in every way; and if thou breakest any [of His commandments], do penance anon. Never suffer the devil to reign in thee through any sin, but have thy thoughts fixed in God, and beg His forgiveness, and humbly entreat Him to give thee might and strength to withstand the devil's temptations and the lusts of thy flesh. Then thou wilt truly abide in God, if thou thinkest more of Him than thou doest of any thing in the world, by day and by night, for thou hast great need that He always be thy shield against all evils, and thy helper to all good. If thou hast thus thy love in God, it then behooves thee, if thou wilt have charity in thee, to be well aware that thou shouldst love thy neighbour, that is, every man who bears thy likeness. Of this the holy apostle Paul warns us, who says thus: *Si distribuero omnes facultates meas in cibos pauperum,* 'If I give all that I have to wretched men, and in addition to that give my body to be burned all to dust for God's love, and I hate a single man, then I have not charity, nor may I be saved in any wise, except I have it.' St. Gregory gives an example of this, that just as no web can be woven without two beams, so charity can never be finished without two loves, that is, God's and man's, and just as many threads are necessary ere it be made, so is much reflecting of thoughts and words and works needful to charity during all thy life-time, ere it be ordained in thee as it is necessary. It is a great pity for many a man who is in great error about himself, and presumes that he is wise and that he has with him love of God and man, but has none. Many a man says in words that he loves God. The true love of God is rather in works than in words. If thou lovest nothing in the world by which thou mayst lose God's love or man's; and wrath does not abide with thee one day's length, but thou either forgivest every trespass [against thee] or requitest [it] with love: if thou doest thus, iwriten, þat is, ðat tu mid rihte ȝeleaue *and* mid faste hope *and* mid soðe luue bie werchind*e* ðat god ðe ðu iliefst. Al ðat ðu wast ðat godd forbett, forbuh hit to donne on alle wise*n* ; and ȝif ðu au(h)t tebrecst, ano*n* siech ðu ðine bote. Ne ðole ðu naure 4 ðat dieuel rixi on ðe for none senne¹, ac fastliche haue ðin iþanc te godd, *and* bide him forȝiuenesse, *and* besiec him eadmodliche ðat he ȝiue ðe mihte *and* strengþe to wiðstanden aȝeanes dieules fondinges *and* ðine flesches lustes. Danne wunest ðu sikerliche 8 on gode, þanne ðu þen[c]st more of him ðanne ðu do of aniȝe þinge of ðare worel d, be daiȝe *and* be nihte, for ðare michele niede ðe ðu hauest þ*at* he æure bie þi*n* sceld aȝeanes alle eueles, *and* þi*n* helpend to alle gode. Danne ðu ðus hauest ðine luue te gode, 12 ðanne behoueð ðe ðat ðu bie wel warr þ*at* tu luuiȝe ðine nexte, ðat is, aurich man*n* ðe berð ðin anlicnesse, ȝif² þu karite scalt habbe*n* on ðe. Herof us warneð ðe holi apostel Paul*us*, *and* ðus seiȝeð: Si distribuero omnes facultates meas in cibos 16 pau*per*um, 'Gif ic dale all ðat ic habbe wrecche mannen, *and* ȝiet ðar uppen ȝiue mine lichame all to barnen to duste for godes luue, *and* ich hatede anlepine mann, ðanne ne habbe ic naht charite, ne ich iboreȝen a none wise ne mai bie*n*, bute ic hes habbe.' 20 Sanc*tus* Gregori*us* seið hier on ane forbisne, þat al swa nan webb ne mai bie*n* iweue*n* wið-ute*n* twa beames, al swo ne mai næure karite bien fulfremed wið-ute*n* twa luues, þat is, godes *and* mannes, and alswo³ ðar behoueð to maniȝe þreades ær hit bie full- 24 wroht, al swo behoueþ to charite on alle ðines liues time michel embeþanc of þohtes⁴ *and* of wordes *and* of werkes, ær hie bie ȝedihd on ðe swa swa hit nied is⁵. Hit is a michel reunesse of mani ma*n*n ðe is on michele dwele on him seluen, wenþ þat he bie 28 wis *and* ðat he haue mid him godes luue and ma*n*nes, *and* ne haueð naht. Mani man*n* seið mid wordes þ*at* he godd luueð. Þe soðe luue of godd, hie is mare on werkes ðanne on wordes. Gif ðu na þing ne luuest on ðare worel d ðurh hwat ðu miht forliesen godes 32 luue oðer ma*n*nes ; ne wraððe mid ðe ne wuneð ones daiȝes længe, ac alchne gylt forȝifst oðe mid luue sah(t)lest: ðanne ðu ðus

¹ sennne *MS.*   ² 3 *corr. from* G.   ³ *page* 24.
⁴ *Corr. from* þoltes.   ⁵ *a letter erased after* s.

then thou hast charity in thee and assuredly God's love and man's. If thou doest not this, do not deceive thyself by believing that Christ abides with thee, or thou with Him, whilst thou hast wrath or envy in thee, or lovest any thing in this false world against His commandment. Of this St. John the Evangelist bears witness, who says thus: *Qui diligit mundum, non est caritas patris in eo*, 'Whoso loveth this world, the love of the Father the Almighty God is not in him.' Woe then to every man who is so much deprived of understanding, that he, through this false love of the treacherous world, should lose the sweet love of Christ and the joy of the everlasting land! It may happen that some one, who sees or hears this, thinks: 'How can I dwell in the world and not love it? Or how can I dwell therein, and also be saved?' According to what holy Writ says: 'Thou who dwellest in the world, and art bound therein with house and with wedded wife and with children, if thou wilt be saved, thou oughtst to follow the righteous and simple Job, who lived in the world with wife and with children, and with great property, which was shared in by all the needful, and who was also tempted with great wealth, and with great distress, and with great sickness, and with many evil upbraidings, both from his own wife and also from his own friends, from relations and from strangers, and from the devil himself; but none could bereave him of this holy virtue which we are speaking about, that is, charity, of God's love or man's, nor break this patience with one intemperate word.' Listen here, listen here, ye proud men, the devil's followers, who follow the devil, that stirs up wrath and strife and bitter words and the forbidden cursings, and will have neither place of rest nor any softness in your heart, on which the Holy Ghost might rest Himself! Cease, cease, if ye will have the Holy Ghost dwelling with you, and drive the fellowship of the cursed spirit from you. Know forsooth, ye worldly men, who are bound in the world, that except ye love the

OF CHARITY. 41

dest, ðanne hafst ðu charite mid ðe *and* iwis godes luue *and* mannes. Gif ðu ðis ne diest, ne beswic ðu noht ðe seluen ðat tu ilieue ðat Crist wunize mid ðe, oðer ðu mid him, all ðare hwile ðe ðu wraððe oðer nið hauest mid te, oðer ani þing on ðese lease worldluuest azeanes his bebode. Hier of berþ zewitnesse *sanctus* Iohannes ðe godspellere, *and* þus seið: Qui diligit mundum, non est charitas patris in eo, 'Se ðe luueð ðese worldes fader luue god-almihtines nis naht an him.' Wa ðan ilke manne ðe is swa¹ swiðe wittes bedæld, ðat he, for ðessere lease luue of ðe swikele world, scal forliesen ðe swete luue of Criste *and* ðe merhðe of ðe liuizende lande²! Hit mai ilimpen ðat sum mann, ðe ðis zeseðh oðer zeherð, þat he þen(c)þ³: 'Hu mai ic on ðane world wunizen *and* naht hes ne luuizen? Oðer hu mai ic ðær on wunizen, *and* ec be zeborzen?' After ðan ðe ðat hali writt seið: 'Ðu ðe wunest on ðære worldes, *and* art ðar inne ibunde mid huse *and* mid weddede wiue *and* mid childre, swa swa ðu wilt bien zeborezen, ðu aust te folzin ðane rih[t]wise *and* onfald Iob⁴, ðe was wunizende on ðare world mid wiue *and* mid children, *and* mid michelere heihte, þe was zemanlich alle niedfullien, ðe was iec fonded mid michele wele, *and* mid michelere nafte, *and* mid michel unhæle, *and* mid manize euele upbreides, aiðer of his azene wiue *and* ec of his auene frienden⁵, of sibbe *and* of framde, *and* of ðe selue dieule; swa nan ne mihte him benemen ðas halize mihte ðe we embe spekeð, þat is, charite, godes luue ne mannes, ne ðis ðolemodnesse tobrecen naht mid one unbehealdene worde.' Hlesteð hider, hlesteð hider, ze modi menn, ðes dieules folzeres, ðe folzið ðe dieule⁶, ðe ararð upp ðe wraððhes *and* þe cheastes *and* te bitere wordes *and* te forbodene werzinges⁷, ðe ne willeð nane reste ne nane soft(n)esse on zeure herte habben, ðar ðe hali gast him mihte resten! Zeswikeð, iswikeð⁸, al swa ze willeð ðes hali-gastes wunienge habben mid zeu, *and* ðas zewerzede gaste(s) felauscipe fram e(u)wz driuen. Wite ze te soðe, ze worldmenn, ðe bieð on ðare world ibunden, bute zie ðeses rihtwises mannes lif luuizen

---

¹ swa *twice in the MS., the first underlined.*
² terra uiuentium, *gloss at the side.*   ³ *page 25.*
⁴ iustus et simplex erat, *added at the side.*   ⁵ friennden *MS.*
⁶ d *corrected from* ð.   ⁷ werzinginges *MS., the last g corr. from e.*   ⁸ -d *MS.*

life of this righteous man and follow [it], ye shall never come to the great happiness which he [Job] has with God Almighty. Those, who have forsaken this deceitful world and serve our Lord in orders, follow Daniel, the holy prophet, who is called *vir desideriorum*, that is, the man who was never overcome by the covetousness of the world, and was never defiled by the lusts of the flesh, and never yearned or cared for, or loved any of the things which were in this world, but his neighbour and the lawful things which God had bidden him to do. Nevertheless, above all things he loved after God *abstinentiam, castitatem*, that is, abstinence from meat, drink, and all kinds of lecheries. None of them could defile him. Although he was long brought up and nourished in [the] king's retinue, it was more agreeable to him to eat beans and peas and such coarse meats, and to drink water, than the costly dishes or the good wines which came from the king. All who have forsaken this world for God's sake, must follow this holy man Daniel in abstaining from all evil things, and in avoiding all kinds of lecheries, if they will attain the great happiness which Daniel has with the angels in Heaven. The spiritual shepherds, who must both guard and direct those who are in the world, and also those who are without, follow Noah, the good steersman, who was very dear and pleasing to God through the great obedience [with] which he wrought for many years, ere he could make the ark; and he afterwards steered it in such a way in the great terrible flood which overflooded all the earth, amidst strong winds and storms, that he lost none of those whom God had intrusted him to keep alive and to bring to land. So ought the spiritual steersmen to steer the ark of the holy Church in such a way that they lose neither a body nor a soul of it, through no wind of human temptation, nor through any storm of devilish temptation; and again, in fair weather, they should not be too sure, because so many little drops of various kinds of carelessness might come into the boat of souls, that they might sink with all

and folʒin, ne cume ʒe næure mo to ðare michele eadinesse ðe he
haueð mid godalmihtin. Do ðe ðese swikele woreld habbeð for-
laten¹ *and* seruið ure drihten *on* religiu*n*, hie folʒið Daniele, ðe
hali profiete, þe is icleped uir desideri(o)ru*m*², ðat is, ðe man*n* 4
ðe naure³ worldes ʒitsinge n(e)⁴ ouerca*m*, ne næure ðe flesliches
lustes hi*m*⁵ ne befielde, ne no*n* ðare ðinge ðe on ðesse worlde
waren⁶ he ne ʒernde, ne he ne rohte, ne he ne luuede, bute his
nexte *and* ðo laʒeliche þing ðe god him hadde ʒehote te don*n*e. 8
Naðelæs, ouer alle þing he luuede under gode abstine*n*cia*m*,
castitate*m*, þ*at* is, wiðheal[d]nesse of metes *and* of dre*n*ches, *and*
of alles ke*n*nes galnesses. Ne mihte hi*m* na*ð*er befele*n*. Swa swa he
was on kynges hyrde lange ifedd *and* ʒefostred, leuere hi*m* was to 1*²*
eten bene*n* *and* pese*n* *and* swilche unorne metes, *and* ðat water to
dri*n*ken, ðan*n*e hi*m* ware ðo derewurðe sondes ðe come*n* fro ðe
kynge, oðer ðe gode wines. Alle ðe ðese woreld for godes luue
habbeð⁷ forlaten, alle hie mote*n* ðisne hali man*n* Daniele folʒin 1*⁶*
mid wiðhealdenesse of alle euele þinges, *and* mid clan*n*esse fram
alles ke*n*nes galnesse(s), swa swa hie willeð cume*n* to ðare michele
eadinesse ðe⁸ Daniel haueð mid ðo angles on heuene. De gastliche hierdes, ðe scule*n* boðe loki*n* *and* stieren ðo ðe bieð in ðare 2*⁰*
woreld, *and* ec (ðo) ðe bieð ute, hie folʒið Noe ðane gode stieres-
ma*n*n, ðe gode was swiðe lief *and* ʒecweme for ðare muchele hersumnesse ðe he maniʒe wi*n*tre swanc, ær he (ða) arche mihte habbe*n*
ʒemaked, *and* seððen hie swa stierde on ðe muchele wilde flode ðe 2*⁴*
ouerʒiede all midden*e*ard, mang stro*n*ge wi*n*des *and* stormes, ðat
he ðarof ne forleas naþing ðe godd hi*m* hadde betaht to liue *and*
to londe to bringe*n*. Swa scule ða gastlich(e)⁹ stieres-men*n* (stere*n*)
ða arche of ðe hali cherche, ðat hie ðarof ne for-liesen ne lichame 2*⁸*
ne saule, for none winde of man*n*liche fandinge,¹⁰ ne for none
storme of dieuliche fandi*n*ge ; *and* eft, on faire wedere, ne bien hie
naht to sikere, forðan swo maniʒe litle dropes of maniʒes ke*n*nes
ʒemeleastes mihte*n* cume*n* in to ðe saule bote, ðat hie mihte*n* sinke*n* 3*²*
mid alle hire biʒeates ; ac lokien¹¹ hie alle ðe wið-i*n*nen scipes borde

¹ *page* 26.   ² *The last* r *on erasure.*   ³ *After this fourteen letters erased.*
⁴ e *red over* no.   ⁵ i *on erasure.*
⁶ was *MS.*   ⁷ habbed *MS.*   ⁸ ð *corr. from* o.
⁹ e *above erasure.*   ¹⁰ *page* 27.   ¹¹ lokieð *MS.*

its contents; but let them all take heed who dwell within the board of the ship, that they be obedient and buxom to their steersman, if they wish to come to the everlasting land with soul and with body. And listen what the Lord who owns the ship says to the steersmen and to all who dwell therein: *Qui vos audit, me audit,* 'Whoso listens to your counsel,' says He, 'listens to Myself; and whoso forsakes you and your lore, forsakes full surely Myself.' This He says to the steersmen. In great peril we all sail who sail *in hoc mare magnum,* 'in this great sea of the bitter world.' Of our steersmen is written: *Ascendunt usque ad coelos, et descendunt usque ad abyssos,* 'They mount up to Heaven' in their spiritual thoughts in order to view the great joy of the kingdom of Heaven, in order to view the winds and the evil storms which come from the devil's blasts, and in order to warn us lest our ropes break, which are woven of three strings, of right belief and of firm hope in God and of the true love which is called charity, which Christ loves most. Again, it is said that 'they go down to the depths' in their thoughts, in order again to warn us against the stone-rocks of the hard heart which never will soften with any water of wisdom, but if a ship comes thereto it breaks up. So does the unwise man who comes to the unbelieving man that neither will nor can understand God's lore through the hardness of his heart: he [the unwise man] breaks up, if he has any good will, for he hurts his good will. And he breaks up with such words: 'What doest thou?' he [the unbelieving man] says, 'thou givest away all that thou hast! If thou listenest to preachers and priests and monks and these ordained men, thou wilt never have any goods. They would swallow all the world, if they could. Be a faithful man and keep thy goods; thou wilt find few who will give thee anything, except they do it for a reason.' The unguarded man who hears this, thinks that he [the unbeliever] gives him good counsel. If he before did little for God, after that he does much less; and so he perishes, because he will neither listen to nor follow his priest's lore nor his counsel. Charity

OF CHARITY.

wuniȝeð, þat hie bien hersum and leðebeiȝe here stieres-manne[1], swa swa hie willeð cumen to ðe liuiende lande mid saule and mid lichame. And hlesteð hwat ðe hlauerd seið, ðe ðat scip auh, to ðe stieresmannen and to alle ðe ðar inne wuniȝeð : Qui uos audit, me audit, 'Se ðe ȝeu(w)er ra(d)[2] hlest,' he seið, 'he hlest me seluen; and se ðe ȝew forsakþ and ȝewere lare, he forsakþ fullȝe-wiss me seluen.' Þis he seið[3] to ða stieresmannen. On michele hahte we fareð alle ðe fareð in hoc mare magnum, 'on ðessere michele sea of ðare bitere woreld.' Of ure stieresman is ȝewriten: Ascendunt usque ad celos, et descendunt usque ad abissos, 'Hie stieð up to heuene' mid here gastliche þohtes for to sceawin ðe michele merhðe of heuene riche, for to sceawin ðe windes and ðe euele stormes[4] ðe cumeð of deules blastes, and for us te warnin þat ure ropes ne to-breken, ðe bieð ibroiden mid þrie strænges, of rihte ileaue and of faste hope te gode and of ðare soðe luue[5] ðe is ihoten carite, ðe Crist mæst luueð. Eft hit seið ðat hie stikð niðer in to nielnesse[6] mid here ðohtes, for us eft to warnin wið ðo stanroches of ðe harde hierte ðe næure ne wile nexin for none watere of wisdome, ac ȝif ðar cumþ scip to hit tobrekð. Alswo doð ðat unwise mann ðe cumþ to ðan unbiliefde manne ðe ne wile ne ne mai godes lare understanden for his herte hardnesse : he to-brekð[7], ȝif he ani god wille hafð, forðan he hert his gode wille. And hie tobrecþ[8] mid þelliche wordes: 'Hwat dest þu?' he seið, 'ðu dalst al ðat tu hafst ! Wile ðu hlesten spelleres and pr(i)estes and munekes and þese hadede mannen, ne scalt ðu næure habben god. Hie wolden for(i)swelȝen all ðe woreld, ȝif hie mihten. Be trewe mann and halt tin god; þu finst feawe ðe wile ȝiuen ðe ani þing, bute hie witen hwarfore.' Þe unware mann ðe ðis ȝeherð, ðingþ ðat he seið him god rad. Ȝif[9] he arrer dede litel te gode, ðar after he doð michel(e) lasse ; and swo he forfarð, for ðan ðe he his priestes lare ne his ræd lesten ne folȝin ne wile. Carite sprat his bowes[10] on bræde and on lengðe swiðe ferr.

---

[1] The 2nd e destroyed. [2] d above erasure. [3] seid MS.

[4] stormes euele MS., with signs of transposition.

[5] Corr. from lirue. [6] abissos on the margin. [7] -d MS.

[8] page 28.—At the bottom of p. 27 in a different hand: qui cum in forma dei e(s)set non rapinam arbitratus est semet.

[9] 3 corr. from G. [10] u altered to w.

spreads its boughs very far in breadth and in length. It has caused me to speak further than I had intended. But now, by God's help, I will turn to the holy virtues just as I had begun before. But methinks that thou lookest wayward, and appearest heavy, and it is [for] me too much labour to think or to speak about them, unless thou wilt listen to it with good will and understand them.

How the Soul answers and says:

I entreat thee for the same Lord who created thee, to help me, that thou wilt bring forth and teach me these holy virtues just as thou hast begun and laid the ground-work of them. For they are very unknown to me because of the many vices which I have had in me too long. But now I will stop them, and with God's help desist from them, and keep my thoughts in thy teaching. For the holy virtue which is called charity, I beseech and beg thee that thou puttest in writing this hallowed lore, because I ponder much whilst I dwell in this wretched body, and often forget what would be good to me to keep; and it will also help some other soul.

How Reason answers and thus says:

Methinks that thou wilt blithely understand and learn God's teaching; and that, I like very well, because it is said in the holy Gospel: *Qui est ex Deo, verba Dei audit,* 'He that is of God heareth blithely God's words.' Now an example comes into my mind which St. Gregory tells us: *Qui virtutes sine humilitate congregat, quasi in vento pulverem portat,* 'He that gathers virtues without humility,' he says, 'he is like the man who bears dust in the wind.' Therefore methinks it is wise, that we first of all things speak of this holy virtue, without which none may be restrained to any advantage or to any good.

Hie me haueð idon speken forðer ðane ic hadde ȝeþouht. Ac nu ic wile wænden to ðe hali mihtes alswo ich ær hadde iȝunnen be godes fultume. Ac me þincþ ðat tu lokest aweiward, *and* heuiliche latst, and hit is me to muchel iswinch ðar embe to þenken[1] oðer to speken, bute ȝif ðu woldest mid god wille ðarto lhesten *and* hes understanden.

Hu andswereð ðe saule *and* seið:

ICH ðe bidde for ðan ilche hlauerd ðe ðe iscop, me to helpe, ðat alswo ðu hauest ȝegunnen *and* ðane grundwall ileid of ðese hali mihtes, ðat tu hes forð-bringe *and* me hes tæche[2]. Forðan hie bieð me swiðe unbecnawe for ðe maniȝe unðeawes ðe ic mid me to longe habbe ihafd. Ac nu ic hes wile leten, *and* mid godes fultume of hem ȝeswiken, and min ȝeþanc to ðine lore healden. For ðare hali mihte ðe cariteð is icleped, ic ðe besechhe *and* bidde ðat tu ðese halwende lore on write sette, for ðan ic am michel þenchinde ðar hwile ðe ic on ðese wrecche lichame am wuniende, *and* ofte forȝete ðat me god wære te healden; and ec sum oðer saule hit wile helpen.

[3]Hu andswereð Scadwisnesse *and* þus seið:

DAS þe me þincþ þu wilt godes lore bliðeliche understonden *and* liernin; *and* ðat me likeð swiðe wel, forði ðat hit seið on ðe hali godspelle: Qui est ex deo, uerba dei audit, 'Se ðe is of gode, he harkeð bleðeliche godes wordes.' Nu me cumþ on iþanke an forbisne þe sanctus Gregorius us seið[4]: Qui uirtutes sine humilitate congregat, quasi in uento puluerem portat, 'Se ðe gadereð mihtes wiðuten eadmodnesse,' he seið, 'he is ilich ðo manne ðe berð dust amidewarde ðe winde.' For ði me þingþ þat is wisdom, ðat we alre ðinge arst speken of ðessere hali mihte, wið[5]-uten hwam non ne mai bien wiðhealden te none freme ne te none gode.

---

[1] *MS.* þennken.   [2] c *corr. from* s.   [3] *page* 29.
[4] *MS.* seid.   *MS.* wid.

Of humility.

This holy virtue about which we speak, is called *humilitas*, that is, humility. The holy apostle calls it *virtutem Christi*, 'Christ's own virtue,' because through His manhood, and through the great humility He showed with it, as an example to all mankind, He overcame [the] devil, and all his power over the deceived world. So thou mayst also, if thou wilt learn this virtue of Him, and follow Him. *Discite a me, quia mitis sum et humilis corde, et invenietis requiem animabus vestris*, 'Learn of Me,' says Christ, 'that am meek, and of humble heart: and so ye may find rest unto your souls.' Hear now the first example He showed to mankind and which we can understand. The apostle says about Him: *Qui cum in forma Dei esset, exinanivit semet ipsum, formam servi accipiens*, 'Though Christ, God's Son, was like God, His Father, in age and in power and in every way, He humbled Himself before man's eyes, with His body of a thrall, which He took, and bore therein the burning light which enlightened all His chosen ones who would follow Him.' If thou canst see this light, full surely the higher thou art, the more cautiously wilt thou humble thyself. If thou wilt not humble thyself for this example, know forsooth that thou shalt see little or naught of this light. Woe be to the blind man, who stands amidst the shining sun and sees naught of it! Again, thou mayst learn more examples of this blessed virtue from Christ. He who lifts up with His finger Heaven and earth, and all the things which are therein, like He who created them all, He made Himself as little as is the child of one night's age. He, through whom kings reign, and from whom all power and strength comes, lay wrapt in rags and bound with swaddling bands; and He who is God's Wisdom, from whom come all understanding and all wisdom, and all speaking tongues, He lay as the child which

Of edmodnesse.

DIES hali mihte ðe we embe spekeð, hie hatte humilitas, þat is, eadmodnesse. Ðe hali apostel hes clepeð uirtutem Christi, 'Cristes awene mihte[1],' forði ðat þurh his mannisnesse, and ðurh ðare michele eadmodnesse ðe he mid hire sceawede, all mannkyn te forbisne, he ouercam deuel, and all his mihte of ðare beswikene woreld. Swa ðu niht alswo, ȝif ðu wilt ðese mihte at him lernin, and him folȝin. Di[s]cite a me, quia mitis sum et humilis corde, et inuenietis requiem animabus uestris, 'Liernið at me,' seið Crist, 'þat ic am softe, and of eadmode hierte: and swa ȝe muȝen finden reste te ȝeure saule.' Harke nu ðe formeste forbysne ðe he mankenn sceawede ðas þe we cunnen understonden. Ðe apostel seið be him: Qui cum in forma dei esset, exinaniuit semet[2] ipsum, formam serui accipiens, 'Do ðe Crist, godes sune, was ȝelich godd his fader on ielde and on mihte[3] and alles kennes wisen, he litlede him seluen to-foren mannes eiȝen, mid his þralles lichame ðe he nam, and ðar inne bar ðat liht barninde ðe lihte[4] alle his ȝecorene ðe him wolde folȝin.' Gif ðu ðis liht miht isien, full[5] ȝewiss ðe ðu heiȝer art, þe warliker[6] ðe seluen wilt neðerin. Gif ðu ðe seluen for ðessere forbisne ne wilt naht neþerin, wite ðu to soðe ðat tu of ðese lihte litel oðer[7] naht ne ȝesikst. Wa mai bien ðe blinde, ðe stant amidewarde ðe scinende sunne and of hire naht ne isikð! Ȝiet[8] ðu miht of ðessere eadi mihte ma forbisne liernen at Criste. He ðe weiȝþ upp mid his fingre heuene and ierðe and alle ðo þing ðe ðar inne beoð, al swo he ðe hes alle iscop, he makede him swa litel swo is ðat child of one niht ielde. He, ðurh hwam kinges rixit, and alle mihtes and alle strengþes of him cumeð, he lai bewunden on fiteres and mid swaðelbonde ibunden; and he ðe is godes wisdom, ðurh hwam bieð alle wittes and ælle wisdomes and alle tungen spekinde, he lai alswa ðat child ðe nan god ne cann, ne speken

---

[1] *a final s erased.*   [2] *m corr. over* n.   [3] *page* 30.
[4] *At side*: erat lux uera que illuminat (*the last* t *corrected from* d).
[5] *A letter erased before* f.   [6] hwarliker *MS.*   [7] tel o *on erasure.*
[8] ȝ *corr. from* G.

knows no good, nor can speak, nor see, nor rule itself, through whom all ears hear, and all men rule themselves, and all eyes see. He to whom all knees kneel, and all men bow, was obedient [to] a mortal man, Joseph the carpenter, and His mother. This same Lord Jesus Christ abode here in this life three-and-thirty winters [years] and a half among sinful men, very God (whom they could not see), and very man (whom they could see), and kept all the laws fully, and was obedient to His Father unto death, for this great humility which He showed to man as [an] example, and ate and drank, and rested and slept, and [did] all things as very man, except without sins. Therefore [the] devil was deceived, and urged the heathen with his wicked admonitions until they doomed Him to death with great injustice, and also the most ignominious death, and the most loathly they could think of, that was on the cross, and also between two thieves. This they did to increase all the shames and the insults which they had done to Him before undeservedly. In such wise Christ, God's Son, overcame the treacherous devil through this blessed virtue; [He] willed to tear mankind away from him by no force, because the devil brought him [man] out of Paradise, not by any force, but by deceiving him; and by right doom of God he [Adam] was put out, because God had warned him before: *In quacunque die comederis ex hoc ligno, morte morieris,* 'In the day,' He said, 'that thou eatest of this tree thou art guilty unto death.' All ye Adam's children who are lustful after new fruits, run, run to the tree which stands amidst Paradise, viz. of the knowledge both of good and evil! For your behoof is planted a blessed tree amidst the holy Church, that is, the holy cross whereon Christ hung, the most precious fruit which ever yet any tree bore. Use this with right belief and with firm hope, and with the true love which is called charity: and to you shall be forgiven the guilt which our father earned, that is, eternal death. And to increase it, then ye shall surely have eternal life, all who ever believe in this true belief, and partake of this holy fruit, which is rightly called *corpus Domini.* Take what ye see, bread and wine without; and in your thoughts believe that which ye see not: that is, Christ's

ne mai, ne isien, ne him seluen wealden, ðurh hwam alle earen
ʒehiereð, and alle menn hem seluen welden, and alle eiʒene isieð.
He ðat alle cnewes to cnelið, and alle menn to buʒeð, he was
buhsum ane deadliche manne, Iosepe ðe smiðe, and his moder. 4
Ðies ilke hlauerd Iesus[1] Crist, he was her on ðese liue wuniʒende
þrie and þrihti wintre and an half mang senfulle mannen, soð
godd, (ðe hie ne mihten isien[2]), and soð mann, ðe hie isien mihten,
and alle ðe laʒwes fulliche hield, and hersum was his fader anon 8
to ðe deaðe, for ðessere muchele eadmodnesse ðe he sceawede manne
to forbisne, and att and dranc, and reste and sliep, and[3] alle ðing
alswo soð mann, wiðuten sennen ane. For ði warð dieuel beswiken and beuall þo haðene mid his leðre menezinges al hwat hie 12
hine fordemden to deaðe mid muchele unrihte, and ec ðane forcu-
þeste deað, and ðane laðlicheste ðe hie beðenchen mihten, þat was
on rode, and iec betwenen twa þieues. Ðis[4] hie deden to echen alle
ðe scames and ðe bismeres ðe hie arrer him hadde idon un-of- 16
earned. On ðelliche wise ouercam Crist, godes sune, ðane swikele
dieuel ðurh ðessere iblescede mihte ; nolde mid none strengþe him
binemen mankenn, for ðan ðe ðe dieuel mid none strengþe ut of
paradise hine ne brohte, ac he him beswoc ; and mid rihte godes 20
dome he was ut ʒedon, for ði ðat godd hadde iwarned him beforen :
In quacunque die comederis ex hoc ligno, morte morieris, 'Hwilche daiʒe,' he sede, 'se ðu etst of ðese trewe ðu art
deaðes sceldi(h).' Alle ʒe Adames children ðe bieð lustfull uppe 24
newe wastmes, ierneð, ierneð to ðe trewe ðe stant amidewarde
paradise, witende boðe god and euel ! Te ʒewere behofde ys ʒe-
planted an iblesced treu amidde ðare hali chereche, þat is, ðe hali
rode ðe Crist on hangede, ðe derewurðeste wastme ðat æure ʒiete 28
ani treu bar. Notieð hier of mid rihte ileaue and mid faste hope,
and mid ðare soðe luue ðe is icleped karite ; and ʒeu scal bien
forʒiuen ðe gelt ðe ure fader of-earnede, þat is, se eche deað. And
to eche, ðan ʒe sculen habben sikerliche ðat eche lif, alle ðe æure 32
belieueð on ðessere soðe beleaue, and of ðese hali wasme notieð,
ðe is mid rihte icleped corpus domini. Notieð ðat ʒe isieð,
bread and win wiðuten ; and on ʒeure iþanke ilieueð ðat ʒe naht ne

---

[1] ihu MS.   [2] added at side.   [3] page 31.   [4] Dis MS.

flesh and His blood. And know forsooth, as truly as bread and wine feed the body, while it dwells in this life, so this holy *corpus Domini* truly feeds both soul and body unto eternal life. And as truly as the tree of Paradise was called 'knowledge both of good and evil,' so this same tree truly bears the fruit which turns many to life, and also some to death, through misbelief and for the irreverence with which one takes it as unworthily as one takes the bread of the board [table], with foul heart and with foul thought and with foul belly. Whoever eats this holy fruit of Him that hung on this tree of life, and is bound with [any] cardinal sin, who can never be unbound but through the mouth of a priest or a bishop, so truly may he know, as it is certainly the flesh and blood of Him who shall judge all mankind, that he there rightly forejudges himself ere he come to the doom. Beware whoso will! I had thought that I should write nought but of these holy virtues, though I myself have none as it behoved me; then I am led aside sometimes, ere I know anything of it, to another thing: for if it does not help one, it helps another. Dear soul, of this holy virtue humility I cannot stop without letting thee hear more of it; because it is so very needful to thee, that thou canst not have nor keep any other virtue, nor be saved in any wise, unless thou hast this. These holy virtues which we speak about are spiritual and invisible, and therefore it is the more difficult to speak about them. They are rightly called God's gifts. Therefore said the angel Gabriel to our Lady St. Mary: *Ave, gratia plena!* 'Hail thou, Mary,' he said, 'full of God's gifts; thou shalt bear in thy womb God's own Son.' Well might she then know that she should be highest over all things in Heaven and on earth (as God's own mother), except Himself. But she declared soon that this holy virtue was in her, when she said: *Ecce ancilla Domini*, 'Look here,' quoth she, 'God's own servant!' Hark, hark, Eve's daughters, ye who think so highly of yourselves, that one calls you ladies, go to

ʒesieð: þat is, Cristes flasch *and* his blod! And wite ʒe te soðe,
all swo soðliche swa bread *and* win fedeð ðane lichame, ðar hwile
ðe¹ he on ðese liue wuniʒeð, swa soðliche fett ðis hali corp*us*
dom*i*ni baðe saule *and* lichame to ðan eche liue. *And* al swa 4
soðliche swa ðat trew of paradise was icleped 'witinde baðe god
and euel,' swa soðliche berð ðis ilche trew ðat wastme ðe maniʒe
want to liue, *and* ec sume to deaðe, for ðare misbileaue *and* for
ðare unwurscipe ðe me nimð hit al swa unwurðliche swa me nimð 8
ðat bread (of ðæ borde), mid fule herte *and* mid fule þanke a*nd*
mid fule buce. Hwa se ðis hali wastme of ðan ðe heng on ðese
liues trewe noteð, *and* is mid heued-senne ibu*n*den, (þe naure ne
mai ben unbu*n*den) bute ðurh priestes muðe oðer ðurh biscopes, 12
al swa soðliche wite he, al swa hit is sikerliche his flesc *and* his
blod ðe scal all ma*n*ken deme*n*, ðat he ðar rihtes for-demþ him
selue*n* ær he to ðe dome cume. Bie war se ðe wile! Ich hadde
iþoht ðat ic naht ne scolde write*n* bute of ðese haliʒe mihtes, ðeih 16
ic me selu none ne habbe swa (swa) me behofd*e*; ðanne am ic
iladd ut oðerhwile, ær ic hit ouht wite, to oðer þinge: for ðan ʒif
hit ne helpð one, hit helpð a*n* oðer. Lieue saule, of ðessere hali
mihte eadmodnesse ic ne mai swa laten ðat tu of hire ʒiet more ne 20
ʒehiere; for ðan hie is þe swa swiðe nedfull, ðat tu ne miht none
oðre mihte habbe*n* ne healde*n*, ne on one wise ʒeborʒen bie*n*, bute
þu ðese habbe. Ðese hali mihtes ðe we embe spekeð, hie bieð
gastliche *and* unaseiʒenliche, *and* for ði hit is ðe strengere embe 24
hem to spekene. Hie² bieð mid rihte godes ʒiues icleped. For ði
sade ðe angle Gabriel to ure lafdi sainte Marie: Aue, gr*a*ti*a*
plena! 'Hail ðu, Marie,' he seide, 'full of godes ʒiues; ðu
scalt beren on ðine wombe godes auwe*n*³ sune.' Wel hie mihte 28
ða (wite*n*)⁴ þ*a*t hie scolde bie*n* heiʒest ouer alle þing on heuene *and*
on ierðe, alswo g*o*des aʒen moder, wið-uten him⁵ selue*n*. Ac hie
kedde sone ðat þies hali mihte was on hire, ða hie sæde: Ecce
ancilla dom*i*ni, 'Loke hier,' cwað hie, 'godes aʒen þralle!' 32
Harkieð, harkieð, Eue dohtren, ʒe ðe telleð swa wel of ʒeu seluen,
þ*a*t me⁶ clepeð ʒeu lafdies, gað to ðare rihte lafdi *and* lierneð ead-

---

¹ *page* 32. ² ie *on erasure*. ³ *page* 33.
⁴ *added red above*. ⁵ m *on erasure*. ⁶ *before* m *an erasure*.

the right Lady and learn meekness! In the time when she was here living in life, it was written: *Maledicta sterilis, quae non peperit*, 'Cursed be the wife who cannot have a child!' They who would not, or could not, bear a child, were very much despised in those days; and nevertheless she would not on that account forbear, but vowed to keep her maidenhood evermore to her Lord God. She would rather be despised here among men, than lose the great honour among the angels. Therefore she said: *Quia respexit humilitatem ancillae suae. Ecce enim ex hoc beatam me dicent omnes generationes*, 'Because my Lord God regarded the humility of His servant, inasmuch as I had made myself despised among my kin of Israelitish folk, because I would not have man's company nor bear children, but offered Him both my body and soul, and promised Him evermore to keep my maidenhood, therefore all mankind will say that I am blessed that I believed in God's message, which He sent to tell me by Gabriel, His high angel, that I should be, through His great mercy, the mother of God's Son, and also ever remain a maiden. This wonder He did to me, *Quia potens est*, 'because He is mighty and holy,' *et misericordia ejus a progenie in progenies timentibus eum*. 'This great mercy He made known in me. Ever more it lasteth with Him from generation to generation, unto all those men who fear Him.' The holy words which I have written in *magnificat*, know thou forsooth that they are of the holy Gospel, which St. Mary said herself to help men, and to warn all those who fear Him, and for His fear forsake all unrighteousness, to have much hope in God's mercy. And as for those who will not so, she says further again: *Dispersit superbos mente cordis sui, et exaltavit humiles*, 'All who are proud and think much of themselves in the imagination of their hearts, if they do not humble themselves ere they go out of this life; just as truly as St. Mary said it with her holy mouth, so truly shall God Almighty destroy them, in soul and in body, as those who are against Him and follow modnesse! On ða time ðe hie was¹ hier² on liue libbende, hit was iwriten: Maledicta sterilis, que non (pe)perit, 'ȝewerȝed bie þat wif ðe child ne mai habben!' Hie ðe child nolden beren oðer ne mihten, hie waren ihealden swiðe unwurð be ðan daiȝe; and naþelæs nolde hie naht ðarfore læten þat hie ne behiet hire maidenhad æure mo to healden hire lauerde gode. Wolde bliðelicor hier bien unwurðed mang mannen, ðanne³ hie scolde forliesen ða michele wurðscipe mang ðo aingles. For ði hie sæide: Quia respexit humilitatem ancille sue. Ecce enim ex⁴ hoc beatam me dicent omnes generaciones, 'For ði ða(t) mi lauerd godd lokede to ðare eadmodnesse of his þralle, þat ic me hadde maked unwurð mang mine kenne of israelisce folke, for þi ðat ic nolde habben wapmannes imone ne childre beren, ac him ic ofrede baðe mine lichame and saule, and min maidenhad him behiet eure mo to healden: for ði seggeð all mankynn þat ic am eadi þat ic beliefde on godes sonde, ðe he me sante seggen bi Gabriel, his heih ængel, þat ic scolde, ðurh his muchele mildce, bien godes sunes moder, and ec æure ðurh-wuniȝen maiden. Ðis selcuð he dede be me, Quia potens est, 'forðan⁵ he is mihti and hali,' et misericordia eius a progenie in progenies timentibus⁶ eum. 'Ðese michele mildce he kedde on me. Eure mo hie ȝelast mid him fro kenne to kenne, to alle ðo mannen ðe him ondradeð.' Ðe hali wordes ðe ic habbe⁷ iwriten on magnificat, wite ðu te soðe ðat hie bieð of ðe hali goddspelle, ðe sainte Marie sæde hire self mannen to helpe, and to warniȝen þat hie michele hope to godes milce hauen, alle ðe him ondreadeð, and for his eiȝhe alle unrihtwisnesse forlateð. And þo ðe swo ne willeð, hie seið ȝiet forðer: Dispersit superbos mente cordis sui, et exaltauit humiles, 'Alle ðe bieð modi and michel læteð of hem seluen ðurh⁸ ðe þanc of here hierte, bute hie⁹ hem seluen neðerien ær ðanne hie of ðese liue faren: al swa soðliche swa sainte Marie hit sade¹⁰ mid hire hali muðe, (swa soðliche) ¹¹ scal goddalmihti¹² hes forliesen, mid saule and mid lichame, al swo ðo ðe bieð aȝeanes him and

---

¹ hie was *twice, the middle was* hie *underlined*.   ² e *corr. from* o.
³ ðannne MS.   ⁴ *Corr. from* hex *by underdotting the* h.   ⁵ *page* 34.
⁶ bus *on erasure*.   ⁷ bbe *on erasure*.   ⁸ rh *corr. from* ch.
⁹ e *corr. from* o.   ¹⁰ de *corr. from* ð.   ¹¹ *added at side*.   ¹² almihtin MS.

the devil, who would glorify himself.' But He sent him very low into hell, and all his followers. Again, she says further : *Et exaltavit humiles*, 'Just as He has cast down into the ground of hell all the proud who in this life followed the devil, so He has raised all those who have loved Christ's meekness and kept it, into the joy of the kingdom of Heaven.' Dear soul, call willingly to our Lady St. Mary, that she, for the great meekness which she had in this life, bear thy errand to Christ, her dear Son, that this holy virtue may reign in thee, ere thou departest from thy body! And how thou mayst know it, I will warn thee. To some men it comes and goes, and with some men it is abiding, and in very few men it is reigning. In the man in whom it is reigning, this is the token : as the worldling lightly laughs at vanities which he sees or hears, so the spiritual man in whom it [humility] reigns, lightly weeps or sobs, sometimes with bitter tears, at other times with very sweet tears, according to what he sees or hears or thinks. Of all the things in which the worldling has consolation and bliss, this spiritual man has nought but grief and sorrow. Though he do better than another, yet let him think worse of himself, than he does of others, who do not so. He thinks in his heart that he is of the same mould as those are who do evil ; and if God had not given it to him, he would full surely do just so or worse ; and as God has mercy and pity on him, He may [also] on them, when it is His will. They are not all humble who live coarsely in meat and in clothes, and go after worldly possessions. Some live coarsely in meat and in clothes, not for God's love, but as it may be natural to them. Reward they shall have, but not such as those shall have who could live exaltedly, but humble themselves in order to have humility and to help God's needy ones. Some others take God's mark upon them, change their clothes and not their manners, judge themselves, and say that they are the most sinful of all men ; but if dieule¹ folȝieð, ðe wolde him seluen herȝen.' Ac he brohte him seluen swiðe neðer in to helle, and alle his folȝeres. ȝiet² hie seið furðer: *Et exaltauit humiles*, 'All swa he hafð ineðered niðer in to helle grunde alle ðe modi ðe hier on liue ðe dieule folȝeden, alswa he haueð iheiȝed alle ðo ðe Cristes eadmodnesse habbeð ȝeluued and ihelden, in to heuene riches³ merhðe.' Lieue saule, clepe ȝierne to vre lafdi sainte Marie, ðat hie, for hire michele eadmodnesse ðe hie hier on ðese liue hadde, ðat hie bere ðin arnde te (Criste⁴), hire lieue sune, ðat ðis hali mihte mote on þe rixin, ær ðu fram ðine lichame scelie! ¶ *And* hu ðu miht hes ȝecnawen, ic ðe wile warnien. To sume menn hie cumð and farð, and mid sume men hie is wunende, and on swiðe feawe menn hie is rixende. On ða manne ðe⁵ hie is rixende, þis [is] ðe tacne: al swo ðe woreld-mann lihtliche lei(c)heð of ydelnesse ðe he isieð oðer iherð, al swa ðe gastliche manu ðe hie on rixeð, lihtliche wepð oðer sobbeð, oðerhwile mid bitere teares, oðerwille mid wel swete teares, after ðan ðe he isiecþ oðer iherð oðer þengþ. Of alle ða þinges ðe ðe woreld-mann hafð frieurenesses and blisses, nafð ðes gastliche mann bute reuneses and sarinesses. Ðeih he betere do ðan an oðer, þeih h(w)eðere he læte wers of him seluen, ðanne he do of oðre, ðe swo ne doð. Ðen[c]þ on his herte þat he is of ðare ilche mo(l)de ðe hie bieð ðe euele doð; and ȝif godd hit him nadde iȝiuen, he scolde fuliwis⁶ don alswa oðer wurse; and alswa godd haueð ore and milsce of him, swa he mai of hem, whanne⁷ his wille⁸ is. Hie ne bieð nauht alle eadmode ðe unorneliche libbeð on mete and on claðes, and draȝeð te world-eihte. Sume libbeð unorneliche on mete and on claðes, naht for godes luue, ac swilch hit hem bie icynde. Lean hie sculen habben, ac⁹ naht swilch swa sculen habben¹⁰ ðo ðe mihte heiliche libben, ac hie neðerið hem for eadmodnesse te habben and for to helpen godes þe(a)ruen. Sume oðre nimeð godes marc (on hem), wandeð here claðes and naht here þe(a)wes¹¹, diemeð hem seluen, seggeð ðat hi bieð senfullest of alle oðre manne; ac ȝif sum mann hes undernimþ mid sume unþeawe, hie cyðeð sone mid bitere answere

---

¹ dieulen *MS.*   ² G *altered to* ȝ.   ³ e *corr. from* o.   ⁴ *written above* gode.
⁵ *page* 35.   ⁶ *On erasure.*   ⁷ w *corr. from* h.   ⁸ willen *MS.*   ⁹ a *on erasure.*
¹⁰ e *on erasure.*   ¹¹ *a letter scratched out between* w *and* e.

anybody reproves them for any vice, they soon show with bitter answer and with evil words that the doom with which they so strongly condemned themselves did not come from a meek heart. Beware, if thou wilt! Thou hast never true humility in thee, until thou canst suffer all harms and shame and insults, that any man may do to thee. And then thou shalt still say, and with the heart believe it: 'All that I have suffered, I am well worthy to suffer that and more, for His love who suffered much more for me, all undeservedly.' Again, beware of one thing! It is written: *Nimia humilitas est maxima superbia*, that is: 'If thou behavest thyself otherwise, than other good meek men, and thou hast [it] not so in thy heart as thou showest outside, know thou then forsooth that that is great pride.' Though thou do a great goodness before many others, it is all lost save humility be with it. Because we have written here before that God's mercy lasteth evermore on all men who fear Him, as St. Mary herself bears witness, therefore, with God's grace, I will tell thee of His fear, after what the holy scriptures say and reveal to us.

Of fear.

Timor domini is another holy virtue, which, as Solomon said, is *initium sapientiae*, 'the beginning of wisdom.' The Holy Ghost speaks through David the prophet, and says thus: *Venite filii, audite me, timorem Domini docebo vos*, 'Come children, [ye] who will learn, and listen to me, and I will teach you the fear of God.' *Quis est homo qui vult vitam?* 'Who is there of you,' he says, 'who will have eternal life, long life, and happy life, who so dearly love this short life?' If thou answerest with heart or with mouth, and sayst: 'I yearn for it and I will have it very blithely, if I may,' he teaches thee yet further, and says: *Prohibe linguam tuam a malo*, 'keep thy tongue from evil, and thy lips that they speak not guile;' *diverte a malo et fac bonum*, 'turn from evil habits, and do good; seek to have peace with God, so that thou *and* mid euele wordes ðat hit ne cam noht of eadmode [1] her*te*, ðe dom ðe hie swa swiðe fordemden hem seluen. Bie war, ʒif ðu wilt! Ne hafst tu næure soðe eadmodnesse on [2] þe, ær ðu muʒe þoliʒen alle harmes *and* scames *and* bismeres, ðat ani man ðe mai don. And ðanne scalt tu ʒiet seggen, *and* mid herte hit ilieue*n*: 'All ðat ic habbe iþoled, ic am wel wurðe ðat *and* more to þolien, for his luue ðe þolede [3] michel more for me, all un-of-earned.' Giet bie war of one þinge! It his ʒewriten: Nimi(a) humilitas (*est*) maxima superbia, ðat is, 'ʒif ðu latst ðe seluen oðerliker ðanne oðre gode eadmode menn, *and* tu ne hafst swa on ðine her*te* swa ðu sceawest wiðuten, ðanne wite ðu te soðe ðat ðat is michel modinesse.' Ðeih þu do ane michele godnesse tefore*n* maniʒe oðre, all it is forloren bute eadmodnesse bie ðar mide. For ðan ðe we habbeð hier te-foren write*n* þa*t* godes milsce last æuremo (to) alle ðo manne*n* ðe him bieð dradinde, swa swa sainte Marie hire self berð ʒewitnesse, for ði, mid god*es* grace, ic ðe wile seggen of his drædnesse, after ðan (ðe) hali writes seggeð *and* us openieð.

4

8

12

16

Of dradnesse.

TIMOR domini is an oðer hali mihte, þa*t* ðe Salamu*n* seide hie is initium sapientie, 'Angi*nn* of wisdom.' Þe hali gast spekð ðurh Dauið ðe profiete, *and* ðus seiþ: Venite fili, audite me, timore*m* domini docebo uos, 'Cumeð children, ðe liernien willeð, *and* (h)lesteð me, *and* ic eu wile tache*n* godes drædnesse.' Quis est homo qui uult uitam? 'Hwa is þa*t*,' he seiþ, 'ðe wile haue*n* ðat eche lif, þa*t* lange lif, ðat eadi lif of ʒeu, ðe luuiʒeð swa swiðe ðis scorte lif?' ʒif ðu audswerest mid herte oðer mid muðe, *and* seist: 'Ic hit ʒ(i)erne *and* ic hit wile hauen swiðe bliðeliche, ʒif ic mai,' he wisseð ðe ʒiet forðer, *and* seið: Proibe linguam tuam a malo, 'forbet ðine tunge fra*m* euele, *and* ðine lippen ðat he ne speken swikedom; diuerte a malo et fac (bon*um*) [4], 'wænd fro euel wune, and [5] do god; siec ðat tu haue pais aʒeanes gode, þa*t* ðu naht ne healde aʒeanes

20

24

28

32

---

[1] *The first* e *on erasure.*   [2] *A letter scratched out behind* n.
[3] *page* 36.   [4] bon*um* *above erasure.*
[5] *an erasure before* a.

hold not against His commandments nor against any man, neither with word nor with deed, which thou canst rule.' When thou hast found this peace, then thou art righteous : and have always the fear of God with thee, lest thou lose this. 'Then will God's eyes be upon thee, that nothing may hurt thee, and His ears open unto thy cries, that He will deny thee nothing.' Thus the Holy Ghost advises thee, who speaks still every day through the psalm which thou seest or hearest. Beware, if thou wilt ! Let him who will not understand, nor keep this holy lore of the Holy Ghost, listen what He says thereafter: *Vultus autem Domini super facientes mala, ut disperdat de terra memoriam eorum,* ' God,' He says, ' looks wrathfully upon them that do evil, and who will not cease through His fear. Therefore will God's wrath come upon them, ere they know it, and cut them off, both body and soul, from this mortal land wherein they dwell and which they love so much.' So they shall also lose the everlasting land, which is eternal life, because they would not listen to God's love nor follow [it]. Again, He says that their remembrance will be so lost, that men will neither speak nor think of them. Again, saith holy Writ : *Qui timet Deum, faciet bona ; qui autem duri cordis est, corruet in malum,* ' He that feareth God, forbeareth always, for awe of Him, to do evil ; he who is of hard heart, feareth not God, and therefore he goeth from evil unto evil and from sin unto sin.' Many men are greatly deceived who fear a mortal man more than they do God Almighty, [they] who for shame of the world or for their short life, forswear themselves wholly, and slay their own soul, and lose eternal life. Therefore Jesus Christ warns us, and says thus : *Nolite timere eos qui corpus occidunt, animam autem non possunt occidere,* ' Fear not,' He said, ' them who can kill your body ; but of Him ye ought to be adread, who can cast both body and soul into the fire of hell.' Again says the Book of Wisdom : *Deum time, et mandata ejus observa,* ' Fear God, and keep His commandments !' Every man ought to do this, because nothing will fail them, neither in this life nor in the other, who fear and love Him

his bebode ne aȝean none manne, ne mid worde ne mid weorke, ðas
ðe ðu muȝe wealden.' Ðanne ðu ðese sibsumnnesse hafst ȝefun-
den, [1] ðanne art tu rihtwis : *and* haue æure godes drædnesse mid
þe, *þat* ðu ðis ne forlies. 'Ðanne sculen godes eiȝen bien uppe ðe,
ðat nanðing ne mai ðe deriȝen, *and* his earen opene to ðine
b(i)enes, ðat naþing he ðe ne wile wærnen.' Ðus ðe ratt ðe halie
gast, ðe spekð ȝiet alche dai ðurh ðene selm ðe ðu ȝesikst oðer
iherst. Bie war, ȝif ðu wile ! Se ðe nele ðese hali lare of ðe hali
gast understanden, (ne wiðealden [2]), hlest hwat he seið ðar after :
Vultus autem domini super facientes mala, ut dispe*r*dat
de te*rr*a memoriam eor*um*, 'Godd,' he [3] seið, 'lokeð wraðliche
uppe he*m* ðe euele doð, ðe for his dradnesse ne willeð iswike*n*.
For ði scal godes wraððe cume*n* on he*m*, ær hie hit aut wite*n*, and
forliesen hem, baðe li(came) [4] *and* saule, of ðese deadliche lande ðe
hie on wunieð *and* swa michel luuiȝeð.' Swa hie sculen iec forliesen ðat liuiende land, *þat* is, ðat eche lif, for ðan ðe hie nolde*n*
godes lare hleste*n* ne folȝin. Giet he seið ðat here ȝemiend scal
swo bien forloren, ðat me of he*m* ne scal neiðer ne speken ne
þenchen [5]. Giet seið ðat hali writ : Qui timet de*um*, faciet
bona ; q*ui* autem duri cordis est, corruet i*n* malum, 'Se
ðe ondrat godd, he lat æure ðe euel to done for his heiȝe ; se ðe is
of harde hierte, he no*n*dratt noht godd, *and* for ði he farð from
euele to euele *and* fra*m* senne to se*n*ne.' Hit bieð maniȝe men
swiðe beswikene ðat more dradeð ane deadliche ma*n*ne ðane he doð
god almihti*n*, ðe for ðare worldes scame oðer for here scorte liue,
hem al forswerieð, *and* sleað here auȝene saule, *and* forlieseð ðat
eche lif. Forði us warneð Iesus [6] Crist, *and* ðus seið : Nolite
timere eos q*ui* corp*us* occidunt, anima*m* aute*m* [7] non
possunt occide*r*e, 'Ne drædeð naht,' he sade, 'hem ðe ȝure [8]
lichame muȝe*n* ofslean ; ac of hi*m* ȝe aweð to be*n* ofdrad, þe mai
baðe lichame *and* saule werpen i*n* to ðe fier of helle.' Eft seið ðe
boc of wisdome : Deu*m* time, et mandata ei*us* obserua,
'Dræd godd, *and* hald his bebode !' Þis auh(t) elch ma*n*n te
do*n*ne, forðan no þing hem ne scall trukien, on ðese liue ne o*n*

---
[1] *page* 37. [2] *On the side.* [3] h *corr. from* s. [4] came *written above* f.
[5] *On the side* : ut dispe*r*dat de te*r*ra memoriam eor*um*. [6] ih̄u *MS.*
[7] *page* 38. [8] *corr. from* ȝeuere *above here.*

E

in truth. After this fear of pain, comes another which is called *timor sanctus*, that is, holy fear, which shall last for ever, world without end, because it is mingled with the true love which is called charity. This fear is as sweet as the son's who fears his father, not for any pain, but fears him lest he lose his sweet love; and therefore he serves his father with great love, mingled with fear. This same fear is needful to us. *Qui timet Deum nihil negligit,* 'He who feareth God, for his carelessness he omitteth to do nought of what he hath to do.' From this fear of God springs another of God's gifts, which is very needful to every man who will be saved.

Of ruth (pity).

Pietas is called one of these holy virtues, that is, ruth (pity) in English. It comes from the wounded hearts which are wounded with God's arrows. Of them says the prophet: *Sagittae tuae acutae,* 'Lord,' he said, 'sharp are Thy arrows;' they wound the guilty man who fought against Thee through the devil's lore. Thou throwest him down, so that he lies stretched upon the bare earth, and esteems himself as earth, weeps and wails that he ever was shaped to man, that he should have misdone so much against his Creator, for which he deserves the pain of hell. Ruth (pity) causes [him] to do this, which is assuredly God's gift. It causes him at first to have ruth (pity) on himself, and then on his neighbour, for all [the] misfortunes which befall him for his sins. If thou canst get this gift of God's, then thou wilt have a soft and good heart, and compassionate to help thyself, and to save thy soul from the pains which it has deserved. Have thou no hope in father nor in mother, in son nor in daughter, in brother nor in sister, nor in any earthly man, when thy body lies under the earth separated from all living men, alone, foul, stinking, full of worms, and in the darkness [away] from all light, and thou, poor soul, in the boiling heat of the hot fire, and again, sometimes, in the shivering chill, so that thou canst not help thyself, until thou have redeemed all thy sins, and be all cleansed ðere oðre, ðe him drædeð *and* luuiʒeð *inne* soðe. After ðesse [1] drædnesse ðe is of pine, cumð an oðer ðe is icleped timor sanctus, þat is, hali dradnesse, ðe æure scal ilasten, on worelde [2] worreld, forðan ðe hie is imæng(d) mid ðare soðe luue ðe hatte kariteð. 4 Dies dradnesse is swete, al swa ðe (sune ðe) drat his fader, naht for none pine, ac drat him ðat he forliese his swete luue; *and* for ði he ðeneð his fader mid muchele luue, imaingd mid dradnesse. Dies ilke dradnesse us behoueð. Qui timet deum nichil ne- 8 gligit, 'Se ðe gode on-dratt, for his ʒemeleste ne latt he naht te [3] donne of ðat he haueð te donne.' Of ðesere godes dradnesse springþ ut an oðer godes ʒiue, ðe is swiðe niedfull auriche manne ðe i-boreʒen scal bien. 12

Of reuhðe [4].

PIETAS hatte on of ðese hali mihtes, þat is, reuhðe [4] *on* engelisc. Hie cumþ of ðare iwundede herte ðe bien iwunded mid godes arewen. Of hem seið ðe profiete: Sagitte tue acute, 16 'Lauerd,' he sæde, 'scarpe bien ðine arewen'; hie wundieð ðane forgilte mann ðe wann ongeane(s) ðe ðurh dieules lare. Þu werpest him ðer niðer, þat he lið istreiht upe ðare bare ierðe, *and* halt him seluen [5] for ierðe, wepð *and* woneð ðat he æure was to manne 20 iscapen, ðat he scolde swa michel habben misdon aʒean his sceppend, for hwat he [6] ofearneð [7] helle pine. Dis doð reuhðe don, ðe is iwis godes ʒiue. Hie dieð him arst habben reuhðe of him seluen, *and* ðanne of his nexten, of alle unʒelimpes ðe him for his sennes 24 to-cumeð. Gif ðu ðese godes ʒiue biʒeten miht, þanne scalt tu hauen nexce herte (*and*) gode, *and* riewsiende ðe seluen to helpe, *and* ðine saule to aliesen fram ðo pines ðe hie ofearned hafð. Ne haue ðu hope te fader ne te moder, te sune ne te dohter, te broðer ne 28 te swuster, ne te nan ier[ð]lich mann, ðanne þin lichame lið under ierðe ʒetwamd fram alle liuiende manne, all-ane, fule, stinkende, full of wermes, *and* on ða þiesternesse fram alle lihte, *and* ðu, earme saule, on ðe wallende brene of ðe hote fiere, *and* eft, embehwile, on 32 ðe chiuerinde chele, ðat tu ðe seluen naht ne miht helpen, ær

---

[1] desse *MS*. [2] *A later hand has inserted* to. [3] t *corr. from* d.
[4] u *corr. from* w. [5] *on erasure*. [6] *page* 39. [7] earned *MS*.

from all thy misdeeds through the pains which thou sufferest, and through masses and prayers and alms which one does for thee. Then thou wilt sorely repent that thou hadst not helped thyself better the while thou couldst. How should God, or any of His saints, or any of thy friends, relation or stranger, have ruth or mercy on thee, since thou thyself hast now here none of thyself? This is God's gift, if thou thus considerest and workest thereafter.

Of knowledge.

After this comes another gift of God, which is called *scientia*, that is, understanding or knowledge. Through it thou canst know all the crafts which are written in books. It teaches thee good manners and to lead [a] good life, how thou shalt turn from evil, and how thou shalt do good works. But there are some who are held very wise through this gift of God, and turn for themselves and also for some others to great harm, what God gave them for their great good. Hereof said the apostle: *Scientia inflat, caritas aedificat.* He says that 'this sharp knowledge puffs up the man who has it without charity.' In such a way it puffs [him] up that he thinks well of himself and despises others who cannot [do] so; and in such a way he loses what should help him best, that is, God's and man's love. Therefore know thou full well, when thou losest man's love through thy pride, it seems to thee that thou needst not honour, nor love, a man lower than thyself, or because he is not so wise as thou, or is not so rich as thou, or of so high family as thou, or not so honoured [a] man as thou in the false world, and for such things thou despisest him and omittest to call on him, or to help him in his need. Full assuredly, thou justly losest here God's love and His grace; and take this for example! Except thou hast God's and all men's love, thou canst not do any good [thing] that will ever be agreeable to God. Of this said the apostle: *Si distribuero omnes facultates meas, et cetera*, 'If I bestow all that I have for God's love, and still, over and above it, ðanne ðu habbe ðine sennes al aboht, and all bie iclensed [1] of alle ðine misdædes ðurh ða pines ðe ðu þolest, *and* ðurh masses *and* bienes *and* ælmesses ðe me doð for ðe. Danne ðe wile sare rewe*n* ðat tu ðe seluen ne haddest betere iholpe*n* ðare hwile ðe ðu mihtest. Hu scolde godd, oðer ani of his halʒen, oðer ani of ðine friend, sibbe oðer framde, haue*n* rewðe oðer mildce of ðe, seððen ðu ðe seluen ne hafst nu hier none of ðe selue*n* ? Þis is godes ʒiue, ʒif ðu dus ðe beþencst *and* ðar after wercst.

Of witte.

HIER after cumþ an oðer godes ʒiue, þe is icleped sciencia, þat is, inʒehied oðer witt. Durh hire ðu miht wite*n* alle craftes ðe on boche bieð ʒewrite*n*. Hie ðe takð [2] gode [3] þeawes *and* god lif to leden, hu ðu scalt fra*m* ðan euele buʒen, *a* hu ðu scalt gode werkes do*n*. Ac hit bieð sume ðe bieð swiðe wise ihealde*n* [4] ðurh ðessere godes ʒiue, *and* want hem seluen *and* iec sumen oðre te michele hearme, þat ðe godd hem ʒaf for here michele gode. Herof sade ðe apostel: Scientia inflat, karitas edificat. He seið þat 'ðis scarpe iwitt swelð ðane mann ðe hes haueð wiðute*n* charite.' On swilche wise hie swelð ðat he latt wel of hi*m* seluen, and forhoweð oðre ðe swo ne cunnen; *and* on swilche wise he forliest ðat hi*m* betst scolde helpen, þat is, godes luue *and* mannes. For ðan (þat) wite ðu te fulle soðe, ðanne ðu forliest mannes luue for ði modinesse, þe þingð ðat þu naust naht to wurðin ne te luue(n) ane wurse mann ðane ðu art, oðer ðat he nis alswa wis alse ðu, oðer he nis na swa riche se ðu, oðer of swa heiʒe kenne swa ðu, oðer naht alswa wurðed mann swa ðu on ðare lease woreld; *and* for ðelliche þinge hine forhowest, *and* forlatst ðat tu ne wilt to hi*m* clepiʒen, ne to his niede hi*m* helpe*n*. Fulʒewis ðu forliest hier rihtes godes luue *and* his grace, *and* nem ðis to forbisne! Bute ðu habbe godes luue *and* alre manne, ðu ne miht don non god ðe æure gode bie ʒecweme. Darof sade ðe apostele: Si distribuero omnes facultates meas, *et cetera*, 'Gif ic deale all ðat ic habbe for godes luue, (*and* ʒiet on-uuen ðan ʒiue mine likame to barnin

---

[1] *An erasure between* l *and* e.   [2] takd *MS.*
[3] *a letter erased after* e.   [4] *page* 40.

give my body to be burned all to dust for God's love, and I hate a single man, then I have not charity, and so I have lost all.' Now some one may say: 'Shall I love the evil man?' Listen what The Most High says to thee: *Diliges proximum sicut te ipsum* 'Love they neighbour as thyself, whatever man he be!' Be he never so much guilty, he is always thy neighbour by nature. Love the [human] nature [in him], and hate his evil! If thou canst mend it, mend it as thou wouldst wish men to mend thine, if thou wert as guilty as he, and think what the Writ says: 'Mercy should always be above righteous doom.' For such things, many very wise men lose God's love and His grace, because they neither have, nor care to have, their fellow-Christians' love, but rely upon their great wisdom; and are often deceived. Would they [only] listen to the holy apostle, they would not stand in this need! *Si quis videtur inter vos sapiens esse, stultus fiat, ut sit sapiens,* 'If any man among you,' says he, 'seemeth to be wise in this world, let him become a fool, and so he may be wise.' The wise worldling esteems it great folly for a man to leave, for God's love, house and home, wife and child, gold and silver, and all worldly wealth, and to become such a great wretch as he who had nothing; [he] says that it is better [for] him to sit in his own [house], and to give alms and to harbour blessed men, than to leave all this, and live by other men's alms. Concerning this, let us listen to Christ's own doom, and so we may be all the more sure in this conflict. It is said in the holy Gospel that a rich young man came to Christ in the days when He was dwelling here in the body, and said: *Quid faciam, Domine, ut habeam vitam aeternam?* 'Lord,' quoth he, 'what shall I do that I may have eternal life?' Our Lord answered him, and said: *Mandata nosti,* 'Thou knowest God's commandments. Thou shalt not slay, nor steal, nor rob, nor commit adultery, nor break the other commandments of God.' 'Oh, Lord,' quoth he, 'all these commandments have I kept from childhood up, and I have broken none.' Then again Christ answered him: 'Good man, thou art as he who has done no cardinal sin.' *Si vis perfectus esse, vade et* al to duste for godes luue)¹, *and* ic hatie on-lepi mann, ðanne ne habbe ic naht kariteð, *and* swa ic habbe all forloren.' Nu seið sum mann: 'Scal ic luuiȝe ðane euele mann?' Hlest hwat se heiȝeste ðe seið: Ðiliges proximum sicut te ipsum, 4 'Luue ðine nexte al swa ðe seluen, hwat manne swo he æure bie!' Ne bie he næure swa swiðe forȝelt, æure he is ðin nexte after ȝekynde. Luue ða ȝekynde, *and* hate his euel. Ȝif ðu miht hit bieten, b(i)et hit alswo ðu woldest ðat me² bette þin, ȝif³ ðu 8 wære swo forȝilt al so he, *and* þenc ðat ðe writt seið þat æure bie ðe mildce ouer ðe rihte dome. For ðelliche þinge maniȝe of ðe wel wise menn forlieseð godes luue *and* his grace, for ði ðat hie ne habbeð, ne ne reccheð to habben, here emcristenes luue, ac 12 hopieð to here michele wisdome, *and* ofte bieð beswikene. Wolden hie hlesten ðane hali apostel, swa hie ne ðorften! Si quis uidetur inter nos sapiens esse, stultus fiat ut sit sapiens, 'Ȝif ȝeure ani,' he seið, 'is ihealden for wis on ðare woreld, becume 16 sott, *and* swa he mai bien wis.' De wise woreld-mann, he halt michel sothade ðat mann forlate, for godes luue, hus *and* ham, wif *and* child, *and* gold *and* seluer, *and* alle worldes wele, *and* becume swo michel wrecche al swo he ðe naht ne hadde; seið 20 ðat him is betere to sitten on his aȝen, *and* ȝiuen almessen *and* herberȝin sæli menn, ðanne he scolde al ðat laten, and libben bi oðres mannes almesse. Hleste we herof Cristes aȝene dom, *and* swa we muȝen bien ðe sikerere of ðese iflite. Hit seið on 24 ða hali goddspelle þat an riche iungman cam to Crist be ðo daiȝen ðe he hier lichamliche was wuniende, *and* seide: Quid faciam, domine, ut habeam vitam eternam? 'Hlauerd,' cwað he, 'hwat mai ic don ðat ic mihte hauen ðat eche lif?' 28 Vre drihten him andswerede, *and* seide: Mandata nosti, 'Ȝecnoust þu godes bebodes. Ne sleih, ne ne stell, ne reaue, ne forliȝe⁴ ðe on hordomes, ne oðre godes forbodes ne tebrec.' 'A, hlaueerd,' cwað he, 'alle ðese bebodes ic habbe ihealde fram 32 childhade, swa ðat ic nabbe nan tebrocen.' De ȝiet him andswerede Crist: 'God⁵ man, ðu art al swo he ðe non heued-senne ne haueð idon.' Si uis perfectus esse, vade et uende omnia

¹ *written above and on the side.* ² *page* 41 ³ Gif MS.
⁴ r *corr. from* l. ⁵ *page* 42

vende omnia quae habes, etc., 'If thou wilt,' He said, 'become a perfectly good man, go and sell all that thou hast, and give it to God's wretched [folk], and follow me!' This young man went away sorry. Here we have learned that it is better to forsake all that one owns, with good will, than to abide until death take it from him, against his will. Listen now what Christ said concerning the rich man who went away sorry, and would not listen to His counsel: 'A rich man can no more,' quoth He, 'enter into the kingdom of Heaven, than a camel can go through the eye of a needle.' *Vae vobis divitibus, qui habetis consolationem vestram,* 'Woe unto you,' quoth He, 'ye rich men, who have so great joy in your great riches, that ye forget God and the salvation of your souls!' Therefore no good seed of God's words can grow in the mould of your hearts, through the great care ye have about your wealth, which ye much covet, and love and like, and dread to lose. Amongst all these thoughts the wretched heart is made so heavy, that no word of God can spring up, nor remembrance of God, nor of His kingdom, nor of the salvation of one's soul. But glee and amusements, and hounds and hawks, and all the things which here may gladden you, ye will blithely see and hear; and ye might have all this if ye loved God more than all this which we have spoken about. Many of you are greatly deceived. Ye fancy that ye love God more than ye do your possessions; but let Him tell what is most true, who is rightly called Truth: *Ubi est thesaurus, ibi est et cor tuum,* 'Where thy hoard is, there is thy heart,' said He. There is thy heart where thy thoughts mostly are, and there is thy greatest love. Understand now well thyself, and look whether thou thinkest more of God than of thy posessions, and know thou forsooth: that of which thou thinkest more, thou lovest more. Woe to the way of the man to whom God has given understanding and wisdom, who will love more the creatures which God created, than he does his Creator, who created him and all things! Dear soul, I warn and beg thee eagerly, that thou, with this gift of God's which is called *scientia,* mayst understand and learn firmly the kinds of sins, whence and when they

OF KNOWLEDGE. 69

q*ue* habes, *et* cet*era*[1], 'Gif ðu wilt,' he seide, 'bie*n* ðurhut god
mann, ga *and* sell all ðat tu hafst, *and* ȝif hit gode(s) wrecche*n*,
and swa folȝe me !' Ðies ȝunge ma*nn* ȝiede a-wei sari. Hier we
habbeð ilierned ðat it is betere to læt*en* all ðat te ma*nn* awh, [4]
mid gode wille, þanne he abide all hwat deað hit hi*m* beneme,
his un]ankes[2]. Hlest nu hwat[3] C*ri*st sade be ða riche manne
ðe ȝiede awei sari, *and* his ræd nolde lesten : 'Ne mai na more,'
cwað he, 'ðe riche ma*nn* cume*n in* to heuene riche, ðanne mai ðe [8]
olu*e*nde cume*n* ðurh ðe nædle eiȝen.' Ve uob*is* diuitib*us*, q*ui*
habetis consolat*i*one*m* ues*t*ra*m*[1], 'Wa ȝeu,' cwað he, 'ȝie
riche m*enn*, ðe habbeð swa michele blisse of ȝeuer michele[4]
richeise, þ*at* ȝie godd forȝete*n and* ȝeu*r*e saule hæle !' For ði ne [12]
mai wex*en* non god sad of godes wordes on ȝeure h*e*rte molde,
for ð*an* michele embeðanc ðe ȝie habbeð on ȝeure michele wele,
ðe ȝie michel ȝitsið, *and* luuieð *and* likeð, *and* dradeð to forliesen[5].
(A)mang[6] alle ðese embeðankes is ðe wrecche hierte swa iheueȝed, [16]
þ*at* no*n* godes word upp ne mai spri*n*gen, ne of godd þenken, ne
of his riche, ne of his saule hale. Ac gleues *and* skentinges, *and*
hundes *and* hauekes, *and* alle ðo þi*n*g ðe ȝeu hier gladien mai,
þ*at* ȝe wille*n* bliðeliche isien *and* ȝehieren; *and* all ðis ȝe mihten [20]
haue*n*, ȝif ȝe godd luuede*n* mare ðanne all ðis ðe we embe haue*n*
ispeke*n*. Maniȝe of ȝeu bien swiðe beswiken*e*. W*e*neð ðat ȝe
luue*n* more godd ðanne ȝe d*o*n ȝeure eihte ; ac læt hi*m* seggen
ðat soðeste, ðe is mid rihte Soð icleped : Vbi es*t*[7] tesaurus, [24]
ibi *est et* cor tuu*m*, 'Ðar ðe ði*n* hord is, þær is þin herte,' he
sæde. Ðar is ði*n* herte ðarof ðe ðu mæst þenkst, *and* ðar is
ði*n* mæste luue. Vnderstand nu wel ðe seluen, *and* loke hwaðer
ðu þenke more of godd ðe of ðin eihte, *and* wite ðu te soþe : [28]
hwarof ðu mare þenkst, ðat tu luuest mare ! Walewa ðas siðes,
þat ani ma*nn* ðat godd hafð iȝiue*n* witt *and* wisd*o*m, scall luuie*n*[8]
more ðe scaftes ðe godd ȝescop, ða*n*ne he do his sceppend, ðe hi*m and*
alle þing[9] ȝescop ! Lieue saule, ic ðe warni *and* ȝierne bidde, ðat [32]
tu, mid ðessere godes ȝiue ðe scientia hatte, understande *and*
lierne fastliche ða ȝekyndes of sen*n*es, hwa*nn*en *and* hwanne[10] (hie

---

[1] *Evangelista on side, red.*   [2] *unstankes MS.*   [3] *hwat twice.*
[4] *i on erasure.*   [5] *an erasure above* n.   [6] A *added red.*
[7] *page* 43.   [8] *liuien MS.*   [9] *þinng MS.*   [10] w *corr. from* a.

will come, that thou mayst guard against them; and when thou art wounded through them, that thou mayst know how to heal thy wounds; and again, concerning those holy virtues, that thou mayst know how to recognise them well, and to keep them with God's help.

Of counsel.

Here comes another of God's gifts, which is called *consilium*, that is, counsel. Of this said Solomon: *Omnia fac cum consilio, et postea non poenitebis*, 'Do all things after counsel; afterwards thou wilt not repent.' Thou hast heard and learned many good things; accordingly take counsel, not from a wise man only, but from one who is both wise and also God-fearing, and tried in religion. What sort of life thou oughtst to lead best, depends much, whether thou hast misdone much, or little; and then, one must look after thy state, and thy body's health or sickness. Because it is a great danger for thee, if thou undertakest such things as thou canst not perform through sickness, which thou hadst promised to God. Again, be aware, if thou hast promised God to do much good, and to keep a holy life: thou canst not keep again the less good life thou hadst before, and be saved. Concerning this says the holy Gospel: *Qui mittit manum suam ad aratrum, et respicit retro, non est aptus regno Dei*, 'Who puts his hand to the plough of the Gospel, and will bear Christ's yoke, and forsakes all the world, and [then] looks back, turning to the world, is not worthy of the kingdom of Heaven.' This is said of the man who forsakes all the world, and follows God's voice, which says thus: *Venite ad me omnes qui laboratis et onorati estis, et cet.*, 'Come unto Me,' says He, 'all ye that labour with evil works, and are heavy laden with many kinds of sins, and I will give you rest unto your souls; and I will lighten your burden, if ye will listen to My counsel. Bear My yoke of obedience upon you, which is soft, and the burden of My commandments is light to hold. With My help ye can do everything; without Me, nothing.' For this sweet calling come both good and evil, and leave all the world, and take Christ's mark of true religion upon them, of whatsoever kind it may

cumen)¹, þat ðu muȝe bien war wið hem; and ðar ðu art ðurh hem
ȝewunded, ðat ðu cunne hes halen; and eft, of ðese hali mihtes,
ðat tu hes kunne wel ȝecnawen, and mid godes fultume wiðhealden.

Of rade.

HIER after cumð an oðer godes ȝiue, ðe is icleped consilium, þat
is, ræd. Herof seide Salomon: Omnia fac cum consilio,
et postea non penitebis, 'Do alle þing after rade, ðer after hit
ne scal þe ofþenchen.' Maniȝe gode þinges ðu hafst iherd and
ilierned; nim ðar after rad, naht at wise manne one, and þe bie
baðe² wis and ec goddfrihti, and ifonded of religiun. Hwilch lif
ðu betst muȝe laden, ðat auþ to benne michel after ðan ðe ðu
hafst michel misdon, oðer litel; and ðanne mot me lokin ðin
ikinde, and ðinne lichame(s) hæle oðer unhale. Forðan, ȝif ðu
undernimst swilch ðat tu for unhale ne miht iforðin, ðat ðu godd
haddest behaten, hit is ðe³ michel⁴ hauht⁵. Eftsones bie warr,
ȝif ðu behatst god michel god te donn, and heih lif te healden:
ðat lasse gode lif ðe ðu arrer hafdest, ne miht tu naht eft healden,
and bien ȝeboreȝen⁶. Hier of seið ðat hali godspell: Qui
mittit manum s(ù)am ad aratrum, et respicit retro,
non est aptus regno dei, 'Se ðe doð his hand to ðere sull
of godspelle, and Cristes ȝoc wile beren, and forlat al ðe woreld,
and loceð abach, wændinde to ðe woreld, he nis naht wurðe⁷
heuene riche.' Dis is ȝesæd bi ða manne ðe forlat al ðe woreld,
and folȝeð godes stiefne, ðe ðus seið: Venite ad me omnes qui
laboratis et honorati estis, et cetera, 'Cumeð to me,' he seið,
'alle ðe swinkeð mid euele werkes, and ȝeheueȝed bieð mid mani-
kennes sennes, and ic eu wile ȝiue reste to ȝeuer saule, and ic wile
lihten ȝeuer berðene, ȝif ȝe mine rad hlesten willeð. Bereð min
ȝoc uppe ȝeu, of hersumnesse, þe is softe, and min berðen is liht,
of mine bebodes to healden. Mid mine fultume alle ðing ȝe
muȝen; wið-uten me, nanþing.' For ðessere swete clepienge
cumeð baðe gode and euele, and lateð all ðe woreld, and nimeð
Cristes marc uppen hem, of soðe religiun, hwilche kennes swa hit

---
¹ *red above; the last word is written* cinneri *or* cinnery.   ² bade *MS.*
³ *page* 44.   ⁴ hit *is te repeated on page* 44; *between* te *and* michel *a
little stroke (like* i) *above the line.*   ⁵ hauth *MS.*   ⁶ *The second* ȝ *corr. from* c.
⁷ wurde *MS.*

be. The Holy Ghost warns them, who says: 'God who hath called you out of the false world into good life, doeth not force you to it, but sayeth: *Si vis perfectus esse,* 'If thou wilt,' He says, 'be a perfectly good man, forsake the world; and if thou wilt not, thou mayst dwell in the world, and also be saved, if thou well keepest thy baptism.' But if thou canst not save thyself well, or thou wilt suffer more, for Christ's love, and lead a better life : listen, I will warn thee concerning it. *Fili, accedens ad servitudinem Dei, etc.,* 'Dear son,' says He, 'if thou comest to God's house to serve Him, be well aware, and prepare thy soul against many kinds of temptations, and stand with great dread, because thou shalt be tried in the holy life as is the pot which is put into the burning oven. If it bursts in it and breaks, it is lost and soon thrown out ; if it remains whole and sound, the potter puts it where it was destined to.' The apostle says that God will not suffer one of His chosen ones to be tried more than he can bear. But they who burst within their dwellings, through the pride with which their heart is as much filled as a bladder is with wind, are thrown out through the devil's lore, not for their own sake only, but also in order to put others to flight. Then they will go again into the world, and be worse than they were before. They will cast away their counsel and their clothes, and betake themselves to the world and are apostates from Christ, forsakers, not with words, but with works, which is worse, if it may be. A monk may go out with leave into a hermitage, or to live in solitude, if he has God to witness that he does so with a pure heart, in order to do better. We find in the Writ that a hermit ought not to live in the wilderness, except he be at first tried through rule and through a master in the spiritual oven that we spoke about before. An anchorite's life is a very spiritual one. These two lives, the hermit's and a solitary life, which we now call an anchorite's, were formerly spent far from men and [those] were much loved and exalted by the holy Fathers who lived so and kept it honourably. So one may still find some— thanked be God!—who lead a very spiritual life according to the world which is now. Also one may find, among men of all kinds of

OF COUNSEL.

bie. Þe hali gast¹ (hem) warneð, *and* seið: 'Godd ðe ȝeu haueð icleped ut of ðare lease woreld *in* to gode liue, he ne nett ȝeu naht ðer to, ac seið: Si uis *perfectus* esse, 'ȝif ðu wilt,' he seið, 'bien ðurhut god man*n*, ðanne forlat ðu ðe woreld; *and* ȝif² ðu³ nelt naht, þu miht wuniȝen *on* ðare woreld, *and* ec bien ȝeboreȝen, ȝif ðu ðin*n*e cristendom wel hal(d)st.' Ac ȝif ðu ne miht ðe naht wel berȝen⁴, oðer ðu wilt, for Cristes luue, more þoliȝen, *and* betere lif laden: lhist⁵, ðerof ic ðe wile warnin. Fili, accedens ad seruitudine*m* dei, *et cetera*⁶, 'Lieue sune,' he seið, 'þan*n*e ðu cu*m*st to godes huse him to ðenin, bie wel war, *and* ȝarke ðine saule aȝen maniȝes ken*n*es fandi*n*ges, *and* stand mid michel dradnesse, forðan ðu scalt bien ȝefonded on ða hali liue al swo is þe pott ðe is idon on ðe barnen*de* ofne. Gif he ðar inne bersteð *and* brekð, he is forloren *and* sone ut-ȝeworpen; ȝif he belæfð hal *and* ȝesund, ðe pottere hine deð ðar to ðe he iscape*n* was.' Þe apostele seið ðat godd ne wile naht þoliȝen of none his icorene more te fondin ðan*n*e he muȝe þolien. Ac ðo ðe bersteð wið-inne here wunienge for here modinesse, hwarof here herte is swa full swa is bladdre of winde, hie bieð ut-iworpen ðurh dieules lare, naht for hem seluen ane, ac for oðre ec awei te affleien. Ðanne fareð hie eft to ðare worold, *and* bieð forcuðere ðanne hie arrer wæren. Hie forwerpeð here ræd *and* here claðes, *and* nemeeð⁷ hem to ðare worold *and* bieð apostate Criste, forsakene, naht mid wordes, ac mid werkes, ðe werse is, ȝif hit mai. Munec mai ut-faren mid ileaue *in* to hermitorie, oðer *in* to onnesse te wunien, ȝif⁸ he godd hafð to iwitnesse ðat he mid hlutter herte hit doð, for bett to donne. We findeð on ȝewrite þ*at* eremite ne owh on wilderne te wu-⁹nien, bute he arst bie ȝefanded ðurh regule *and* ðurh maistre in ðan gastliche ofne ðe we ær embe spaken. Ancer is swiðe gastlich lif. Ðese¹⁰ twa lif, hermite *and* ansæte lif, ðe we nu clepeð anker, hie wæren hwile ferr fra*m* mannen wuniende, *and* wæren swiðe iluuede *and* iheiȝed ðurh ða hali faderes ðe ðar inne wuneden *and* hit orliche hielden. Swa me mai ȝiet sume finden—iþanked¹¹ bie godd!—ðe swiðe gastlich lif lædet after ðare worold ðe nu is. Al

---

¹ *a letter erased*, hem *on the side*. ² ȝis *MS*. ³ *page* 45. ⁴ bergen, *MS.*
⁵ lihst *MS*. ⁶ Salamon *written against this at side*.
⁷ *Between* neme *and* eð *a slit in the vellum*. ⁸ Gif *MS*. ⁹ *page* 46.
¹⁰ s *corr. from* d. ¹¹ iþandked *MS*.

lives, some good and some evil. He knows it, who knows everything. If thou wilt remain in the world, and have wife and children, and till land and weary thyself, thou shalt have all the more toil. But if thou hast a good counsellor, thou mayst well live there, and also earn good reward from God. Do all the things which thou hast to do, with counsel; and let the counsel be such, that thou doest nothing against the holy Writ. Christ warns us of this, who says thus: *Dum es cum adversario tuo in via, etc.*, 'Whiles thou art in the way with thine adversary, grant him what he will have done, lest he take thee and deliver thee to the dun (creditor), and he afterwards deliver thee to the tormenters and to the killers!' Follow this Gospel, if thou wilt. God's word, God's counsel is thy enemy, because it does not say all that thou wouldst wish. But if thou wilt listen to God, thou must be obedient to the holy Writ, the little while thou art with it here in this road, in this short life; and know forsooth, except thou agreest to it here whatever it advises thee to do: when thou comest into the higher way, when thou art separated from thy body, it will deliver thee up to the dun (creditor), who will claim thee for each sin, and maintain his right after God's own word, that thou hast to follow him to hell, because thou hast been disobedient to God as he [is]. Therefore listen now to what God advises thee: *Divitiae si affluant, nolite cor apponere,* 'If the world's riches much increase towards thee, set not thy heart upon them, but set it on Me. Riches will fail thee, I will never fail thee. Why is thy coffer dearer to thee than I? Did I not send to thee, saying by the writ of the Gospel that thou shouldst make thy hoard above in the kingdom of Heaven, and not upon earth? Why wilt thou not be obedient to Me?' Listen still further to Christ's advice, what He says in the holy Gospel: *Cum facis prandium aut coenam, noli vocare amicos tuos, etc.*, 'When thou wilt make a dinner,' Christ says, 'call not thy friends, nor thy brethren to it, neither thy kinsmen, nor thy neighbours. If any of these can repay thee for thy dinner, do not call them. But call the poor and the weak, the blind, the dumb, the deaf, the halt, who cannot repay thee for it; then thou art blessed: [for] thou shalt be recompensed *in*

swa me mai, mang alles kennes liues menn, sume gode and sume
euele finden. He it wot, ðe all wot. ȝif ðu wilt on ðare woreld
beleauen, and wif and childre hauen, and land teliȝen and weriȝen,
ðu scalt hauen ðas te more iswink. Ac ȝif ðu hauest godne rad- 4
ȝiue, ðu miht ðar wel libben, and ec at gode god lean ofearniȝen.
Alle ðo þing ðe ðu hauest te donne, do it mit ræde; and ðe rad bie
swulch, ðat tu noht ne do aȝenes ðe holi write. Hierof us warneð
Crist, and ðus seið: Dum es cum aduersario tuo in ui(a), et 8
cetera, 'Ðarhwile ðe ðu art mid þine wiðerwine on ða weiȝe, bie
him teiþinde ðat ðe he wile hauen idon, læste he ðe niɲe and
betæche ðe ðe crauiere, and he seððen betache ðe ðe pineres and
ðe cwelleres!' Ðis godspell folȝe, ȝif ðu wille. Godes word, godes 12
ræd is ðin unwine, forðat hit ne seið noht al ðat tu woldest. Ac
ȝif ðu wilt lesten godd, þu scalt bien ðe hali write buhsum, ðo litle
hwile ðe ðu art mid him her on ðese weiȝe, on ðese scorte liue;
and wite ðu te soðe, bute ðu him bie hier teiðinde hwat swa hit ðe 16
ratt[1] to donne: ðanne ðu cumst on ða hei(g)ere[2] weiȝe, ðanne ðu
art itwamd fram ðine lichame, hit te wile betachen ðe crauiere[3],
ðe ðe wile crauen of elchere senne, and betellen riht after godes
awene worde, ðat tu aust him to folȝin to helle, forðan ðe ðu art 20
godd unhersum al swa he. Forði hlest nv hwat godd ðe ratt:
Diuicie si affluant, nolite cor apponere, 'Worldes eihte, ȝif
hie is swiðe rixinde to ðeward, ne do ðu náht ðine herte ðerto, ac
do hes to me. Ðe richeise ðe scal trukien, ic ne truke ðe naure. 24
Hwi is te ðin hucche[4] trewer ðanne ich? Ne sente ic ðe seggen bi
ða write of goddspelle ðat tu scoldest makie ðin hord up in heuen-
riche[5], and naht upen ierðe? Hwi ne wilt tu me bien buhsum?'
Hlest ȝiet furðer Cristes rad, hwat he seið on ða hali godspelle: 28
Cum facis prandium aut cenam, noli[6] uocare amicos tuos,
et cetera, 'Ðanne ðu wilt makien gestninge,' seið Crist, 'ne clepe
ðu naht ðine friend, ne ðine breðren ðarto, ne ðine kenesmen, ne
ðine neihibures. Gif æni of ðesen ðe muȝen forȝielden ðine 32
gestninge, ðane ne clepe ðu hes naht. Ac clepe ðo wrecches and
to unmihti, þe blinde, ðe dumbe, ðe deaue, ðe halte, ðe ne muȝen
naht hit te forȝielden; ðanne art tu isæli: hit te scal bien forȝolden

[1] page 47.   [2] g rcd above i.   [3] deuele at side.
[4] u on erasure.   [5] c corr. from another letter.   [6] Corr. from Nolite.

resurrectione justorum, that is, when the righteous will arise, and thou among them, on God's right hand.' If thou doest not so, the devil cannot well maintain that thou art disobedient to God. Who does this? Who keeps this? Why do men say that one cannot well be saved in the world? Why wilt thou not follow God's counsel and His teaching? This is truly one of the holy virtues which God divides among His chosen ones, that He gives them good counsel through the holy Writ, which He sends them in order to say how they may work His will, and so be saved. Let him listen and follow whoso will! *Omni petenti te, tribue,* 'Give to every man that asketh of thee, if thou hast what he has not, as thou wouldst that he should do to thee, if thou hadst not.' Therefore He says: 'If thou givest to the man who gave to thee, or whom thou knowest will give to thee, what reward oughtst thou to have from God? Do not so the sinful men who know nothing of God? If thou lovest the same that love thee: do not so the worst men of the world? Do not so the heathen? But love thy enemies for the love of God; thou shalt have great reward for it from God; and let Him revenge who is a righteous judge over the living and over the dead! If a needful man will borrow from thee of thy property, lend him blithely, as to thy fellow-Christian, without any reward, and thou shalt have the reward from God.' If thou lendest him anything of thine, and thou takest again more than thou lentst him: surely thou actest against God's commandment, and deservest His wrath, except thou repairest it. For after the holy Writ, every reward is reckoned for usury; and the usurers will never come into the kingdom of Heaven; for, though they would divide all that they have got with usury and with unrighteousness, it is not agreeable to God, who is righteous. The rich men who lend their property upon churches and upon the church-lands, or upon towns, or upon other things which yield rents, and keep them longer than until they have as much as they lent upon them, full assuredly they are doomed as usurers; and they shall have all such reward for it as usurers, that is, the pain of hell, except they repay it. And the amendment is no other than to repay what they have taken unjustly, and with penitence. Concerning this said the prophet: *Domine, quis habitabit in tabernaculo tuo, aut quis, etc.,* 'Lord,' said he, ' who in resurrectione iustorum, ðat is, ðanne ðe rih(t)wise sculen arisen, *and* tu amang¹ hem, on godes swiðre.' Gif ðu naht herof ne dest, ne mai ðe deuel betellen wel ðat tu art gode unhersum. Hwa doð þis? Hwa halt þis? Whi seggeð men ðat me ne mai naht wel bien ʒeboreʒen on ðare woreld? Hwi ne wilt tu folʒin godes rad *and* his lore? Þis is iwis on of ðe hali mihtes ðe godd scift mang his ʒecorene, ðat he ʒifð² hem god ræd þurh ðe haliʒe writes, ðe he sent hem seggen hu hie muʒen his wille werchen, *and* swa bien ʒeboreʒen. Hlest *and* folʒih se ðe wile! Omni petenti te, tribue³, 'Ælche manne ðe ðe bitt ðu aust to ʒiuen, ʒif⁴ ðu hafst ðat te he ne haueð, swa ðu woldest ðat he dede ðe, ʒif ðu ne hafdest.' Forðan he seið: 'ʒif ðu ʒifst ðo manne ðe gaf ðe, oðer ðe wost ðat wile ʒiuen ðe, whilch lean aust ðu te hauen of godd? Ne don swa ðe senfulle men ðe of gode noht ne cunnen? Gif ðu luuest ðo ilche ðe ðe luuiʒeð: ne don swa ðe werste menn of ðe woreld? Ne don swa ðe heðene? Ac luue þine unwines for ðe luue of godd; ðarof ðu scalt hauen michel lean of godd; *and* lat him wreke ðe is riht deme ouer ðe liuiende *and* ouer ðe deade. ʒif nedfull mann wile borʒin at te of ðin eihte, lean him bleðcliche, al swa ðin emcristen, wiðuten elchere mede, *and* ðu scalt hauen ðe mede of god.' Gif ðu him lanst ani þing of ðinen, *and* tu nimst aʒean more ðanne ðu him lændest: iwis ðu art aʒeane(s) godes bebode, *and* his wraððe of-earnest, bute ðu hit ib(i)ete. Forðan after ðe hali writes, ealch miede is iteld for gauele; *and* þe gaueleres ne cumen neure into heueriche; for ðan, ðeih hie dælden all ðat hie mid gauele biʒeten⁵ habbeð *and* mid unrihtwisnesse, hit nis naht gode icweme, ðe is rihtwis. Ða riche menn ðe laneð here eihte uppe chierches *and* uppe ða chirch-landes, oðer uppe tu-⁶nes, oðe uppe oðre þinges þe rentes ʒiueð, *and* healden hes lenger ðanne hie hauen al swa michel swa hie ðar uppe lænden, fullʒewiss hie bieð idemd for gouleres; *and* al swulch lean hie sculen ðarof habben alse gaueleres, ðat is, helle pine, bute hie hit biete⁷. *And* ðe bote nis nan oðer bute ʒielden ðat hie habben mid unrihte inomen, *and* mid scrifte. Her of sæde ðe profiete: Domine, quis habitabit in tabernaculo tuo, aut quis, et cetera⁸, 'Hlauerd,' he sæde, 'hwa

¹ amanʒ, *MS.*   ² *page* 48.   ³ Ewangeli*sta at side, over a red* lu *or* lif.
⁴ Gif *MS.*   ⁵ biʒetenð *MS.*   ⁶ *page* 49.   ⁷ *an erasure above* te.
⁸ psalmi*sta written at side, red.*

shall abide with Thee in Thy house, or who shall rest himself on Thy holy hill of the kingdom of Heaven?' The Holy Ghost answered him, after other things, and said: *Qui jurat proximo suo, etc.*, 'He that sweareth truth to his neighbour, that is, his fellow-Christian, and deceiveth him not with any bargain or with any other thing; and he that putteth not out his money to usury, nor taketh reward from the *innocentes*, that is, harmless men who intend no evil to anybody: these shall abide in God's tent, and rest themselves on His hill.' And those who take reward, shall never come there, if they are taken away with it. Now there are some others who esteem themselves wise and crafty, and entrust their money to the heathen, in order to have gain from it; and some lend to their fellow-Christian for half-gain, who travels with it by land and by water in great danger of life and of soul, and with great toil: and they [themselves] sit at home and have no trouble for it, except in their thoughts and in their speeches. Clerics and laymen see and hear this; but through the evil custom it seems to them no misdeed, but those are esteemed wise and crafty men. Of such said God through the prophet: *Vae, qui sapientes estis in oculis vestris, et coram vobismet ipsis prudentes*, ' Woe unto you that esteem yourselves wise, and are prudent in your eyes! Ye deceive My people by your evil example, and by your sharp intellect. Ye understand how to defend yourselves by your manifold speeches; ye justify the wicked for reward, and take away the righteousness of the righteous from him!' Therefore he is now esteemed a fool, except he gets much property; and ye justify those who get much property by your great property, and say that they are worthy and good men. The prophet says still further: *Vae, qui dicitis bonum malum, et malum bonum*, 'Woe unto you who say that it is good to get much property, which cannot be got without unrighteousness!' Therefore it is called by God's mouth *Mammon of iniquity*. Woe unto you who say that he is unhappy who has no worldly property, who will get none by any injustice, and who, after having

mai wunen mid ðe on ðine huse¹, oðer hwa mai him resten upe ðin
haliȝe munte of heueneriche²?' Ðe hali gast him andswerede, after
oðre þinges, and sæde: Qui iurat proximo suo, et cetera, 'Se
ðe swereð soð his nexte, þat is, his emcristenn, and him naht ne 4
beswikð mid none chiepinge ne mid nan oðre ðinge; and se ðe ne
ȝifð naht his eihte te goule, and se ðe ne nimð none mede of ða
innocentes, ðat bien uneilinde menn ðe none manne euel ne
willeð: ðese muȝen wuniȝen on godes telde, and uppen³ his munte 8
hem resten.' And ða ðe mede nemeð, hie ne sculen ðar neure
cumen, ȝif hie bien ðar mide ȝenomene. Nu bien sume oðre ðat
healden hem seluen wise and ȝeape, and befasteð here paneȝes ðe
haðene menn, for to habben of hem biȝeate; and sume, hi læneð 12
here emcristen te halue biȝeate, ðe fareð ðar mide be londe and
be watere on michele hahte on liue and on saule, and mid michele
swinke: and hie sitteð at ham and ne hauen ðarof non ȝeswink,
bute on here ðohtes and on here spaches. Ðis ȝesieð and ȝehiereð 16
hadede and leeavede; and for ðare euele ȝewune ne ðin(c)ð hit hem
no misdade, ac bieð ihealden for wi-⁴se menn and for ȝeape. Of
swilche sade godd ðurh ðe profiete: Ve, qui sapientes estis in
oculis uestris, et coram uobis met⁵ ipsis prudentes!⁶ 'Wa 20
ȝeu ðe healdeð ȝeu seluen for wise, and to-foren ȝeu seluen bieð
ȝeape! Ȝie beswikeð mi folk mid ȝeure euele forbisne, and mid
ȝeure scarpe witt. Ȝie cunnen ȝeu bewerien mid ȝeuere manifelde
spaches; ȝerihtwisið ðane forȝelte for medes, and ðe rih(t)wisnesse 24
of ðe rihtwise manne ȝe him benemeð.' For ðan he is ihealde nu
for sott, bute he michel eihte beȝete; and þo ðe michel eihte
biȝeteð mid ȝeure michele eihte, hem ȝie rihtwisið, and seggeð þat
he bien auhte men and gode menn. He seið ȝiet forðer, ðe profiete: 28
Ve, qui dicitis bonum malum, et malum bonum⁶, 'Wa ȝeu
ðe seggeð ðat it is god te biȝeten michel eihte, ðe ne mai bien
biȝeten wið-uten⁷ unrihtwisnesse⁸!' For-ði hie is icleped of godes
muðe Mammona iniquitatis. Wa ȝeu ðe seggeð ðat he is 32
unsali ðat none wordles eihte ne hafð, ðe mid nane unrihte none ne
wile biȝeten, and ða ðat he hadde mid maniȝe unrihtes biȝeten

---

¹ use on erasure.   ² riche(s) MS.   ³ the stroke above e is red.
⁴ page 50.   ⁵ t corr. from ð.   ⁶ propheta red at side.
⁷ a letter erased behind ē.   ⁸ unirht- MS.

lost what he had got by much unrighteousness, suffers it with patience, and thanks God. God says in another place: *Vae, qui ridetis, quia plorabitis,* 'Woe unto you that laugh now for the vain bliss of this world, and for your great wealth which ye have now! Woe unto you that tax your fellow-Christian, and turn the right into wrong, and the wrong into right, and that take reward for your deceitful speeches, that speak on either side, as if ye were friend of both of them!' If thou wilt dwell in the world, and keep in mind these words of God, and follow the blessed Job, who was a good worldly man, thou canst save thyself with God's help.

Of strength.

Here follows another of God's gifts, which is called *fortitudo*, that is, strength of God. It is very needful; be thou never so wise, nor so cunning, nor so prudent to do what thou shalt do: except thou hast this strength of God, thou canst do no good. Thou canst see many a very wise clerk, who certainly does not instruct himself, and thinks that he has enough in his knowledge which he understands, and does not beg this strength from God; therefore he remains among them who understand no good, and is like them in works. Just as easily he sometimes will misdo, as he who understands no good. Whoso for fear of God keeps himself from all cardinal sins and from all the things which God forbids him, has this strength of God. David the king lost this holy virtue, when he committed adultery with Bath-sheba, Solomon's mother, who was wedded to Uriah. But he never ceased until he had [got] it again. *Miserere mei, Deus,* this precious psalm he made anon, and cooled God's wrath by it. 'Lord,' quoth he, 'according to Thy great commiseration, have mercy upon my great sin! And according unto Thy manifold mercies, which Thou hast had towards mankind, do away from me this great unrighteousness, so that Thy tender eyes may never see in me what mislikes them! But let the stream of Thy sweet mercy, which never ceases, run to me, so that I may understand when it comes, through the flowing tears which it brings with it unto the dried-

(he haueð forloren)¹, and ðat ðoleð mid ðolemodnesse, and gode þankeð. An oðer stede he seið, godd: Ve qui ridetis, quia plorabitis², 'Wa ȝeu ðe nu leiheð for ðese³ wordles lease blisse, and for ȝeure michele wele ðe ȝe nu hauen! Wa ȝeu ðe beplaitið ȝeuer emcristen, and wændeð ðat rihte te w(r)ohȝe⁴, and ðat wohȝe te rihte, and ðe nimeð mede for ȝeuer swikele spache(s), ðe spekeð an aiðer half, swilche ȝie here beire friend wære.' Ȝif ðu wilt on ðare world wuniȝen, and ðurh ðese godes wordes war bien and ðane eadie Iob folȝin, ðe was god worldmann: ðu miht mid godes fultume ðe seluen berȝen⁵.

Of stren[g]ðe.

HIER after cumþ an oðer godes ȝiue, ðe is icleped fortitudo, þat is, strengþe of gode. Hie is swiðe niedfull; ne bie ðu næure swa wis, ne so ȝeap, ne swa witti to donne ðat tu scalt don: bute ðu habbe ðese strengþe of gode, ne miht tu non god don. Ðu miht isien sum wel wis clerec, ðe wisliche him seluen naht ne wisseð, and þincþ ðat he hafð inohȝ on his witte ðe he cann, ne ðese strengþe ne besekð (nauht) at gode; for ði he belæfð among ðan ðe non god ne cunnen, and hem he is ilich of werkes. Alswa lihtliche oðerhwile he misdoð, al swo he ðe non god ne cann. Se ðe for godes eiȝhe him halt fram alle heued-sennes and fram alle ðe forbodes ðe god him forbiet, he hafð ðese strengþe of gode. Ðese hali mihte forleas Dauið kyng, ða ðe he forlaiȝ mid Bersabee, Salomones moder, ðe was bewedded Vrie. Ac he naure ne ȝeswoc⁶ ær he hes eft (h)afde. Miserere mei deus, ðane derewurðe salm anon he makede, and godes wrað he ðar mide acolede. 'Hlauerd,' cwað he, 'after ðat ðe ðin mildce ys michel, haue ore of mine michele senne! And after ðine manifealde mildces ðe ðu hafst ihafd to mankenne, do awei fram me ðese michele unrihtwisnesse, ðat næure ðine milde eiȝen ne ȝeseo on me ðat hem mislikie. Ac let ðane wellstream, ðe næure ne trukeð, of ðine swete mildce iernen to me, swa (ðat)⁷ ic muȝe understanden hwanne he cume⁸ ðurh ðe flowinde teares ðe he

---
¹ On the side.   ² Ewangelista, red at side.   ³ s corr. from d.   ⁴ r red above.
⁵ page 51.   ⁶ a underdotted before o.   ⁷ written above, red.   ⁸ cumen MS.

up heart. And besprinkle me with the hyssop of the holy cross, of the holy water which came out of the right side of Thy holy temple. Then shall I become cleansed from all my sins, and whiter than any snow. Lord, still I have more need! *Cor mundum crea in me, Deus*! My heart is much defiled with foul thoughts, for the sin which I first thought to do, and I know that Thou neither wilt nor canst dwell in it. But make it pure and clean, so that Thou mayst dwell within me, and renew a right spirit within me. For my spirit is grown very old, and wasted away, through the great error when it went out of Thy right way, and followed the devil's doctrine, and rejected Thine. *Ne projicias me*, because, my dear Lord, I am well conscious that I have deserved to be rejected by Thee, as I rejected Thee and Thy teaching. But now I beg Thee, through Thy great goodness, that Thou mayst not reject me from Thy face, as the lord who is wrath against his servant, and drives him from his face. And never take from me Thy Holy Ghost that Thou hast given me through Thy great goodness! Sorry and sorrowful am I, night and day, until I have Him. *Redde mihi laetitiam*, Lord, give me now again the same bliss of Thy salvation which I had before, ere I sinned! Thou hadst made me glad and blithe; but I have lost it because of my weakness. And fasten in me the spirit of strength, and make me strong through Thy power! I fancied to have strength of myself, and therefore I fell. But if Thou now wilt raise me, and bestow upon me a right and strong spirit: *docebo iniquos, etc.*, [then] will I teach the unrighteous Thy ways, and tell them how great mercy Thou hast [had] on me, who was all guilty against Thee; and the merciless who never yet had mercy on themselves nor on others, shall turn to Thee, and believe in Thee, and praise and bless Thee, and become holy men by Thy grace, who were the devil's before. Lord, I now thank Thee above all things! I feel my heart consoled through Thy great mercy, that Thou hast sent upon me, sinful man, the spirit of consolation, which fills my sorry heart with the sweet bliss of its dear vision, through the tears which come running, brinkgð mid¹ him to ðere fordruȝede hierte. And spræng me mid tare ysope of ðare holi rode, of ðan holie watere ðe ȝiede ut of ðe riht² side of ðine hali temple. Ðanne wurð ic iclansed of alle mine sennes, and hwittere ðane ani snaw. Lauerd, ȝiet ic habbe more niede. Cor mundum crea in me, deus³! Min herte is swiðe hefeld mid fule þohtes, for ðare senne ðe ic arst þohte to donne, and ic wat ðat þu ne wilt ne ðu ne miht on hire wuniȝen. Ac make hes hlutter and clene, þat tu muȝe wuniȝen mid me, and rihtne gost newe inne me. For ðan min gast is swiðe for-⁴ealded and forwurðen, for ðe michele dwele, ða ðe he ȝiede ut of ðe rihte weiȝe, and folȝede dieules lare, and forwarp ðine. Ne proicias me³, for ði, min leue lauerd, ich am wel bicnawe ðat ic habbe ofearned þat ðu scoldest me forwurpen, swa swa ic forwarp þe and ðine lore⁵. Acc nu ic bidde ðe, for ðine michele godnesse, ðat tu ne forwerp me fram ðine ansiene, al swa ðe lauerd ðe is wrað wið his þralle, and drifð him ut of his ansiene. And ðine hali gast ðe ðu me hafst iȝiuen for ðine michele godnessse, ne benem ðu me næure. Sari and sorhfull am ic, niht and dai, al hwat ic hine habbe. Redde mihi leticiam⁶, Hlauerd, ȝif me nu aȝean ðe ilche blisse þat ic (h)adde ær, ar ic sineȝede, of ðire hale. Þu hafdest me imaked glad and bliðe; ac ich hes haue forloren for mine wocnesse. And faste on me ðane gost of strengþe, and make me strong ðurh ðire mihte. Ic wende habben strengþe of me seluen, and for ði i fell. Ac ȝif ðu nu me wilt aræren, and rihte gost and stronge me betachen, docebo iniquos, et cetera⁶, ic wile tache ðo unrih[t]wisen ðine weiȝes, and hem kyðen hu michel mildce ðu hafst of me, ðe was all forȝelt aȝeanes þe; and to orelease ðe næure ȝiete ne hadden ore of hemseluen ne of oðren⁷, hie sculen wænden to ðe, and ȝelieuen on ðe, and ðe heriȝen and blescien, and mid þine grace hali menn becumen, þe ærrer waren ðes dieules. Lauerd, nu ic ðe þanki ouer alle þing. Ic ȝefele min herte ȝefrieured ðurh þine michele mildce, ðe on me senfulle hafst ȝesænt ðane froure gost, ðe felð mine sari herte mid ðare swete blisse of his lieue sune, ðurh ðo

---

¹ min MS.   ² page 52.   ³ Psalmista written at the side, red.
⁴ between for and e a letter erased.   ⁵ and ðine lare repeated.
⁶ Psalmista red at side.   ⁷ page 53.

with great bliss, on the dried-up land. Lord, now I would praise Thee, and offer a sacrifice, if I had anything which would be agreeable unto Thee. But I know well that *bonorum meorum non eges*, Thou hast no need of any of the goods which I have. But if it is Thy will that I must offer Thee a sacrifice, for Thy worship and my salvation, then Thou must do as Thou hast always done to all Thy people. Thou hast sent them their sacrifice, just as the good lord who sends offerings to his men for his own worship, and for their service. *Sacrificium Deo spiritus contribulatus*, according to what Thy Holy Ghost says: "The most agreeable sacrifice which one can offer Thee, is the spirit and the heart that are greatly afflicted with humility and with manifold thoughts of true repentance, which make the heart sorry and sob, and the eyes wet with running tears." St. Peter offered this sacrifice, when he had great guilt by forsaking Thee. He went out, *et flevit amare*, and bewept his sin very bitterly, and Thou forgavest it him. Mary Magdalene offered this sacrifice upon Thy precious feet, and she left there all her sins. Hannah offered Thee this sacrifice, who was barren, and despised among the people of Israel; and she was soon heard, and Thou answeredst her prayer, so that she might have a child and brought forth Thy prophet Samuel. We find written in the Holy Scripture that everyone was heard according to his need to whom it was Thy will to send this sacrifice.'

Dear soul, I have written this in order to console thee when thou hast need. Look and read; as for this holy virtue, it will please thee by night and by day, if thou wilt think of it with all thy heart.

Of understanding.

After this comes another of God's gifts, which is called *intellectus*, that is, understanding. This holy virtue makes [thee] understand God and all spiritual things, as much as thou canst understand while thou art bound in thy wretched body. God speaks of it through the prophet, and says to thee: *Intellectum tibi dabo, et instruam te, etc.*, 'I will give thee understanding, and I will instruct thee in this way which thou goest now. Because thou hast forsaken thy sins and thy evil customs, and learnest so teares ðe cumeð ierninde, mid michele blisse, uppe ðe fordruȝede londe. Hlauerd, nu ic ðe wolde wurðiȝen, *and* loc ofrien, ȝif ic hadde ani þing þat ðe icweme wære. Ac ic wot wel ðat bon*orum* meor*um* non eges[1], ðu nehafst none niede of non *ðare gode ðe ic habbe. Ac ðanne hit is þin wille ðat ic ðe loc ofrin mote, ðe to wurðscipe[2] *and* me to hale, ðanne most þu don al swa ðu hafst aure idon bi alle ðinen. Ðu hafst isænt hem here ofrende, al swa ðe gode hlauerd ðe sent his menn ofrende for his aȝene wurscipe, *and* for here seruise. Sac*rif*icium deo spi*ritus* contribulatus[1], after ðan ðe ðin hali gast seið: "Þat icwemeste loc ðat (mann ðe) mai ofrin, ðat is ðe gast *and* ðe hierte ðe bieð swiðe ȝeswæint mid eadmodnese *and* mid manifealde pohtes of soðe bereusinge, ðe makieð ðe herte sari *and* sobbiende, *and* ðe eiȝene wæte mid teares ierninde." Ðis lac offrede sanc*tu*s Pet*rus*, ða ða he was swa swiðe forȝ(i)elt ðat he hadde ðe forsaken. He ȝiede ut, et fleuit amare, *and* beweop hi(s) senne swiðe biterliche, *and* þu hes him forȝaue. Ðis loc offrede Marie Magdalene upe ðine derewurðe fiet, *and* alle hire sennen hie ðar forliet. Ðis loc ðe ofrede Anna, ðe was unberinde, *and* unwurð mang Israele folke; *and* hie was sone iherd, *and* hire biene ðu hire teiðedest, þat hie chilt moste habben *and* brohte forð ði³ne profiete Samuel. On ða haliȝe write we hit findeð, hwam swo ðin wille was te senden ðis loc to ofrien, he was ȝeherd of his niede.'

Lieue saule, ðis ic habbe iwriten for ðe te frieurien ðanne ðu niede hafst. Loke *and* ræd; ðis holi mihte, hit te wile likin be nihte oðer be daiȝe, ȝif[4] ðu mid alre herte hier embe wilt þenchen.

Of andȝet.

HIERAFTER cumð an oðer godes ȝiue, ðe is icleped intellec-tus, þat is, andȝeat. Dies halie mihte, hie dieð understonden of gode *and* of alle gostliche þinges, swa michel swa ðu miht under-stonden ðe hwile ðe ðu art on ðine wrecche lichame ȝebunden. Hier of spekð godd ðurh ðe profiete, *and* seið to ðe: Intellect*um* t*ibi* dabo, *et* instruam te, *et* cet*era*, 'Ich ðe wile ȝiuen an[d]ȝeat, *and* ic ðe wile wissin on ðese weiȝe ðe ðu nu gost. For ði ðat tu

---

[1] Psalm*ista*, *red al side*.   [2] wurd- *MS*.   [3] *page* 54.   [4] ȝ *corr. red from* t.

blithely these holy virtues and receivest them well: My eyes shall be upon thee, and I will shield thee from all evil, as long as thou art conscious that thou hast no good but from Me.' Through this gift of God thou canst know all the thoughts which come from thy heart; which are of God, and which are of thy flesh, and which are of the devil. It is great need for thee to understand well the thoughts which come from God. Concerning this said the prophet: *Audiam, quid loquatur in me Dominus Deus,* 'I will listen to and understand what my Lord God speaketh in me.' Sometimes He will reprehend thee and make thee think thus: 'Why wilt thou continue in thy sins until death? Why can I have no dwelling with thee? Thy sins separate Me from thee; I can never dwell in a foul heart. As often as thou thinkest of Me, or hearest speak of Me: then I am with thee. Thou wast created, and afterwards hallowed, to My use, and that I, for thy profit, might dwell in thee. But thou drivest Me out of thee through thy manifold lusts which thou wilt follow, against My will. Unless thou ceasest, thou wilt repent it the more bitterly for ever!' At another time, when thou thinkest that God has forsaken or forgotten thee, He will say: *Numquid potest mater oblivisci filium uteri sui,* 'How can the mother forget the child which she bore in her womb? Though she forget it, I never forget thee.' At another time come many thoughts of God's threat, concerning the pains of hell; at another time He promises thee great joy in Heaven; at another time He consoles thee about thy sorrow for thy sins. But that is a great danger, except thou take much care of it, and thank Him much for it. The thoughts which come from thy flesh are always weak, either of meat, or of drink, or of clothes, or of sleep, or of some idleness. God forbids us to be either anxious or full of cares. He will find for all of us what is needful, if we first make Him rest in ourselves. *Primum quaerite regnum Dei, et haec omnia adjicientur vobis,* 'Seek ye first the kingdom of God,' and afterwards, says He,

hauest þine sennen[1] and ðine euele þeawes forlaten, *and* ðese hali
mihtes swa bleðeliche liernest[2] *and* wel undernimst: mine eieʒene
sculen bien uppe ðe, *and* ic ðe wile scilden fram alle euele, swa
longe swa ðu wilt bien icnawen ðat tu nan god ne hauest bute of 4
me.' Đurh ðessere godes ʒiue ðu miht alle ðo ðohtes icnawe ðe
cumeð fram ðire herte; hwilche bieð of gode, *and* hwilche of ðine
flesche, *and* hwilche bieð of ðe dieule. Đa ðohtes ðe cumeð of
gode, ðe is michel nied ðat tu wel understande[3]. Hier of sade 8
ðe profiete: A u d i a m, q u i d l o q u a t u r i n m e d o m i n u s d e u s,
'Ic wile lesten *and* understanden hwat min lauerd godd spekð in[4]
me. Oðer hwile he ðe wile undernemen *and* ðus ðe don[5]
þenchen: 'Hwi wilt ðu ðurhwuniʒen on ðine sennes anon to 12
ðin(e)[6] deaðe? Hwi ne mai ich none wuniʒenge habben mid ðe?
Đine sennes me[7] twameð fram ðe; ich ne mai næure wuniʒen on
fule herte. Swa ofte swa ðu ðenchst on me, oðer ihierst speken
of me: þare hwile ich am mid ðe. Đu ware ʒescapen, *and* eft 16
ʒehalʒed, to mine behofte *and* for ðine freme me ontewuniʒen. Ac
ðu me drifst ut of te for ðine manifealde willes ðe ðu folʒin wilt,
aʒeanes mine wille. Bute ðu iswik, ðe hwatliker hit te scall æure
ma rewen.' Oðerhwile, hwanne ðu ðencst ðat godd ðe hafð 20
forlaten oðer forʒeten, ðanne seið he: N u m q u i d p o t e s t
m a t e r o b l i u i s c i f i l i u m u t e r i s u i, 'Hv mai ðat moder
forʒeten ðat child ðe hie bar in hire wombe? Þeih hie hit forʒete,
ic næure ne forʒete ðe.' Oðerhwile cumeð maniʒe þohtes of godes 24
þreatt of helle pines. Oðerhwile he behat ðe michele merhþe[8] on
heuene. Oðerhwile he ðe frieureð of ðine sarinesse for ðine
sennes. Ac ðat is michel hauht, bute ðu hierof neme michele
ʒieme, *and* him hierof michel ðanki. Đa ðohtes ðat cumeð of 28
ðine flesce, æure hi beð nexse, oðer of mete, oðer of drenkch, oðer
of claðes, (oðer of slape)[9], oðer of sume idelnesse. Đis forbet
godd, þat we houhfull ne care-full ne scule bien. All he wile us
finden ðat nied is, ʒif we arst him makieð reste on us seluen. 32
P r i m u m q u e r i t e r e g n u m d e i, e t h e c o m n i a a d i c i e n t u r
u o b i s, 'Arst secheð godes riche,' *and* sið ðen he saið ðat alle

---

[1] sen-nnen *MS*. [2] liernedest *MS. with dots under* ed. [3] understanden *MS*.
[4] i *corr. from* o. [5] speken *underlined between* don *and* þ.
[6] in *corr. from* m. [7] *page* 55. [8] mehrþe *MS*. [9] *on the side*.

we shall have all these things. Against such thoughts thou shalt answer: *Non in solo pane vivit homo,* 'Man liveth not by bread alone, but liveth by the words that proceed out of the mouth of God.' If thou wilt know what the kingdom of God is, which thou shalt first seek: the holy apostle instructs us, who says: *Regnum Dei non est esca et potus, sed justitia, et pax, et gaudium in spiritu sancto,* 'The kingdom of God is not meat and drink; but righteousness, and peace, and joy in the Holy Ghost.' That is the kingdom of God!

Dear soul, I beg and warn thee to have no hope in thy fasting, nor in thy watching, nor in any other good. Except thou have these three things, God will never reign in thee, nor thou evermore with Him, viz. that thou be righteous towards God and towards all men. Give to each what he ought to have! Again, [it is necessary] that thou have peace with God and with all men; and if thou breakest it, may God shield thee! Do thou not so. Thou hast no longer respite than the apostle says: *Sol non occidat super iracundiam vestram,* 'On the same day that thou breakest [peace], see that thou be reconciled, ere the sun goes to rest!' Take now great care of this third thing: that is, let thy bliss not be in any earthly thing, but in the Holy Ghost alone. Woe, Eve's children, how are ye deceived, who seek bliss without Paradise, where no bliss is! Turn back, turn back, and go home, otherwise you will never have any! Even the thoughts which come from the devil are always bitter, except thou givest way to his deceitful admonition; at first it seems sweet to thee, but in the end it is very bitter. When thoughts of avidity, or of luxury, or of covetousness, or of wrath, and of envy and indignation, or of vain boasting, or of haughtiness and pride come to thee, know thou forsooth that it is the devil or his messenger. The will of the flesh holds sometimes with him; do not love either of them! *Nolite fieri, etc.,* 'Be not like the horse or the mule, which have no understanding,' but above all take heed of your heart. Every day thoughts come to it, as flies to a sore. Let him resist who will! As long as thou art in this poor life, thou art in a great fight. Those who fight not, are all trodden down under the devil's feet. Be prudent ðese þing we sculen habben. Onȝeanes ðelliche ðohtes ðu scalt andsweriȝen: Non in solo pane uiuit homo, 'Ðe mann ne leueð[1] naht he bread ane, ac leueð bi ða wordes ðe gað ut[2] of godes muðe.' Ȝif ðu wilt witen hwat bie godes riche, ðe du arst scalt siechen : þe hali apostel us wisseð, and seið[3] : Regnum dei non est esca et potus, seð iusticia, et pax; et gaudium in spiritu sancto, 'Godes riche nis naht mete and drench, ac is rihtwisnesse, and sibsumnesse, and blisse in ðe hali gaste.' Þat is godes riche.

   Lieue saule, ic ðe bidde and warni ðat tu none hope ne haue upe ðine fastene, ne upe ðine wæcche, ne uppe non oðre gode. Bute ðu ðese þrie ðing habbe, ne rixit næure god on ðe, ne ðu næure mo mid him. Ðat is, ðat tu bie rihtwis aȝeanes gode and aȝenes alle mannen. Gield ælche ðat he auh te habben. Eftsones, ðat tu haue pais aȝeanes godd and aȝeanes alle mannen; and ȝif ðu brekst, scilde ðe godd! Ðat tu ne do. Ne hafst tu no lengere f(i)erst ðanne ðe apostele seið: Sol non occidat super iracundiam uestram, 'On ðan ilche daiȝe ðe ðu tebrecst, ær ðe sunne go te reste, loce ðat tu bie sahtled!' Of ðese ðridde þing nim nu michele ȝieme. Þat is, ðat tin blisse ne bie of non ierðliche þinge, bute of ðe haliȝe gast ane. Waleawa, Eve children, hu ȝie bieð beswiken, ðe secheð blisse wiðuten paradise, ðar ðe nan nis! Wændeð aȝean, wændeð aȝean and fareð hom, elles ne wurð ȝew næure mo non! Do ilche ðohtes ðe cumeð of ðe dieule, æure hie bieð bitere, bute ȝif ðu teiðest his swikele meneȝinge; hie ðe ðingþ arst swete, ac hie is at ten ænde wel bitter. Ðanne ðe ðohtes cumeð of ȝiuernesse, oðer of galnesse, oðer of ȝitsinge, oðer of wraððe, and of nið and of ande, oðer of idel ȝelp, oðer of modinesse and priede, wite ðu to soðe ðat it is dieuel oðer his sånde. Ðes flesces iwill halt oðer-h(w)ile mid him; ne lief[4] þu here noðer. Nolite fieri, et cetera, 'Ne bieð ȝelich ðe horse ne ðe mule, ðe ne habbeð non andȝet!' Ac nemeð ȝieme ouer alle þing te ȝeure[5] herte. Al dai ðar cumeð to þohtes, al swo doð fliȝen to sare. Weriȝe se ðe wile! All ðare hwile ðe ðu art on ðese earme liue, ðu art on muchele ifihte. Þa ðe noht ne fihten, he bieð al te-treden under dieules fiet. Bie ȝeap aȝean

---

[1] an erasure between e and u.   [2] t on erasure.   [3] page 56.
[4] page 57.   [5] to ȝeure before it, underlined.

against all the thoughts which I named to you before, and withstand them just as thou wouldst so many devils, if thou couldst see them. Take thy sword, that is, God's Word, and say: *Vade retro, Satana,* 'Go back, thou Satan, with all thy cursed spirits, not through my strength, but through His who overcame thee and drove thee away!'

Of wisdom.

After this comes another gift of God, which is called *sapientia*, that is, wisdom. Solomon says that *sapientia aedificavit sibi domum, etc.,* 'Wisdom,' says he, 'reared up herself a house, and she carved herself seven posts.' These are the seven holy virtues which we before have spoken about, beginning with that which is called the fear of God, which is the beginning of this wisdom. Here is gathered such timber as can never rot, and this precious virtue is work-master over it. *Vere, non est hic aliud, nisi domus Dei et porta coeli,* 'Verily, here is nothing else among such timbering but the house of God and the gate of the kingdom of Heaven!' This is certainly the holy virtue which is called God's wisdom, God's word. He says in the holy Gospel: *Si quis diligit me, etc.,* 'Whoso loveth Me will keep My words: and My Father will love him, and We will come unto him,' *et mansionem apud eum faciemus,* 'and We will make our abode with him.' Courage, thou dear soul, be now glad and blithe in the Holy Ghost, as I said before! Because thou hast gathered fair timber of these holy virtues, and God's own Wisdom is work-master over it, and says that He will dwell there with thee, because thou lovest Him and His words. We must now let thy wretched body rest, which is very weak and very frail. Its head aches, its eyes relax, its sustenance is little, for it has nothing but through its hand-work to live upon, and what men will give it, for the love of God, who have pity on it. It has toiled much about this: may God Almighty repay it, for it has now need to rest.

alle ðe ðohtes ðe ic ȝeu hier te-fore[1] nænnede, and wiðstond hem al
swa ðu woldest aȝeanes al so fele dieulen, ȝif ðu hes isien mihtest.
Nim ðin sweord, ðat is, godes word[2], and seiȝe : Vade retro,
satana, 'Go abach, (þu)[3] sathanas, mid alle ðine awerȝede [4]
go(st)es[4], naht þurh mine strengþe, ac ðurh his ðe ðe ouercam
and awei ðe drof!'

Of wisdom.

HIER after cumð anoðer godes ȝiue, ðat is sapiencia ȝe- [8]
namned, þat is, wisdom. Salemon seið þat sapiencia
edificauit sibi domum, et cetera, 'Wisdom,' he seið, 'ararde
hire an hus, and hie karf hire seuen postes.' Þat bieð ðo seuen
hali mihtes ðe we hier teforen habbeð ȝespeken, þe anginneð at [12]
tare ðe is icleped godes dradnesse, ðe is anginn of ðese wisdome.
Hier is igadered swilch timber ðe næure rotien ne mai, and þis
derewurðe mihte is wrihte ðerover[5]. Vere, non est hic aliuð,
nisi domus dei et porta celi, 'Fullȝewiss, nis her nan oðer [16]
mang þelliche timbringe bute godes hus and heueneriches gate.'
Ðis[6] is ȝewiss ðe holiȝe mihte ðe is icleped godes wisdom, godes
word. He seið on ðe holiȝe godspelle: Si quis diligit me, et
cetera, 'Se ðe luueð me he wile lokin mine wordes, and min fader [20]
him wile luuiȝen, and to him we willeð cumen,' et mansionem
apud eum faciemus, 'and mid him willeð ma[7]kien wunienge.'
Ælle, ðu lieue saule, bie nu gladd and bliðe in ðe hali goste, all
swo ic ær sade! Forðan þu hauest fair timber ȝe(i)gadered of ðese [24]
hali mihte(s), and godes auȝen wisdom is ðar ouer wrihte, and seið
ðat he wile ðar mid ðe wuniȝen, for ði ðat tu luuest him and his
wordes. Wit mote nu læte resten ðine wrecche lichame, ðe is
swiðe unstrang and swiðe brusel. His heaued him acþh, ðe[8] eiene [28]
him trukieð, his bilif is litel, forðan he ne hafð bute ðurh his
handiswinke bi to libbenne, and ðat menn, for godes luue, him
giuen willeð, ðo ðe of[9] him rewðhe habbeð. He hafð michel hier
abuten iswunken, ȝielde him godalmihtin, for ði him is nied nu to [32]
resten.

[1] e corr. from i.   [2] þat is godes word repeated.   [3] On the side.
[4] d underdotted before e.   [5] ð corr. from h.   [6] D crossed red.
[7] page 58.   [8] a letter erased after e.   [9] f crossed red.

Now answers the soul:

I beg thee and conjure thee, too, upon the Holy Trinity, which is Father and Son and Holy Ghost, one true God, that thou leave not this work, because I have much help and good strength by it, God be thanked! Just as the body can have no strength without bones, so can I have no strength of soul, no power, without these holy virtues. Do thou not spare for our body! One cannot easily believe it; it has often deceived me. I have followed its will ever too long; I shall never [do] so again. But one ought to do with it as with the ass: *Ut jumentum factus sum apud te, et ego semper tecum*, that it may tell this truth: 'I am made as a beast toiling before Thee, that I may rest again with Thee.' Again, this same prophet said: *Sitivit in te anima mea, corpus multipliciter*, 'My soul was thirsty,' he said, 'after Thee, Lord, and my flesh much more, for the manifold labours of fasting and of its sustenance, which I got for my sins with my sweat.' Think of, and seek very willingly after these holy virtues, and put them into writ, so that they may do good to some other soul.

Reason.

Dear soul, if thou hast well understood, God's temple is reared upon thee, after what the apostle says: *Templum Dei, quod estis vos*, 'God's temple is holy; and that ye are yourselves.' But he says after this very awfully: *Si quis autem violaverit templum Dei, disperdet eum Deus*, 'Whoso defileth the temple of God with any foul sin, him shall God destroy, both body and soul.' Right belief is the ground-work of this holy temple. Concerning this the apostle says: *Fundamentum aliud nemo potest ponere, praeter idem quod positum est, quod est Jesus Christus*, 'Other foundation can no man lay than that is laid, which is Jesus Christ,' when Peter said: 'Thou art the Christ, the Son of the living God'; and all Christians who believe in Christ ought to believe and say so. The posts which

Nu andswereð þe saule:

ICH ðe bidde *and* ec halsiȝe, uppe ðare hali þrinnesse, ðe is fader *and* sune *and* hali gost, on soð godd, þat ðu þis weork naht ne forlate, for ðan ic habbe ðarof michel help *and* gode stre[n]gþe, 4 ȝeþanked bie godd! Riht alswo ðe lichame none strencþe ne mai habben wið-uten bonen, al swo ne mai ic ne non saule stre[n]gþe ne mihte habben wið-uten ðese hali mihten. Ne wonde ðu naht (for) ure lichame! He nis naht lihtlich to ilieuen. He me hafð ofte 8 beswiken. Ic habbe ifolȝed his iwill eaure to longe; swo ne scall ic næure mo eft. Ac me scal don bi him al swo bi ðan asse: Vt iumentum factus sum apuð te, *et* ego s[emper] t[ecum][1], þat he muȝe (ðis) soð seggen: 'Ich am imaked al swo a dier 12 swinkende beforen ðe, ðat ic eft muȝe resten mid ðe.' Eft sæde ðes ilke profiete: Sitiuit in te anima mea, corpus multipli- citer, 'Mi saule was ofþerst,' he sæde, 'after ðe, hlauerd, *and* min flesch michele swiðere, for ðo manifelde swinche(s) of fasten *and* of 16 his biliue, ðe ic for mine sennen mid mine swote [2] biȝatt.' Dench *and* siech well ȝ(i)erne after ðese hali mihtes, *and* sete hes on ȝewrite, ðat bie muȝen sum oðre saule don god [3].

Ratio.

LIEUE saule, ȝif ðu wel hafst understonden, godes temple is ȝerard uppe on (ðe), after ðat ðe apostel seið: Templum [4] dei, quod estis uos, 'Godes temple is hali, *and* ðat ȝe bieð ȝeu seluen.' Ac he seið ðar after swiðe eisliche: Si quis autem 24 uiolauerit templum dei, disperdet illum deus, 'Se ðe bifeleð godes temple mid ani full senne, godd him scal forl(i)esen, baðe licame *and* saule.' Of ðese hali temple ðe rihte beleaue is grundwall. Herof seið ðe apostele: Fundamentum aliuð 28 nemo potest ponere, preter idem quod positum est, quod est Iesus Christus [5], 'Ne mai no mann leiȝen oðer grundwall [6] þanne ðat ðe is ileid, þat is, Iesu Crist,' þar ðe Peter sade: Tu

---

[1] s. t. *MS.*   [2] *page* 59.   [3] *a letter erased between* g *and* o.
[4] Tempilum *MS.*   [5] iħc x̄p̄c *MS.*   [6] gruundwall *MS.*

are to bear this work are named before. Charity rises up from the foundation, and encircles all the walls, and all those who are dwelling in the holy house; and it rises up to the roof, for all the rafters of the holy virtues are fastened to it. Steadfast Hope has its place on high, because it is the roof, and covers all who are beneath it with the shingles of holy thoughts, which Wisdom finds for it. This holy virtue is wholly work-master of this blessed temple. It locks it within and without, so that He, who is King of all kings, may have His rest within. Therefore He begs that peace shall be as well in body as in soul, and that this holy virtue Peace shall be reigning in both of you; and the Justice of God shall pass sentence upon that of you who breaks it.

Now answers the body, and says:

I am very much surprised at thee, Reason, who shalt after God's ordinance instruct and direct, as well the soul as the body, that thou doest not understand that I and the soul are not of one nature, though both of us had one Creator. I am heavy, as one who is made of earth; and she is light as the air, which is called *spiraculum vitae*, that is, 'the breath of life.' She is a spirit, and I am dust; she is heavenly, and I earthly; she is of high nature as one who is God's own likeness, I am the likeness of the guilty Adam, through whom I am in great difficulties: in hunger and in thirst, in watches and in toils, and in many kinds of wretchedness, sorry and sorrowful, wailing and weeping. He knows it who knows all things, that scarcely could I write this through the tears which came running from the well-spring of repentance. Weep, weep along with me all who esteem yourselves guilty, and let us wash out the spots of our evil manners! There is no lye so good as tears: they make a face bright. Well is he who is made clean, and has the fair shroud of charity all beset with gem-stones of good works! He may come, with God's help, to the bridal before the bridegroom, and abide with Him in great joy and in great happiness. Dear Reason, this is my comfort, that I think (though you,

es *Christus*[1], filius dei uiui, *and* þis sculen ilieuen *and* seggen
alle Cristene ðe on Criste belieueð. Ðe postes þat sculen beren up
ðis weorc, he bien inamned hier te-foren. Cariteð arist up fram ðe
grundwalle, *and* beclepð all ðe wouh, (*and*) alle ðe bieð in ðo hali 4
huse wuniende; *and* hie arist up anon to ðe roue, forðan to hire
bieð ifastned alle ðe raftres of ðe hali mihtes. Ðe faste hope hafð
hire stede[2] up an heih, for ði hie is rof *and* wrikð alle ðe hire bieð
beneðen [3] mid ðe scincles of holie þohtes, þe sapientia[4] hire fint. 8
Ðies hali mihte is all wrihte of ðesen eadi temple. Hie hit belokeð
wið-innen *and* wiðuten, þat he, ðe is alre kiningene kyng, muȝe
hauen his reste wið-innen. For ði he bitt ðat pais bie aiðer on
licame *and* on saule, *and* ðat þies hali mihte sibsumnesse bie rix- 12
ende on ȝeu baðe; *and* hwaðer ȝunker hes tobrecð: justicia dei
scall ðar of don riht.

NV andswereð[5] ðe lichame, *and* seið: 'Swiðe ich am ȝewundred
of ðe, Ratio, þe scalt[6] after godes isetuesse wissin *and* stieren 16
ȝe ðe saule ȝe ðe lichame, þat ðu ne undernemst þat ic *and* ðe
saule ne bieð nauht of one ikende, ðeih wit boðe anne sceppend[7]
hadden. Ic am heui, al so he ðe is imaked of ierðe; *and* hie is liht
alswo ðe left, ðat is icleped spiraculum uite, þat is, ' ðe blast 20
of liue.' Hie is gost, *and* ic am dust; hie is heuenlich, *and* ich
ie(r)ðlich; hie is of heiȝe kenne al swo hie ðe is godes aȝen anlicnesse,
ic ham ðes forȝeltes Adames anlicnesse, þurh hwam ic am on
muchele aruednesses, on hungre *and* on ðurste(s), on wacches *and* 24
on swinkes, *and* on maniȝe(s) kennes wrecchades, sori *and* sorhfull,
woninde *and* wepinde. Þat he wot ðe wot alle þing, þat unneaðe
ich mihte ðis writen for ðo teares ðe comen iernindefrom ðare well-
riðe of rewnesse. Wepeð, wepeð forð mid me alle ðe healdeð ȝeu 28
seluen forȝelte, *and* waschen ðe spottes of ure euele ðeawes! Nis
ðar non swo god leiȝe se teares: hie makieð scene ansiene. Wel
him ðe is clene iþrowen, *and* hafð ðat faire scrud of charite all
besett mid ȝimstanes of gode werkes! He mai cumen, mid gode(s) 32
fultume, in to ðe bredale to-fore ðe bredgume, *and* mid him
wuniȝen on michele merhðe *and* on michele ædinesse. Lieue Racio,

---

[1] χρс MS.   [2] sted *on erasure.*   [3] *a letter erased before* m.
[4] *underlined, and* vvisdom *written at side by another hand.*   [5] -d *MS.*
[6] *page* 60.   [7] d *corr.from* t.

with good right, esteemed me unworthy) my hope is nevertheless always steadfastly on Christ, God's Son, who shaped Himself after my likeness, and became true Man ; who was, and is, and evermore will be, true God. Thanked be He! He brought my nature, after much unworthiness which He suffered here for me, to great worship, and set it very high on His Father's right hand; and He has promised me forsooth that, as truly as He came hither and took my humanity and my nature, as truly shall I come to Him, and receive of His Godhood and His nature, through His great mercy, if I will listen to Him and follow His advice. For His love I beg you to forbear me and so to instruct and to guide me, that I may follow and be obedient to both of you in all good works; the little while that we dwell together.

Reason.

Now answers Reason, and says thus: Let it not seem strange to thee, that I begged thee to have peace in thee and in thy soul. I know well that God cannot abide in any soul which is in discord through sins. The prophet bears witness of it, who says: *In pace factus est locus ejus,* 'In peace is made His stead, wherein He shall dwell.' I know well what the apostle says about both of you: *Caro concupiscit adversus spiritum, et spiritus adversus carnem,* 'The flesh,' says he, 'lusteth against the spirit, and the spirit against the flesh.' And nevertheless ye may have peace, for he says afterwards: *Ut non quaecunque vultis, ita faciatis,* 'Because,' says he, 'ye strive between you, so that neither of you shall have his will.' But ye shall both, through this strife, follow God's will; then there will soon be peace over all thy land. But help now all that thou canst, that thy soul may have a little rest, and that this holy temple be reared on both of you, so that God, your Creator, may dwell therein; then you are certainly blessed. We must still work a little, that it may be, with God's help, still better stored.

THE BODY'S SPEECH AND REASON'S ANSWER.

ðis is min froure, ðat ic þenche, þeih ȝie be gode rihte unwurð helden of me, naðeles (min [h]ope is aure fastliche) upe Criste, gode(s) sune, þe scop him seluen after mire andlicnesse, *and* becam soð ma*nn*; se ðe was, *and* is, *and* æuremo bieð, an soð godd. 4 Iþanked bie he! Mine ikynde, after maniȝe unwurðscipes ðe he for me hier þole*d*e, he brohte to muchele wurðscipe, *and* sette hes wel heiȝe on his fader swiðer hand, *and* hafð me soðliche behoten þ*at*, al swa soðliche swa he ca*m* hider *and* underfeng[1] 8 mine ma*n*nischnesse *and* mine ȝekynde, swa soðliche ic scal cume*n* to hi*m*, *and* underfon of his goddcu*n*dnesse *and* of his ȝekynde, ðurh his michele mildce, ȝif ic hi*m* wile hleste*n and* his rad folȝi*n*. For his luue ic ȝeu bidde þ*at* ȝe me forbere*n and* swa wissie*n and* 12 swa stiere*n*, þ*at* ic mote folȝi*n and* buhsum bien ȝing bam on alle gode werke(s), þe litle hwile ðe we tegedere wunieð.

Ratio.

NV andswereð Ratio, *and* ðu(s) seið: Ne þenche ðe no selcuð, 16 ðat ic ðe badd habbe*n* pais on ðe *and* on ðire saule. Ic hit wat wel ðat godd ne mai bie*n* wuniȝende on none saule ðat unfrið is of se*n*nes. Herof berð iwitnesse ðe profiete, ðe seið: In pace factu*s* est locu*s* eiu*s*, 'On sibsumnesse is imaked his stedel ðe he 20 on scal wuniȝe*n*.' Ic wot wel hwat ðe apostel seið be[2] ȝeu baðe: Caro co*n*cupiscit aduersu(s) sp*i*ritu*m*, et sp*i*ritu*s* aduersus carne*m*, 'De flæsch,' he seið, 'hit ȝitsið aȝea*n* ðe goste, *and* ðe gost aȝean ðe flesche.' *And* naðelas ȝit muȝe*n* habbe*n* pais, forða*n* he seið after: 24 Vt non quecunque uultis, ita faciatis, 'For ði,' he seið, 'ȝit winneð ȝung betwen, ðat ȝunker noðer ne scal habbe*n* his ȝewill.' Ac ȝit scule*n* baðe, ðurh[3] ðese ȝewi*n*ne, folȝi*n* godes wille; ðanne is sone pais ouer al ðine londe. Ac help nu ðat 28 ðu miht, ðat ðin saule hadde a litel reste, *and* ðat ðis[4] hali temple (be)[5] arard on ȝinc, þ*at* godd, ȝinker scepp*end*, mihte ðari*n*ne wunien; ðanne bie ȝit iwiss isali. Wit moten ȝiet a litel swi*n*ken, ðat hit bie, mid godes fultume, ȝiet bet astored[6]. 32

---

[1] *page* 61. [2] e *on erasure.* [3] r *corr. from* w.
[4] *an* i *erased after* s. [5] be *written above* is. [6] *on erasure.*

Of peace.

Dear soul, this same virtue that is called Peace, about which we now shall speak, is very necessary for thee to keep and have, because, though thou hast toiled never so much in God's temple, He will never dwell in it, except peace be there. He brought this peace with Him from Heaven to earth, and gave it to all men who were *bonae voluntatis,* ' of good will,' that is, none save those who follow God's will. Because nobody is neither good nor righteous, but those who [are] God's and follow Him. Nobody can be full of wrath against him who has this blessed virtue. Of this says the prophet: *Pax multa diligentibus legem tuam, et non est illis scandalum,* ' Great peace have all who love Thy law: they are never wrathful.' Charity is God's law, which can hate no man, on account of any of the things one may do [against] it. Again, when Christ sent His disciples into the world, to teach them [viz. mankind] the way to the kingdom of Heaven, He then commanded them to say thus in each house where they would come: *Pax huic domui,* that is: ' Peace be unto this house !' If they found in it the man of peace, then their peace should remain there ; and if they did not, it should turn again to them.

Of prudence.

After this it behoves thee to have one of the holy virtues that well knows how, and is able to look after the gates and the doors of this holy temple. If thou couldst get *prudentiam,* [as] one [of them] is called, it [viz. prudence] would be very profitable to thee to look after this office. It is justly called Prudence. It is wise and prudent anent all thoughts, anent all words, anent all works. It will know all that they seek and that they wish for. If there comes any thought or any word on the part of God, they are very welcome to it. If they come from the devil, Prudence knows them soon, and drives them shamefully away. They can have no entrance there. If they come from men, Prudence can quickly find out, on whose behalf he is come, and receives him accordingly. For

Of sibsumnesse[1].

LIEUE saule, þies ilche mihte ðe is icleped pax, ðe we nu embe spekeð, hie is swiðe niedfull ðe to healden and to habben, for [2] ðan, ne haue ðu næure swo michel iswunken on godes temple, bute ðær bie pais inne, ne wuneð he ðar næure. Ðas sibsumnesse he brohte mid him fram heuene to ierðe, and ȝaf hes alle ðo mannen ðat waren bone voluntatis, 'of gode wille,' (ðat nis non bute se ðe folȝið[3] godes wille). For ðan non nis god ne rihtwis, bute godes and ða ðe him folȝið. Se ðe hafð ðese eadi mihte, him ne mai no mann wraðhin. Herof seið ðe profiete: Pax multa diligentibus legem tuam, et non est illis scandalum, 'Michel sibsumnesse is allen ðe luuieð ðine laȝe, ne bieð hie naure wroðe.' Charite is godes laȝe, ðe ne mai nanne man hatien, for non ðare þinge ðe me hire do. Efsones, ðo ðe Crist sente his lierning-(c)nihtes in to ðe world, hem to tachen ðane wei to heuene riche, ðo hiet he hem ðat hie scolden in to ælchen huse ðar hie comen, ðus seggen: Pax huic domui, þat is: 'Sibsumnesse bie te ðesen huse!' Ȝif hie funden ðar inne ðane mann of pais, þanne scolde here pais belæuen ðerinne; and ȝif h(i)e ne deden, hie scolde aȝean wanden to hem.

Of ȝepnesse.

HIER after ðe behoueð ðat tu habbe on of ðe holie mihtes ðe wel cunne and wel muȝe ðo gaten and ðo duren wel bilokin of ðis holi temple. Ȝif ðu mihtest biȝeten prudentiam, [swa] hatte an, hie ðe ware swiðe beheue ðese wike to lokin. Hie is ȝeapnesse inamned mid gode rihte. Heo is wis and ȝeap aȝean alle ðohtes, aȝean alle wordes, aȝean alle werkes. Hwat hie siechen and hwat hie willen, all hie wile iwiten. Ȝif ðar cumþ ani þoht oðer ani word a godes half, hie bieð hire swiðe welcume. Ȝif hie cumeð fram dieule, prudencia hes icnauð sone, and drifþ hes awei scandliche. Ne muȝen hie ðar habben non infare. Ȝif hie cumeð fram mannen, hie cann hwatliche underfinden, an hwos half he[4] is icumen, and ðar after hie hine underfengð[5]. [6] Forðat hit ilimpð

---

[1] i corr. from u. [2] page 62. [3] folȝid MS. [4] corrected from hie.
[5] g and ð connected. [6] page 63.

it often happens that God sends a man to help another one, or to instruct him; and again, it happens that a man comes to another through the devil's admonition, though he may not know it. If thou wilt know a man, keep this Prudence with thee! Listen what he speaks most and oftest. If it is of God, or of things which belong to thee, he is to be loved and to be retained. If he speaks of sins and foolishness, then it is as if God said Himself: *Ex abundantia cordis os loquitur,* 'That of which the heart is full, the mouth speaketh.' The same man who is bound by a cardinal sin, and loves it, and speaks most about it, is not to be retained, unless he will listen to the words of God. If somebody comes there who asks for anything which is necessary for body or soul, advise him, help him, if thou canst! If thou canst not, have pity on him, and pray for him and all who help him. If anyone comes and brings tidings of idleness, and is speaking foolish words which raise laughter, he shall have no dwelling with thee, as thou lovest God and peace. Jesus Christ commanded us to be prudent, and said: *Estote prudentes sicut serpentes,* ' Be prudent as adders,' He said. The prudence of the adder is, that it lies down all rolled up, and its head in the middle, in order to save the head. The head is ever the beginning of all things which thou wilt do. Turn thyself all about! First think whether the thing which thou wishest to begin will be agreeable to God, or profitable to thee, or will become harmful to thy neighbour. If a righteous man has done so before thee, and if the holy Writ does not contradict thee, and bears witness to thee: do then what thou wilt do so. And [mind] that the beginning of all things be ever begun in God's name! Again, it [the adder] has another prudence, which we ought to follow : it has its hole. As soon as anything will do harm to it, it creeps into its hole, and so it saves its life. Just so do thou, after God's own counsel, when the devil, or any evil man, or anything which displeases thee, will harm thee; anon creep thou into thy hole, into Christ's open side, with thy good belief, and say unto thy Saviour: *Sub umbra alarum tuarum protege me, Domine,* ' Lord,' say, ' under the shadow of Thy wings, of Thy arms, which were fastened on the holy

ofte ðat godd sant ane mann an oðer to helpe, oðer him to wissin;
and eft hit ʒelimpð ðat a mann cumþ tan oðer ðurh dieules meneʒinge, þeih he hit naht ne wite. ʒif ðu wilt mann icnowen, haue
ðese ʒeapnesse mid ðe! Hlest hwat he speke mest *and* oftest.
ʒif it is[1] of gode oðer of þinges ðe to ðe belimpeð, he is to luuiʒen
and to wiðhealden. ʒif he spekð of sennes *and* of sothades, ðanne
hit is alswo godd sade him self: Ex habundantia cordis os loquitur, 'Of ðat ðe herte is full, ðarof spekð ðe muð.' Đe ilke
mann ðe is ibunden mid heaued-senne, *and* hes luueð, *and* mast
ðar embe spekð, nis he noht to wiðhealden, bute ʒif[2] he wolde
godes wordes lesten. ʒif ðar cumþ sum ðe sehþ of aniʒere niede
ðe belemð to lichame oðer to saule, ræd him, help him, ʒif ðu miht.
ʒif ðu ne miht, haue rewðe of[3] him, *and* bide for him *and* for alle
ðe him helpen. ʒif ani cumþ and bri[n]gþ tidinges of idelne(s)ses,
and is spekende sotwordes ðe aræreð up hleitres, none wunienge
ne haue he mid ðe, swa se ðu luuest godd *and* sibsumnesse. Iesv
Crist hiet ðat we scolden bien ʒeape, *and* sæde: Estote prudentes sicut serpentes, 'Bieð ʒeape al swa næddre,' he sade.
Đare næddre ʒeapnesse is, ðat hie lið al abuten itrand, *and* hire
heaued on midden, for to berʒen ðat heaued. Of alle þing ðat tu
wilt don, æure is ðat anginn ðat heaued. Bewænt te all abuten!
Đenc arst whaðer hit wile bien gode icweme, ðat ðing ðe ðu wilt
aginnen, oðer ðe beheue[4], oðer ðine nexte to none harme ne wande.
ʒif rihtwis mann habbe swo ʒedon te-fore ðe, ʒif ðat hali writ ne
wiðseið ðe naht, *and* berð þe iwitnesse: ðat tu wilt so don, do hit
ðanne. And æure of alle þinge ðat ðe anʒinn bie a godes name
ʒegunnen![5] ʒiet hie haueð an oðer ʒeapnesse, ðe we sculen folʒin:
hie haueð hire hol. Swa raðe swa ani þing harm hire wile don,
swo hie crepþ in to hire hole, *and* swo hie berhð hire lif. Riht
alswo do ðu, after gode(s) awene rade, ðanne dieuel ðe wile derien,
oðer ani euel mann, oðer ani þing ðat te misliki; anon crep ðu in
to ðine hole, in to Cristes opene side, mid ðine gode ileaue, *and*
seiʒe to ðine aliesende: Sub umbra alarum tuarum protege
me, domine, 'Lauerd,' seiʒe, 'vnder ðare scadewe of ðine fiðeres,

---

[1] s *corr. from* h. [2] gif *MS.* [3] os *MS.*
[4] *corr. from* behieue. [5] *page* 64.

cross, shield me from all kinds of evils that come from the devil (whom Thou overcamest there), and cool my wretched heart, which is envenomed by his manifold temptations! Cool the great heat of my sorrows with the blessed stream which comes out of Thy holy side!' If thou believest this, and doest so, be sure, nothing can be of harm to thee. Though thou mayst suffer harm, all that thou sufferest for God's love will turn out to be good for thee.

Of foresight.

Providentia, that is, foresight, is another holy virtue, which thinks of and looks after all things ere they come. Therefore it repents nothing which it has done. Before the city of Jerusalem is a great hill, which is called Zion, that means 'Sight.' Upon it were the watchmen who looked after the holy city, and guarded it against all its enemies. So does this virtue upon the hill of great Consideration. It spies and looks from afar, and says thus : 'Well, thou wretched soul, which, I say, takest no heed of thyself! Couldst thou see all thy enemies who are round about thee, as I do, sorry wouldst thou be, eagerly wouldst thou cry to God to save thee! I warn thee before. Thou wilt not long be dwelling here; forsake thy sins! If thou forsakest them not here, ere thou goest out of the world, certainly they will never forsake thee, ere they bring thee to their parents. These are the cursed spirits which here above in the clouds wait for souls. If they find upon thee any of their deeds, no angel may help thee from going into pain, and paying the penalty there. *Quia nullum malum impunitum,* " No evil shall be unpunished, either here or there." It sees and hears a merry song of the good soul: *Veni, sponsa Christi, accipe coronam,* " Come, thou Christ's own bride, and receive the great worship and the great joy of the kingdom of Heaven, which He has prepared for thee to have for evermore for the good fidelity which thou borest in Him!" '

of ðine armes, ðe waren ifast(n)ed on ðare hali rode, scild me fram
alle ðes kennes eueles¹ ðe cumeð fro ðe dieule, ðe ðu ðar ouercome,
and kiel mine wreche herte, þe is iattred of his manifealde fondinges!
Kiel ðe muchele hate of mine sarinesses mid ðan eadiȝe well-streme
ðe cumþ of ðine halie side!' Gif ðu ðis ȝeliefst, *and* swa diest,
bie ðu siker, ne mai þe non þing to harme [bien]. Þeih ðu harm
all hit want (ðe) to gode² ðat tu for godes luue þolest.

Of forscea[w]nesse³.

PROUIDE*N*TIA, þat is, forsceawnesse⁴, is an oðer hali mihte,
ðe þencþ *and* lokeð alle þing beforen (ar ðanne hie cumen).
For ði ne rewð hire naht after hire dædes. To-foren ðare burh of
Ierusalem is an muchel dune, ðe hatte Syon, þat is tokned 'Scea-
winge.' Þærupen weren ðe sceaweres ðe lokeden ðe hali burh, *and*
warneden fram alle here unwines. Al swo doð ðies mihte upe ða
dune of muchel embeðanke. Hie sceaweð *and* lokeð ferrene to,
and ðus seið: 'VVelle⁵, ðu earme⁶ saule, ðe, ic segge, ðe none
ȝieme ne nemst of ðe selucn! Mihtest tu isien alle ðine unwines
ðe bieð⁷ aᵇbuten þe, also alse i do, sari woldest tu bien, ȝierne
woldestu⁹ clepien to gode þat he ðe aredde! Ic ðe warni te-foren.
Ne biest ðu naht hier lange wuniȝende; forlat ðine sennen! Ȝif
ðu hier he(s) ne forlatst, ær ðanne ðu fare of ðare woreld, full
ȝewiss ne forlateð hie ðe næure, ær ðanne hie ðe bringen to here
eldren. Dat bið ðo werewede gostes ðe waitið ðo soules hier
buuen on ðe wolkne. Þ(o)¹⁰ þe hie findeþ upe ðe of here werkes,
ne¹¹ mai þe helpen non angel ðat tu ne scalt in to pine, *and* ðar
abeggen. Quia nullum malum inpunitum, "Ne scall non euel
bien unpined, oðer hier oðer ðar." Of ðare gode saule hie ȝesieð
and iherð merigne song: Veni, sponsa *Christi*, accipe coronam, "Cum, ðu Cristes awen bried, *and* underfoh ðe michele
wurðscipe *and* ðe michele merhþe of heueue riche, þe he ðe haueð
iȝarked æurema to habben for ðare gode trewðe ðe ðu him
bere!"'

---

¹ *an* i *erased after* s. ² ȝode *MS*. ³ w *has disappeared by the binding;*
ȝap *is written black above* scea *in another hand.*
⁴ *The first* s *and* e *underdotted,* ȝ *written over* ce. ⁵ *The first* e *corr. from* l.
⁶ wrecche (*with* w, *not* p) *written over* earme. ⁷ bied *MS*. ⁸ *page* 65.
⁹ woldest stu *MS*. ¹⁰ o *inserted after* þ. ¹¹ *a* ð *at side and a stroke before* n.

Of righteousness.

Another holy virtue is called *justitia*, that is, righteousness. Certainly it desires that God should first pass His judgment on all His creatures, and that afterwards every creature should have its right, according to what is prepared for them. Truly, it ought to be justice within God's temple. *Justitia et judicium praeparatio sedis ejus*, this is written of it : 'Righteousness and judgment make God's seat.' *Anima justi sedes sapientiae*, 'The soul of the righteous is verily God's seat.' The same holy virtue *justitia*— that is, the justice of God's temple—asks right and judgment of all our misdeeds, because all creatures which God has created keep their nature better than man alone. Anent this said the prophet : *Non intres in judicium cum servo tuo, Domine*, 'Lord,' said he, 'enter not into judgment with Thy servant, because all that is living in Heaven and on earth could not be justified before Thee.' This same justice threw out him who was [a] bright angel in Heaven. It threw Adam out of Paradise ; it brought Christ to death, for God had said to Adam : *Morte morieris* ! There shall none escape who comes from him, so that he shall not suffer death. Since this is true, that it [justice] spared not, either the angel, or the man, or Christ Himself : how may it spare thee ? Here we are affrighted. But the holy apostle consoles us : *Si nosmet ipsos judicaremus*, 'If we sift ourselves in penitence with true repentance, and judge ourselves with right satisfaction, we shall nevermore again be doomed.' The strength of this holy virtue takes up into Heaven and down into hell, and spreads as wide as the earth. For all the wrongs which are done on earth, it will have right. It takes no reward for holding up wrong, nor for pulling down right. Those who will revenge themselves for wrong which is done to them, take its judgment away from it, because it says : *Mihi vindictam*, 'Let me avenge, judgment is mine !' I cannot believe that anybody suffers death without the judgment of this awful virtue, be the death as it may. Neither devil nor man can have any power or strength over others, except in so much as this mighty

Of rihtwisnesse.

AN oðer hali mihte is icleped i*u*sticia, þat is, rihtwisnesse. Fulȝewis hie wile ðat godd a-forewarde habbe his ȝerihte of alle his iscafte, *and* seððen aurich ȝescafte here rihte, after ðan ðe hem iscapen is. Hie awh wel to bene i*u*stise i*n*ne godes temple. I*u*sticia *et* iudicium preparati*o* sedis ei*u*s, ðis is ȝewrite*n* be hire: 'Rihtwisnesse *and* dom, hi makieð godes sate.' A*n*ima i*u*sti sedes sapie*n*tie, 'Das rihtwises saule iwis is godes sate.' Des ilche hali mihte i*u*sticia, þat is, godes temple-rihtwisnesse, hie acseð riht of alle ure misdades *and* dom, forðan alle ðe scaftes ðat godd haueð ȝescapen, alle hie healdeð bet here ikynde þanne mann one. Hier aȝean sæde ðe profiete: Non intres i*n* iudicium cum seruo tuo, domi*n*e, 'Hlauerd,' he sade, 'ne go ðu noht i*n* to dome mid ðine þral'le, forðan all ðat is liues on heuene *and* on ierðe ne mihte bie*n* irihtwised onȝeanes þe.' Dis ilche i*u*stise warp ut him ðe was briht angel on heuene. Hie warp ut Adam of para(d)ise; hie brohte Criste to ðe deaðe, for ði ðat godd isæd[2] hadde to Adame: Morte morieris! Ne scall ðar non atbersten ðe cum*þ* of him, þat he deað ne scal ðoliȝen. Seððen þis is soð, þat hie ne wandede, ne ðe angele, ne ðe manne, ne Crist self: hu mai hie wonde ðe? Her we bieð offeruht. Ac ðe hali apostel us freureð: Si nosmet[3] ipsos iudicarem*u*s, 'ȝif we seiȝeð us seluen on scrifte mid soðe birewnesse, *and* we deme*n* us selue*n* mid[4] rihte deadbote, ne sculen we næure mo eft bien idemd.' Se strengþe of ðessere hali mihte, hie takð up i*n* to heuene *and* niþer i*n* to helle, *and* spratt swo wide swo middenard. Of alle ðe unrihte(s) þe bieð idon on ierðe, hie wile habben riht. Ne nimð hie none miede for unriht to healde*n*, ne for riht to leien. Þa ðe willeð hem seluen wreke*n* of unrihte ðe hem is idon, hie benemeð hire hire dom, forðan hie seiȝeð: Mi*h*i uindictam, 'Læt me wreken, (d)om[5] is min!' Ne mai ic ilieue ðat ani man*n* deað þoliȝe wið-uten ðe dome of ðessere eisliche mihte, bie hit swilch deað swo hit eure bie. Ne dieuel ne mann none mihte ne none strengþe habben ne muȝen ouer oðren, bute alswo michel swo ðis

---

[1] *page* 66.   [2] a *altered to* æ.   [3] með *MS.*
[4] o *underdotted before* m.   [5] d *corrected over* ð.

virtue will give them. Thou must love and follow this holy virtue, that is, be righteous in thyself and towards all others, if thou wishest to be saved.

Of strength.

Fortitudo, that is, God's strength, is another holy virtue, which is needful to shield God's temple from all enemies. The prophet said of it: *Esto nobis, Domine, turris fortitudinis*, 'Lord, be our tower of strength against all enemies!' This same holy virtue is the tower and strength to all the virtues which dwell in it, and so it is to all the chosen ones of Christ.

[Of moderation.]

Temperantia is another holy virtue, which has very great discretion and moderation in all kinds of things. It will not suffer any overdone thing; [and] on the other side, neither too little nor too much. Whoso will listen to its counsel, shall neither eat too much, nor drink too much, nor too little; nor shall he rest or sleep too much, nor too little; nor shall he speak too much, nor [be] too much silent; nor shall he be clad too proudly, nor too coarsely; nor shall he be too glad, nor too sorry. As one regulates a bath, so that it is neither too hot nor too cold, so this holy virtue regulates all the manners of the man who loves it and knows how to keep it. He is happy who keeps it! This one regulates all these blessed virtues; and those who will not listen to it, become powerless, and they shall ever repent it. It regulates all the temptations and all the displeasures and all the unwillingness, which come from man, and withholds [him] from misdoing.

Of obedience.

Another virtue is called *obedientia*, that is, obedience. This is very profitable in God's house. All who love God ought to love maini mihte hem wile ȝiuen. Ðese hali mihte ðu most luuiȝen *and* folȝien, *þat is, þat þu* bie rihtwis on ðe seluen *and* aȝean alle oðren[1], swa swa ðu wilt bien iborewen.

Of stren[g]ðe. 4

FORTITUDO, *þat* is, godes strengþe, is an oðer hali mihte, ðe is niedfull to scilden godes temple fram alle unwines. Of hire sade ðe profiete: Esto nob*is*, domine, turris fortitudinis, 'Hlauerd, bie ure tur of strengþe aȝean alle[2] unwines!' Ðies 8 ilche haliȝe mihte, hie is tur *and* strengþe to alle ðo mihte(s) ðe ðar inne bieð wuniȝende, *and* swa hie is alle Cristes ȝecorene.

TEMP*ER*ANTIA is an oðer hali mihte, ðe cann swiðe michel scile *and* mæðe of alle kennes þinge. Hie ne wile ðoliȝen 12 non ouerdon þing; an oðer halue, ne to litel ne to michel. Se ðe hire ræd hlesten[3] wile, ne scal he noðer eten to michel, ne drinken to michel, ne to litel; ne he ne scall resten ne slapen to michel, ne to litel; ne he ne scal to michel bien spekende, ne to michel swi- 16 (g)ende; ne he ne scal to prudeliche bien isc(r)edd, ne to unorneliche; ne he ne scal bien to glad, ne to sori. Al so me tempreð an baþ, ðat hit ne bie to hot ne to cold, also deð ðis haliȝe mihte alle ðes mannes ðeawes ðe hes luuiȝeð *and* healden cann. He is isali 20 ðe hes halt! Alle ðese eadi mihtes ðes one atempreð; *and* ðo ðe[4] hire ne wyle[5] ilesten, hie becumeð to unmihte[6], *and* eure hit hem scal rewen. Alle ðe foudinges *and* alle ðe unluste(s) *and* alle[7] unwilles ðe cumeð of ðe manne, ðies hes atempreð, *and* wiðhalt te 24 misdon.

Of hersumnesse[8].

AN oðer mihte is ȝehoten obediencia, ðat is, hersumnesse[9]. Ðies is swiðe behieue on godes huse. Alle ðe godd luuiȝeð 28

---

[1] odren *MS*. [2] *page* 67. [3] leshten *MS*.
[4] ne *MS*. [5] *over erasure*, w = w, *not* p. *Also an erasure on the margin*.
[6] *a letter erased after* e. [7] *The first* l *on erasure*. [8] buh *is written above*
her *in another hand, black*. [9] her *underdotted*, i-buh *written above it*.

and keep it. As all mankind had death through disobedience, so it came to life through obedience. This holy virtue makes the man pliant and obedient to God and to his parents; and afterwards, to old and young and every man. After this, as to what he can perform, he takes no heed whether it is fair or loathsome, or hot or cold, or heavy or light; he thinks all to be good, for His love who was obedient to His Father even until death, Jesus Christ. This is very profitable to every man whoever will be saved, that he be obedient to God, and, for His love, to the bishop, and to his priest, and to his lord. But one ought not to be obedient except in good [things]. If a man commands or bids to do a sin, one ought not to be obedient to it. Where God gives this virtue, it soon shows itself. A man may be of never so high a family, it makes him become a servant. Just as it does these monks, who are obedient to a mortal man as if it were God Himself, so it does them who dwell in the world. They are very eager to learn God's laws, and then to work after them, and they beseech him who knows well how to instruct them, and listen blithely to and follow his counsel, lest they fall with the blind into the pit which Christ Himself spoke of. He called them dumb dogs through the prophet, who said: *Canes muti, non valentes latrare,* 'They are the dumb dogs which cannot or may not bark.' For the love of God I beg, do not look unworthier on this account, because thou knowest who it is. Through this holy virtue and through his good belief Abraham was blessed by God, and it was promised to him that One should come of his kind through whom all mankind should be blessed. Thus spoke God to Abraham: *Exi de terra tua, etc.,* 'Go,' quoth He, 'out of thy land and out of thy kindred and out of thy father's house, and come into the land that I will show thee.' Abraham believed what God said to him, and was obedient to Him. This same says God to them whom He wishes to be obedient to Him: 'Go out of thy land!' Thy land is thy flesh, which is nothing but earth. Go out of the lusts of thy flesh and follow them no more. 'And out of thy kindred!'

OF OBEDIENCE.

hes aʒeð to luuien *and* to healden. Al swa al mankinn ðurh un-
her*s*umnesse haf*d*en deað, al swa ðurh hersumnesse hit cam to liue.
Ðies holi mihte makeð ðane mann leðebeih *and* hersum gode *and*
his eldre*n*; *and* ðar after ealde *and* ʒunge *and* alle manne. After 4
ðat, ðe he iforðen mai, ne nim*þ* he none ʒieme hwaðer hit bie fair ðe
loðlich, ðe hot ðe cold, ðe heui ðe liht; all hi*m* ðingð god, for
his luue ðe was hersum his fader ano*n* to ðe deaðe, Iesv Cri*s*t.
Ðies is swiðe[1] beheue æurilch mann ðat æure i-boreʒe*n* scal bie*n*, 8
þ*at* he bie hersum gode, *and*, for his luue, ðe biscope, *and* his prieste,
and his louerde. Ac me ne auh to bie*n* hersum bute of gode. ʒif
ma*n*n hat oðer bitt[2] senne[3] to donne, þar to ne awh me naht to
bien hersvm. Whar ðe godd ʒifð ðese mihte, hit kydh hit sone. 12
H(i)e makeð ðane mann—nis he of swo heie ke*n*ne, þ*at* hie hi*m*
ne makeð—þreall. Al swa hie deð ðese munekes, ðe bieð her*s*um ane
deadliche ma*n*ne al swa hit wære godd self, swa hie dieð hem ðe
on ðare woreld wuniʒe*n*. Hie bien swiðe ʒiernfull godes laʒe to 16
liernin, *and* ðanne ðar after werche*n*, *and* him ðe hem wel ca*n*n
wissin hie beseke*ð*, *and* his ræd[4] bliðeliche hlisteð *and* folʒið, ðe
laste hie falleð mid ða blinde i*n* to ða*n*[5] pette ðe Cri*s*t self embe
spak. He he*m* clepede du*m*be hundes ðurh ðe profiete, ðe sade : 20
Canes mu(ti), no*n* ualentes latrare, 'Hie bieð ðe dumbe
bundes ðe ne cu*n*nen oðer ne muʒen berken.' For ðe luue of godd
ic bidde, ne latt tu herfore no*n* ðe unwurþere, for ða*n* ðu wost
hwo it is. Ðurh ðesse holi mihte *and* ðurh[6] his gode ileaue*n*[7] was 24
Abraha*m* iblesced of godd, *and* him behoten ðat on scolde cume*n*
of his ke*n*ne ðurh hwa*m* all ma*n*nke*n*n scolde bien iblesced. Ðus
spak godd to Abrahame : Exi de *t*erra tua, *et* cetera, 'Ga ut,'
cwað he, ' of ðine lande *and* ut of ðine ke*n*ne *and* ut of ðines fader 28
huse, *and* cu*m* in to ðo londe ðe ic ðe wile sceawi*n*.' Abraham
iliefde ðatt godd[8] hi*m* sæde, *and* was him hersum. Ðis ilche seið
godd to hem ðe he wile ðat bie hi*m* hersum : 'Ga ut of ðine lande!'
Þi*n* land ðat is ðin flesc, ðe nis bute ierðe. Ga ut of ðines flasches 32
lustes, ðat tu[9] hem na[10] more ne folʒe. 'And ut of ðine ke*n*ne!' Þat
bieð alle ðine euele ðeawes ðe ðu mide ware ibore*n* *and* ec ifedd.

---

[1] *page* 68.   [2] oðer bitt *double, the first time crossed with red colour.*
[3] señne *MS.*   [4] *or* rad?   [5] *or* ðæm?   [6] *an erasure above* r.
[7] *or* ileaue? *The little line over* ue *very short and curved.*   [8] g *corr. from* d.
[9] *an erasure over* t.   [10] *page* 69.

H

That are all thy evil manners wherewith thou wast born and also fed. 'And out of thy father's house!' The while the man lies in cardinal sins, he is the devil's son, as the good man is God's son when he loves and follows God. All this world was the devil's house ere Christ came, who cast him out. Thereof He said: *Nunc princeps mundi hujus ejicietur foras*, 'Now shall the prince of this world be driven out.' Here God teaches thee that thou shalt forsake the world voluntarily, ere death takes it from thee against thy will, and come to the land which He will show thee, that is, the land of the heavenly Jerusalem. Again He tried him [viz. Abraham], and found him true. *Tolle filium tuum, quem diligis, Isaac*, 'Take thy son, whom thou lovest so much, and offer him to Me on the hill which I will show thee!' Abraham had no son by his right spouse but one, and that was begotten in his great age. Therefore he was called Isaac, that is, Bliss. So says God to thee: 'Offer me thy son Isaac, that is, the thing which thou lovest most!' Understand now well what that may be, and look whether thou couldst be obedient in this respect to God Almighty. If thou lovest thy own will most of all, it is very wholesome for thee to offer this to thy Lord God, because it is a very agreeable sacrifice to Him that thou forsakest thy own will and followest His. This thou shalt offer upon the high hill of Obedience. There is no virtue in God's temple which has not lot and part with this blessed virtue.

Of mercy.

Another holy virtue is called *misericordia*, that is, mercy, which is very agreeable to God. He showed it Himself to all the needful who besought Him. So were Mary and Martha, who besought Him for their dead brother, Lazarus, whom He soon raised from a double death, [viz.] of the soul and of the body. So He soon had pity on the adulterous woman, who was to be stoned to death, after the old law. He forgave her the death, and all her sins He forgave. So He did St. Peter, who had forsaken Him. Anon, when He looked upon him, he began to weep, and his sins were forgiven him. How [did] the thief, who never had done good? This mercy made him come from the cross anon into Paradise. There is none who

OF OBEDIENCE AND MERCY. 111

'*And* vt of þines fader huse!' Ðar hwile ðe mann lið *on* heaued-
sennes, he is ðes dieules sune, al swo ðe gode mann ðe is godes
sune þanne he godd luueð *and* folʒeð. All ðis woreld was ðes
dieules hus ær Crist come, ðe him ut warp. Ðerof he sade : N u n c 4
p*r*inceps mu*n*di huiu*s* eicietu*r* fora(s), 'Nu scal ðe alder
of ðis woreld ut bie*n* ʒedriuen.' Hier ðe lærð godd ðat tu scule
ðe woreld forlate*n* ðines aʒenes þankes, ær ðe deað hes te benime
þines unþankes, *and* cume*n* to ðo lande ðe he ðe wile sceawi*n*, þat 8
is, ðat lond of ðare heuenliche Ierusalem. Efsones[1] he him fondede,
and fond him treuwe. T o l l e f i l i u *m* t u u *m*, q*u*em diligis,
Isaac, 'Nim ðine sune, ðe ðu luuest swa michel, *and* offre hine
me upe ðare dune ðe ic ðe wile sceawi*n* !' Abraam ne hadde 12
nanne sune be his rihte spuse bute ænne, *and* ðat was biʒeten on
his michele ielde. For ði he was icleped Isaac, þat is, blisse. Al
swo seið godd to ðe : 'Offre me þine sune Ysaac, þat is, þat þing
ðe ðu mast luuest!' Vnderstond nu wel what ðat bie, *and* loke 16
hwæðer ðu muʒe ðerof bie*n* hersum goddalmihtin. ʒif ðu luuest
ðin aʒene wille alre mast, þanne is ðe swiðe holsum ðat ðu þis
ofri ðine louerde[2] god, forðan hit is (him) swiðe ʒecweme loac
ðat ðu lat ðine aʒene wille and folʒe his. Ðis ðu scalt ofrien upe 20
ðare (heiʒe)[3] dune[4] of hersumnesse. Nis no*n* mihte o*n* godes
temple ðat ne hafþ lott *and* dole mid ðessere eadiʒe mihte[5].

Of milce.

MISERICORDIA hatte an oðer hali mihte, ðat is, milce, 24
ðe gode is (swiðe) icweme. Ðat he sceawede him selu to
alle nied-fulle ðe him besohte*n*. Also was Marie *and* Martha, ðe
him besohte*n* of here deade broðer, Lazarum, ðe he sone arearde of
tua deaðes, of saule *and* of lichame. Swa he hadde sone mildce of 28
ðe forleiene wiue, ðe scolde bie*n* ofsteand te deaðe, after ðare
ealde la(u)ʒe. He forʒaf hire ðane deað, *and* alle hire sinnen he
forʒaf. Swa he dede seinte[6] Petre, ðe hine hadde forsaken. Anon,
ðo ðe he lokede upe*n* him, he agann to wepe*n*, *and* his sennen him 32
wæren forʒiuene. Hu ðe ðeof[7], ðe næure god nadde idon ? Ðis

---

[1] *an erasure between* E *and* f.   [2] *o corr. from* d.   [3] *on the marg'n.*
[4] ðune MS.   [5] *page* 70.   [6] seintre MS.   [7] *o corr. over another letter.*

could know all the mercies which God has done, and does still, ever through this blessed virtue. Of this Jesus Christ reminds us, who says: *Estote misericordes,* 'Be merciful, as your Father is in Heaven!' Again, He says Himself: *Beati misericordes, quoniam ipsi misericordiam, etc.* 'Blessed are the merciful, for they shall have mercy from God, as they have mercy on men.' Of this holy virtue is written in the Psalter: *Misericordia et Veritas obviaverunt sibi,* 'God's Mercy and Truth, that is, God, met together.' All that ever is in the holy Writ, is all a prefiguration of God. It says that these two, Mercy and Truth, met one another, and I shall write as if Mercy spoke with Truth; and thus she says: 'Tell me, Truth, what is thy counsel concerning guilty Adam, and all his offspring? Can he nevermore come back? Wherefore was he ever shaped to man? Why was he not shaped to have ever, with the angels, the joy of the kingdom of Heaven?' Then answered Truth: 'No injustice is done to him. I warned him, and said forsooth, that the day on which he would break God's commandment, he should suffer death; and he had [his] own choice to do whichsoever he would. The devil used no force against him.' Then answered *Misericordia* again: 'Consider that just as thou saidst that he should suffer death, so thou saidst [also]: "Let us make man in our own image, after our likeness!" After thy likeness thou shapedst him. Never let thy own likeness perish, but let him come, through thy great goodness, to the happiness for which he was created, although his great evilness has not earned it!' Truth was compliant, as her custom ever is, and said to Mercy: 'Let us go before God and His Justice and His Judgment and before all His holy Virtues, and complain there. All that I can do to help thee I will [do] blithely.' *Misericordia* took with her *Pietatem* and *Pacem,* and they came before God, and very meekly besought Him, and the happy Mercy soon stretched herself down before God, and said thus: 'Holy, holy Lord, have mercy and pity on Adam, Thy guilty man, who so many hundred years has suffered the darkness

OF MERCY. AN ALLEGORY. 113

mildce him dede cumen fram ðare rode anon in to paradise. Nis
ncn ðe mihte witten alle ðe milcen ðe godd hafð idon, and ʒiet
dieð, æure ðurh ðessere eadi mihte. Herof us meneʒeð Iesu Crist [1],
and seið: Estote mi(sericordes), 'Bieð mildciende, al swo ʒeuer 4
fader is on heuene!' Eft he [2] seið him self: Beati [3] misericordes,
quoniam ipsi misericordiam [4], et cetera, 'Eadi bieð ðe milde,
forðan hie sculen hauen milce of gode, swo swo hie habbeð milce of
mannen.' Bi ðessere holi mihte is iwriten on ðe saltere: Miseri- 8
cordia et Uerita(s) obuiauerunt sibi, 'Godes Mildce and Soð,
þat is, godd, ʒemetten hem to gedere.' All ðat æure is on ðe hali
write, all [5] hit is forbisne of gode. Hit seið þat ðese two, Mildce and
Soð, hem imetten, and ic write swilch [6] Mildce speke wið Soðe, and 12
ðus seið: 'Sei me, Soð, hwat is ðin rad of ðe forgilte Adame, and
of all his ofsprenge? Ne mai he nauere mo aʒean cumen? Hwarto
was he aure iscapen te manne? Hu ne was he iscapen for to hab-
benne forð mid ðo aingles hueneriches merhþe?' Da andswerede 16
Soð: 'Nis him idon non unriht. Ich him warnede, and soð sade,
hwilche dai ðe he tobreke godes forbode, he scolde [7] deað þoliʒen;
and he hadde auʒene kere te donne hwaðer swo he wolde. Ne dede
dieuel him none strengþe.' Þa andswerede ʒiet Misericordia: 'Be- 20
þenc þat alswa swa ðu sadest ðat he deað scolde þoliʒen, alswa ðu
sadest: Faciamus hominem ad ymaginem et similitudi-
nem! After ðine anlicnesse ðu hine scope. Ne latt ðu naure
forfaren ðine aʒen anlicnesse, ac to ðare eadinesse ðe he to was 24
iscapen, lat him ðarto cumen, for ðire muchele godnesse, þei his
miche[le] euelnesse hit nabbe noht ofearned!' Soð was leðebei, alse
hire iwune is aure, and sade to Mildce: 'Cume we te-fore gode and
his Rihtwisnesse and his Dome and beforen alle his holi mihtes, and 28
bemæn ðe ðar! Al ðat ic mai ðe bien te fultume ich wille bleðeliche.' Misericordia nam mid hire Pietatem and (Pacem),
and comen before gode, and swiðe eadmodliche him besohten, and se
eadiʒe Mildce hire astrehte sone teforen gode, and ðus sæde: 'Hali, 32
hali lauerd, haue are and milce of Adame, ðine forgilte manne, ðe
swo maniʒe hundred wintre hafð iðoled þo ðesternesse of helle, ðe

---

[1] jhu crist in luca *written above* ðapostel.   [2] h *on erasure.*
[3] in Math qc. *written above.*   [4] m *written over the following* &.
[5] a *over* &.   [6] an e *erased after* h.   [7] *page* 71.

of hell, who was shaped to the great happiness of Thy kingdom! But the devil has not him alone, but all his offspring so in his power, that none can come into the kingdom for which they were shaped; but he brings [them] all into hell, both good and evil. Lord, have mercy and compassion and pity on Thy handiwork! Ever they have hope that thou wouldst have pity and mercy upon them.' Anon Pity complained, and said: 'Ay, Thou, Lord, beginning and source of all goodness, have mercy and pity on wretched Adam's soul, that was shaped after Thy likeness, and on Thy patriarchs and on Thy prophets, and on many thousand holy souls, which all suffer pain through Adam's guilt, with good right, for his disobedience! They all weep and wail, and hope in Thy great mercy and look to Thee, until Thou shalt send them some release. I am so sorry for them that I cannot have rest.' 'Lord, if it is Thy will,' said Peace, 'this cannot be in Thy kingdom. Thy peace is so very great that not a single thought can exist there except with all softness and with all meekness. Make reconciliation between Mercy and Justice, and make Judgment and Pity [to do] well together! Nevertheless, I know well that Thou wilt have pity on mankind. Thy goodness cannot help it.' Then said Justice: 'With much right Adam suffers what he suffers, for he was disobedient to his Creator. He disdained God when he allowed His adversary to overpower him, without force. To his Lord he did first great harm, he slew first himself, and since all mankind, and for his disobedience he bereft God's kingdom of himself and of all his offspring, so that he nevermore can come again [here] by right doom.'

Then said Truth: 'That is right that God's mercy is ever higher and more than His right judgment. Lord, it is truth that Thou promisedst to Abraham, Thy dear friend, that through One of his kin all mankind should be blessed. Afterwards, thou promisedst to David, the righteous king: *De fructu ventris tui ponam super*

OF MERCY. AN ALLEGORY. 115

was iscapen to ðare muchele eadinesse of ðine riche! Ac noht
he one¹, ac all his ofsp(r)eng hafð dieuel swo on his walte, ðat non
ne mai cumen into ðare riche ðe hie to waren iscapen; ac alle he
bringþ in to helle, baðe gode and euele. Hlauerd, haue ore and 4
rewhþe and mild(c)e² of ðin handiwerc! Æure hie habbeð hope
ðat tu scule habben ore and milce of hem.'

Anon hire bemande Rewðe³, and sade: 'Ælle, ðu, lauerd, angin
and welle of alle godnesse, haue rewðhe and milce of ðe wrecche 8
Adame(s) soule, ðe was iscapen after ðine andlicnesse, and of ðine
patriarches and of ðine profietes, and mani þusend hali saules, ðe
alle þolieð pine for Adames gelte, mid gode rihte, for his un-⁴her-
sumnesse! Alle hie wepeð and wonið, and hopieð to ðire 12
muchele milce and to ðe lokið, all hwat ðu send hem sume
aliesendnesse. Hi me reweð (swa)⁵ swiðe ðat ic reste ne mai
habben.'

'Lauerd, ȝif hit is ðin wille,' sæde Sibsumnesse, 'þis ne mai noht 16
bien on ðine riche. Ðin sibsumnesse is swo (swiðe) michel ðat on
lepi þoht⁶ ne mai ðer bien bute mid alle sof[t]nesse and mid alle
eadinese. Make seihte betwen Milce and Rih[t]wisnesse, and Dom
and Rewðe make wel to-gedere! Naðelæs, ic hit wot⁷ wel ðat tu 20
wilt hauen ore of mankenne. Þin godnesse⁸ hit ne mai noht læten.'

Ðat sede Rihtwis-nesse: 'Mid michel riht ðoleð Adam ðat he
ðoleð, for ðan he was his sceppend unhersum. Godd he unwurðede
ða þa he ðolede ðat his wiðerwine him ouercam, wið-uten strencþe. 24
His louerd he dede arst michel harm, he slou arst him seluen, and
seððen all mankenn, and for his unhersumnesse he bereauede godes
riche of him seluen and of all his ofsprenge, þat naure mo he ne
mai aȝean cumen be rihte dome.' 28

Ða sade Soð: 'Ðat is riht ðat godes milce bie aure heier and
more ðanne his rihte dom. Hlauerd, hit (is)⁹ soð ðat tu behete
Abraham, ðine lieue frend, þat þurh an of his kenne scolde bien
iblesced all mankenn. Eft ðu behete Dauiðe, the rihtwise kyng: 32
De fructu uentris tui ponam super sedem tuam, "Of ðo

---

¹ an erasure above o. ² e over two erased letters.
³ pieta(s) written on the margin. ⁴ page 72. ⁵ on the margin.
⁶ ne mai ðoht erased. ⁷ a letter erased after t.
⁸ an erasure before g. ⁹ r i d above t.

sedem tuam, "Of the fruit of thy body will I set upon thy throne." Again, he says in another place: "The Lord hath said unto me: Thou art My Son; [this day have I begotten Thee]."'

Then spoke Almighty God, and said: 'This day has ever been with me and evermore will [be]. It is true that thou sayest: "On this day have I begotten Thee in Heaven, without mother." So Thou shalt be begotten on earth, without father, by a mother. Thus Thou shalt become a true Son of Man as Thou art the true Son of God. I demand no other sacrifice for Adam's guilt but Thee. *Postula a me,* and ask of Me as much folk as Thou wilt long for, and I shall give [it] Thee for Thine inheritance, and Thou shalt rule all the earth and all what therein is.'

Tunc dixi: ecce, venio! Then said Truth: 'Lord, Father, Thou wouldst no other sacrifice nor other offering but that I accepted man's body and soul, and that I offered Thee here for their guilt. *Ecce venio,* look, I am ready to work Thy will, and to release mankind.'

That said God's Justice: 'Now Thou wilt become man, Thou shalt suffer death after Thy own doom, if that wonder can be true that Eternal Life may suffer death; and Thou shalt in every way atone for what he has broken. Hail Thy goodness!'

That said Truth: 'For this I am all ready, to be obedient to God even until death in order to release mankind.' *Justitia et Pax osculatae sunt*; the prophet says that 'Justice and Peace have kissed each other.' When this was done, Truth sprang out of the earth, and as true kind of earth. Our earth was cursed through Adam's guilts. *Maledicta terra in opere tuo,* 'Cursed be the earth in thy work,' quoth God to Adam. Now says the prophet: 'Lord, Thou hast been favourable unto Thy land.'—*Benedicta tu in mulieribus, et benedictus* ... 'Blessed be thou,' said the angel, 'on God's behalf among all women, and blessed be the fruit of thy womb, which is true God and true Man!' Through this Man Jesus Christ, who was of Adam's kind, the earth became blessed, which was before cursed. He paid for all the harm which had come through Adam, very wisely as He who was Wisdom Himself. Through Eve, who was still virgin, all mankind was lost; through

wastme of ðine wombe ic wille setten uppe ðine setle." Eft he
seið an oðer stede : Dominus dixit ad me : filius meus.'
Ða spac almihti godd, *and* sade : ' Ðies dai haueð aure ibien mid
me *and* æure ma wurð. Hit is soð ðat tu seiest : " On ðese daiʒe 4
ic ðe habbe istriend *on* heuene, wið-uten moder." Swa ðu scalt *on*
ierðe, wið-uten fader istr(i)end of moder. On ðelliche wise ðu
scalt becumen soð mannes sune swo swo ðu art soð godes sune¹.
Ne bidde ic non oðer loc for Adames gelte bute ðe. Postula a 8
me, *and* besiech at me swo muchel folc swo ðu wilt after ʒiernen,
and ic ðe wile ʒiuen to ðin eruename, *and* ðu scalt wealden all
middeneard *and* all ðat ðar inne is.'

Tunc dixi : ecce, uenio. Ðo sade Soð : ' Hlauerd, fader, ðu 12
ne woldest non oðer loac ne oðer ofrende bute ðat ic underfenge
mannes lichame *and* his saule, *and* ðat ic ðe her offrede for here
gelte. Ecce venio, loke, ic am (i)radi ðine wille to werchen, *and*
mankenn to aliesen.' 16

Ðat sade godes Rih[t]wisnesse : ' Nv ðu wilt mann becumen, ðu
scalt deað þolien after ðine auʒene dome, ʒif ðat wunder mai bien
soð þat eche lif mai ðoliʒen deað; *and* ðu scalt *on* alle wise bieten
ðe he haueð tebroken. Hoal ði godnesse ! ' 20

Ðat sade Soð : ' Hierto ic am all iradi, te bien hersum godd anon
to ðe deaðe for mankenn to aliesen.' Iusticia et Pax osculate
sunt ; ðe profiete seið ðat ' Rih(t)wisnesse *and* Sibsumnesse
kesten hem to-gedere.' Ðo ðis was ʒedon², Veritas de terra orta 24
est, *and* swo swo soð ʒekynd of ierðe. Vre ierðe was ʒewerʒed
ðurh Adames geltes. Maledicta terra in opere tuo, 'ʒewerʒed
bie ðe ierðe *on* ðine werke,' cwað godd te Adame. Nu seið ðe
profiete: Benedixisti, domine, terram tuam.—Benedicta tu 28
in mulieribus, et benedictus, 'Iblesced bie ðu,' seide ðe angel, '*on*
godes half mang alle wiues, *and* iblesced bie ðat wasme of ðine wombe,
þe is soð godd *and* soð mann ! ' Ðurh ðese manne Iesu Crist, ðe
was of Adames kenne, warð se ierðe iblesced, ðe was arer iwerʒed. 32
All he ʒeald ðane harm ðe was ʒecumen ðurh Adam, swiðe
wisliche al swo he ðe was wisdom him self. Ðurh Eue, ðe was
ʒiet maiden, was all mankenn forloren; ðurh Marie, ðe eadi

---

¹ *page* 73.   ² ʒedon and *MS.*

Mary, the blessed Virgin, it became saved again. Through the tree and its fruit all mankind was doomed to death; through the tree of the dear holy cross and through the blessed fruit which hung thereon, it came again to eternal life. Through obedience concerning the tree, the devil overcame Adam; through obedience Christ overcame the old devil on the holy cross. Because He was obedient to His Father until death, although He Himself had not deserved it, for He never did a sin; and nevertheless He suffered the cross, as if He were guilty. Adam saw with his eyes the fruit of the tree which he liked, but Christ suffered that one blind-folded Him. His feet bore him [Adam] to the forbidden tree, but Christ's feet were bored through with iron nails to the cross. His hands took the fruit of the tree, but Christ's hands were nailed through to the holy cross. The fruit in his mouth seemed sweet to him, but God received the bitter gall in His mouth. Adam's heart was poisoned through the devil's admonition, so that he both liked it well and also yielded, but Christ suffered that one stung through His heart; and for the two great [sins of] liking and granting, two great blessings came to us from the holy wound, that was, water and blood. In the water we are washed from all sins; by the fruit which hung on the holy cross, and by the blood which came out of it, we taste on [our] palates all kinds of poison of the devil, and so we cool our wretched heart, which is often scorched by the great burning of the devil's temptations. Thus our Saviour Jesus Christ healed us, thus our Redeemer redeemed us; and afterwards, He arose from the dead as He who was true life, and bore our sacrifice and our offering up to Heaven, His holy body, which He took of our kind, and offered to His Father a very agreeable sacrifice, by His own witness who said: *Hic est filius meus dilectus, in quo mihi bene complacui,* 'This is my beloved Son, in whom I am well pleased.' He has opened the gate of the kingdom of Heaven to all who believe in Him and will

OF MERCY.

maiden, hit warð eft ȝeboregen. Đurh ða trowe *and* his wastme werð al mankenn idemd to deaðe¹; þurh ðe trowe of ðe lieue halie rode *and* ðurh ðare iblescede wastme ðe ðar on heng, hit cam eft te ðan eche liue. Đurh unhersumnesse of ðe trowe ouercam ðe dieuel Adam; þurh hersumnesse of ðe hali rode ouercam Crist ðane ealde dieuel². For ðan he was hersum his fader anon to ðe deaðe, swa swa he him self hit ne hadde noht ofearned, forðan he neure senne ne dede; *and* naðelæs þolede o³ ðe rode, swilch he ware forȝ(e)ilt. Aȝeanes ðat Adam mid his eiȝene iseih ðat⁴ wastme of ðe treuwe ðe him likede, aȝeanes ðat þolede Crist ðat me blindfallede his(e)⁵. Aȝeanes þat his fiet him baren to ðe forbodene treuwe, aȝeanes ðat waren Cristes fiet ðurhborede mid isene nailes to ðare rode. Aȝeanes ðat his honden namen ðas trewes wastme, aȝeanes þat waren Cristes handes ðurhnailed te ða hali rode. Aȝeanes þat him ðuhte swete ðat wastme on his muðe, aȝeanes þat underfeng godd ðe bit(r)e ȝalle on his muðe. Aȝeanes ðat Adames hierte was i-attred ðurh dieules meneȝinge, swa ðat him baðe hit wel likede *and* ec teiþede, ðolede Crist ðat me þurh-stong his hierte; *and* aȝeanes⁶ ða twa michele likinge *and* teiþinge, us comen twa michele gode⁷ of ðare hali wunde, þat was, water *and* blod. On ða watere we bieð iwascen of alle sennes; of ða wastme ðe hangede on ðe hali rode, *and* of ða blode ðe ðar⁸ utȝiede, we notieð on ȝomes alles kennes attre of dieule, *and* swa we kylieð vre wreche hierte, ðe his ofte forswald of ðan michele brene of dieules costninges⁹. Đus us halde ure halend Iesu¹⁰ Crist¹¹, þus us aliesde ure aliesend, *and*¹² seððen aros of deaðe, alswo he ðe was soð lif, *and* bar up to heuene ure loac *and* ure ofrende, his hali¹³ lichame, ðe he nam of ure ȝekynde, *and* ofrede his fader swiðe icweme loc, be his aȝene iwitnesse ðe sade: H*ic* *est* f*i*l*iu*s m*eu*s d*i*lect*u*s, *i*n q*u*o m*i*h*i* b*e*n*e* compl*a*c*u*i, 'Đis is mi leue sune, on him me likeð swiðe.' Heueneriches gate he haueð iopened alle ðe on him (leueð)¹⁴ *and* him folȝin willeð. Alle his ikorene he hafð

¹ *page 74.*   ² *an erasure above* d.   ³ *o red inserted.*   ⁴ treu *underlined.*
⁵ *e is red inserted.*   ⁶ *Here begins another hand.*   ⁷ ȝode *MS.*
⁸ dar *MS.*   ⁹ costninȝes *MS.*   ¹⁰ jhu *MS.*
¹¹ *end of second hand, old hand goes on.*   ¹² þu *underdotted.*
¹³ his hali *once more, underlined.*   ¹⁴ *Added red on the margin.*

follow Him. He has promised to all His chosen, as truly as He arose from the dead, that they shall dwell so with body and with soul, both with the holy angels and with Him evermore. Amen.

Of penitence.

When Christ first began to preach, that was, when He went from the river Jordan, He said: *Poenitentiam agite, appropinquabit enim regnum coelorum,* 'Repent of your sins, the kingdom of Heaven approacheth.' Full surely a clean soul is Christ's kingdom. Therefore our Lord admonishes us first of all things about this blessed virtue, that we should repent of our sins, and so look to us with His help, that we may not fall into sin again. That says St. Jerom: *Est autem poenitere peccata ante acta deflere, et flenda non repetere,* 'So shall,' says he, 'a man repent of his sins, that he do not again what he again needs to repent of.' This says St. Austin: *Poenitere est poenam tenere,* 'That is true repentance,' says he, 'to hold oneself ever in some pain.' Again, we find in the holy Writ that neither the knight who bears weapons unlawfully, nor the chapman who buys and sells with unrighteousness, can ever do true repentance, the while they defile this office; nor he who perseveres in wrath, nor he who habitually lies in whoredom, nor gleemen, nor usurers, nor witches, nor unjust judges, nor any of those men who lie in cardinal sins and love them. Let a man who will be very repentant, not only repent of his sins, but moreover repent that through his carelessness he has not done good in the time which he nevermore will recover again, and [which] is gone by. Those who are in a religious order are ever under penance, as it also behooves us.

Of confession.

Here follows another holy virtue, which is called *confessio,* that is, confession; that is, when the man opens his heart, and tells his confessor his sins through his mouth, which were before concealed bihoten, swa soðliche [1] swa he aros of deaðe, þat hie sculen al swo mid lichame *and* mid saule, *and* mid ðe hali angles *and* mid him aure mo wunizen. Amen.

Of scrifte. 4

DA ðe Crist gann (arst) to spellen, ðat was, ðo ðe he ziede fram flumen Iordan [2], ða sade he : Penitenciam agite, appropinquabit enim regnum celorum, 'Nimeð scrifte of zewer sennes, hit neiheð [3] heuene riche.' Fullzewis is clene saule Cristes 8 riche. For ði us menezeð allre þinge arst ure lauerde of ðesre eadi mihte, þat we scolden beon rewsende [4] ure sennen, *and* swa hus l(o)kin [5] mid his fultume, þat we eft ne befallen on senne. Dat seið *sanctus* Ieronimus : Est a*utem* penitere peccata 12 ante acta deflere, *et* flenda non repetere, ' Swa scal,' he seið, 'mann his senne berewsen, ðat he eft ne do ðat he eft ðurue be-riwsin.' Dis seið *sanctus* Augustin*us* : Penitere est penam tenere, ' Dat his,' he seið, ' soðe berewsinge, ðat mann him healde eure on 16 sumere pine.' Eft we findeð on ða hali writt ðat ðe cniht ðe weapne berð unlawliche, ne chapmann ðe beið *and* selð mid unri[h]twisnesse, ne muzen neure soðe scrifte don, ðare [h]wile ðe hie ðese wike befeleð ; ne he (ðe) ðurhwuneð on wraðþe, ne he ðe 20 wuneliche lið on hordome, ne glewmen, ne gau(e)leres, ne wi(c)chen, ne uuriht domesmann, ne non ðare manne ðe on heaued-senne lið *and* ða luuieð. Mann ðe wel wile bien riwsinde, ne rewe him nauht ane hise sennes, ac zet ðat (he) for [h]is zemelaste ne hafð 24 god [6] zedon on ða time ðe he naure mo eft nacoureð, *and* is forð zegan. Da ðe bieð on religiun, hie bieð aure under scrifte, swa bihoueð [7] us alswa.

Of andetnesse. 28

HIER after cumeð an oðer hali mihte, ðe is icleped confessio, ðat his, andetetdnesse ; ðat is, ðanne ðe mann undett [h]is herte, [8] *and* seið his scrifte his sennes ðurh his muðe, ðe

---

[1] *page* 75.   [2] *Here begins a new hand which goes on to end.*
[3] *Some letters erased behind* ð.   [4] s *corr. from* h.
[5] o *corrected above* i.   [6] *a half* g *before* z *underdotted.*
[7] bihoued *MS.*   [8] *and* seið *twice, the first time underdotted.*

in his heart. Of this said God: *Dic tu iniquitates tuas, ut justificeris,* 'Tell thou thy unrighteousness, if thou wilt be justified.' Concerning it said St. Austin: *Qui per vos peccatis, per vos erubescatis,* 'Ye who sin of your own accord, be ashamed of yourselves. And know ye forsooth that same shame is a lot of the forgiveness.' *Fit enim veniale per confessionem, quod criminale fuerat per operationem,* 'It is a pardonable sin through confession what was before a cardinal sin through work.' But it behooves it to be well clear, and that no venom be concealed. Of this said the prophet: *Confitemini Domino, quoniam bonus,* 'Confess your sins,' he said, 'to God Almighty, because He is good, because His mercy is here in the world.' He who gets God's mercy not here will never get it elsewhere. We find in the holy Writ that if a man were suddenly upon his death, and he could have no priest, he ought to confess his sins to him who is nearest to him, and he should have mercy, except it were that he contempted the priest; or if he were alone, then he must [confess] to God only. And let every man look that he never mistrust in God's grace nor in His mercy, nor, again, be no man too bold to sin, and say: 'More can God forgive than we can sin.' *Non adjicies peccatum super peccatum et dices: quoniam misericordia Domini magna est!*

Of cleanness.

Another blessed virtue is called *munditia,* that is, cleanness, which is much loved within God's house. It cannot suffer any uncleanness in God's temple, neither beneath in thy body, nor above in thy soul, neither in thoughts—for it knows well that thoughts are more open before God than speeches are before man— nor can it suffer aught of foul speeches—for it knows that God hears them and mislikes them all—nor can it dwell near to evil works, for God bids to shun them. *Mundamini qui fertis vasa Domini,* 'Make yourselves clean who bear God's vessels!' Cleanse thy heart, because it ought to be God's vessel. One shall bear in waren arrer ȝedett on his herte. Hier of sade godd: Dic tu iniquitates tuas, ut iustificeris, 'Sei ðu þine unrihtwisnesses, ȝif ðu wilt bien irihtwised[1].' Herof sade *sanctus* Avgustinus: Qui *per* uos peccatis, *per* uos erubescatis, 'ȝie ðe seneȝin be ȝew seluen, doð scame ȝew seluen. *And* wite ȝie to soðe ðat ilke scame is on lott of ðare forȝifnesse.' Fit enim ueniale *per* con-fessione*m*, quod criminale fuerat *per* operacionem, 'Hit is forȝiuenliche senne ðurh andettednesse ðe was arrer heaued-senne ðurh weorke.' Ac hit be[h]oueð ðat hie bie wiel (h)lutter, *and* ðat ðar ne bie forholen non atter. Hier of sade ðe profete: Confitemini d*omi*no, qu*onia*m bonus, 'Andettið ȝewer sennen,' he sade, 'goddalmihtin, for ðan ðe he is god[2], for ðan his mildsce is hier on world.' Se ðe her godes mildsce ne beȝett, ne wurð hie hi*m* naure mo calles hwer. We findeð on ðe hali write ðat ȝif mann ware firliche[3] uppen (h)is deaðe, *and* he prest ne mihte habben, andette his sennen him ðe ware necst him, *and* he scolde habben mildsce, bute ȝif hit ware ðat he ðane prest forhowede ; oððer ȝif he ware all hone, ðanne most he to godd ane. *And* belokie elch mann ðat he naure nortriwi godes are ne his mildsce, ne eft sones ne bie no mann to þrist to seneȝin, *and* segge : 'Mare mai godd forȝiuen ðanne we muȝen seneȝin.' Non adicies peccatu*m* super peccatu*m et* dices: qu*onia*m misericordia d*omi*ni magna est!

Of clennesse.

AN oðer eadi mihte his ȝehaten mundicia, þat is, clannesse, ðe is inne godes huse swiðe ȝeluued. Ne mai ȝie iðolien none unclannesse on godes temple, ne beneðen on ði likame, ne abuuen on ðire saule, ne on ðouhtes, for ðan hie wat wel ðat openlicor ben þouhtes to-foren gode ðanne beð spaches be-foren manne ; ne of fule spaches hie ne mai nauht ðolien, for ðan h(i)e wot ðat god his ȝehiereð *and* alle mislikið; ne euele workes hie ne mai nieh wunien, for ðan ðat godd his hat scunien. Mundamini qui fertis uasa d*omi*ni, 'Makieð ȝew clane ðe bereð godes faten !' Clanse þine hirte, for ðan þe hie owh to be*n*ne[4] godes fatt. On

---

[1] page 76.   [2] ȝod MS.   [3] The 1st i corr. from a.   [4] page 77.

it God's message, God's word. *In corde meo abscondi eloquia tua, ut non peccem tibi,* 'In my heart I hid Thy words, Lord, lest I should sin against Thee.' So did St. Mary; she bore God's words in her heart, that she often might think of Him whom she loved much, *conferens in corde suo.* She bore in her heart what God said: *Beati mundo corde, quoniam ipsi Deum videbunt,* 'Blessed are the pure in heart, for they shall see God.' God cannot be seen with any other eyes but with the heart's. Wash and wipe well clean the eyes, because it is true what they tell thee. If thou wilt know which eyes the heart may have, they are named *intellectus et ratio*. These can see about as well at mid-night as at mid-day. Intellect and reason are the two eyes. Through intellect thou understandest all things, and through discernment thou shalt discern the evil from the good. All that thou thinkest thou seest with these eyes. But ever too many are short-sighted with the one of these eyes, and too many with both. Of all the blessings which God promised in His preaching, there is none so high as is 'who is pure in heart.' May he get it whoso can ! I warn thee, thou never gettest it clean whilst thou doest not care what thou thinkest, nor what thou speakest, nor what thou hearest speak. And except thou gladly makest it clean as much as possible, with God's help, thou shalt never see God Almighty with these eyes with which thou seest sun and moon. Love this holy virtue *munditiam,* and it will make thee pure in heart. Amen.

Of lore.

Disciplina is another holy virtue, which God Himself bids us to take through the prophet, who says: *Apprehendite disciplinam, etc.,* 'Take discipline of all the misdeeds which ye do, lest God be angry, and ye perish from the right way!' Except thou doest justice to thyself for the misdeeds which thou misdoest, with fasting, or with watching, or with wailing and sore repentance, or with weary-

OF CLEANNESS AND LORE.

hire me scal beren godes sande, godes word. In corde meo abscondi eloquia tua, ut non peccem tibi, 'On mine hierte ich hedde þine wordes, hlauerd, þat ich nolde naht seneȝin aȝeanes ðe.' Swa dede *sancta*¹ Maria; hie bar godes wordes on hire hierte, þat hie ofte mihte þenken on him ðe hie michel luuede, conferens in corde suo. Hie bar on hire hierte þat þe godd sade: Beati mundo corde, q*uonia*m ipsi deum uidebu*n*t, 'Eadi bieð ða clane-hierte menn, for ðan hie sculen gode ȝesen.' Godd ne mai ben ȝesiȝen mid none oðer eiȝen ðanne mid þare hierte. Wassce *and* wipe wol clane ða eiȝene, for ðan soð is ðat hie ðe siggen. Gif² þu wilt witen wilke eiȝene ðe hierte muȝe habben, hie bieð ȝenamned intellect*us* et racio. Ðese muȝen ȝesen alswa wel onbuten mid-niht alswa on mid-daiȝ. Andȝeat *and* skele bieð ða twa eiȝene. Ðurh andȝeat þu unde(r)stanst alle þing, *and* ðurh scadwisnesse þu scalt skilien ðe euele fram ðe gode. All ðat ðe þu þencst þu ȝiesichst mid þese eiȝen. Ac aure to fele bieð bisne mid þan onen of þese eiȝen, *and* to fele mid baðe. Of alle ða edmodnesses ðe godd³ behet on his spelle, nis ðar non swo heih swa is 'ðe is⁴ clane-hierte.' Beȝiete se ðe muȝe! Ich⁵ þe warni, ne beȝiethst ðu his naure clane ðar wile ðat þu ne recst wat þu þenche, ne wat þu speke, ne wat ðu ȝehire speken. And bute þu his ȝier[n]e make clane after þine mihte, mid godes helpe, ne scal tu naure ȝesen mid ðase eiȝene ðe þu mide ȝesiest sunne *and* mone, godd almihtin. Luue ðese hali mihte mu*n*diciam, *and* hie ðe makeð clane-hierte. Amen.

4

8

12

16

20

24

Of lore.

DISCIPLINA is on oþer hali mihte, ðe goddself us hat nemen⁶ ðurh⁷ ðe p*r*ophete, ðe seið: Apprehendite disciplinam, *et cet.*, 'Nemeð discipline of alle ðe misdades ðe ȝe deð, þe las te godd him wraðþi, *and* ȝie forfaren of ða rihte weiȝe!' Bute ðu neme riht of ðe seluen of ðe misdades ðe ðu mis-dest, mid fasten, oððer mid wake, oððer mid wope *and* sare beriwsinge, oððer mid weringe⁸,

28

32

---

¹ *an* i *underdotted after the 2nd* a.   ² G *with a* j *inserted above*.
³ gode *MS*.   ⁴ ðeies *MS.*   ⁵ ic *inserted red above between* ich *and* þe.
⁶ *page* 78.   ⁷ *and* ðurh *MS.*   ⁸ þeringe *MS., a letter erased between* r *and* i.

I

ing [thyself], or with kneeling, or with toil, or with pure prayer, or with pure alms, with the counsel of thy confessor: God's wrath will come upon thee, so that thou losest the one right way which goes to Heaven. That is a great wrath of God that man is so blind that he goes to hell laughing. Though he much misdo, he is therefore not more sorry, than if he had not misdone. *Excaeca cor populi hujus, ne videant et intelligant.* Of them said God : ' Blind the heart of this people, lest they see or understand the right way to the kingdom of Heaven.' Their hard heart and their evilness have deserved it that the blind leads the blind. That is, he who should instruct him, does the same sins and gives an example of them, and he also teaches him and says that [neither] for eating nor for drinking nor for woman, whom God has shaped as companion to man, anybody ever shall be lost. Woe to this lore and this deed! Do thou not so, dear soul. But when thou feelest that thou hast neither God's love nor His fear as thou shouldst, cry to Him and say with the prophet: *Illumina oculos meos, Domine,* 'Lord, open my eyes and lighten them with the true light, so that I never be sleeping in the soul's death, nor that the devils may boast that they had the upper hand over me.' *Bonitatem et disciplinam et scientiam doce me, etc.,* ' But Thou, Lord, teach me goodness, through which I may be good, and teach me such discipline, that I may soften Thy wrath, and such knowledge, that I may know and please Thee !'

Of patience.

Patientia is a holy virtue, that is, patience, which God Himself taught us with word and also with example. In His Gospel He said: *Qui te percusserit in maxillam, praebe ei et aliam,* ' Whosoever shall smite thee under the ear, suffer it for My love, and turn to him the other. Whosoever shall take away thy coat, give him thy mantle. Whosoever shall compel thee to go with him two miles, go with him three.' This seems foolishness to the fool, but nevertheless Wisdom said it. The blessed man who has this virtue will suffer, for God's love, all kinds of things which one may do him, oððer mid cnewlinge, oððer mid swinke, oððer mid clane bede, oððer mid hlutter almesse, mid ðe rade of þine scrifte : godes wraððe cumþ uppen ðe, swa þat ðu forliest ða ane rihte weiȝ þe gað to heuene. Ðat is michel godes wraðþe þat mann is swa blind 4 ðat he farð to helle leiȝinde¹. Þeih he michel mis-do, nis for ði na mare sori, þanne ȝif he nadde naht mis-don. Exceca cor populi huius, ne uideant et intelligant. Of hem sade godd : 'Bland ðies folkes hierte, þat hie ne sien ne understande ðe rihte weiȝe to 8 heuene riche.' Heare harde hierte and here euelnesse hit haueð of-earned þat ðe blinde latt ðane blinde. Þat is, se ðe him wissin scolde, deð ðo ilke sennes and haueð ðar of forbisne, and ec he him lareð and seið þat for ates ne for drenches ne for wifmanne, ðe 12 godd haueð ȝescapen manne to ȝemoane, ne scal man naure ben forloren. Walawa þessere lare and ðesere dade ! Swa ne do þu naht, lieue saule. Ac þanne ðu ȝefelst þat ðu godes luue ne his eiȝe ne hafst swa swa ðu scoldest, clepe to him and seih mid ðe 16 prophete : Illumina oculos meos, domine, 'Hlauerd, opene mine eiȝene and liht his mid þe soðe lihte, þat ich naure ne bie slapinde on ðare saule deaðe, ne ðat ðe dieule(s)² muȝen beȝelpen þat hie hafden ðe heiȝere hand ouer me.' Bonitatem³ et disci- 20 plinam et scienciam doce me, et cetera, 'Ac ðu, hlauerd, tach me godnesse, ðurh wan ich god muȝe bien, and tach me swilche discipline, þat ich þine wraððe muȝe softin, and swilch andȝet, ðat ich ðe muȝe ȝecnawen and ȝecwemen !' 24

Of Ðolemodnesse.

PACIENCIA is an hali mihte, ðat is, ðolemodnesse, ðe godd⁴ self us tahte mid worde and ech mid forbisne. On his spelle he sade : Qvi te percusserit in maxillam, prebe ei 28 et aliam, 'Se ðe smit þe under ðat (e)are, þole⁵ hit for mine lune, and wand him to þat oðer. Se þe benimð ðe þine kiertel⁶, ȝif him þine mantel. Se ðe net þe to gonne mid him twa milen, ga mid him þrie.' Þis þincð ðe sott sothade, ac naðelas wisdom hit 32 sade. Ðe sali mann þe ðese mihte hafð, alleskennes þing ðe

---

[1] an erasure under de. [2] s inserted above, red. [3] page 79.
[4] godð MS. [5] e corr. from a. [6] kie on erasure.

except sin only. That said Solomon: *Melior est patiens viro forti*, 'Better is,' he said, 'the patient man than the strong who taketh castles.' Because to do evil is no strength, but is impotence, for he is esteemed as stronger who overcomes his own mood, than he who slays and takes castles. Dear soul, all the while thou dwellest in the smoke-house of thy body, whence many kinds of smokes of impatience come, it is very great need to thee to have this virtue with thee; and full surely it will bring thee to the kingdom where thou never more shalt find anything which thou mayst dislike.

Of maidenhood.

Virginitas is a very precious virtue, that is, maidenhood, which follows the holy Lamb, and is nearest to it. For the great purity this same holy virtue is hallowed in Christ, St. Mary's Son, who was and is evermore maiden. She promised to keep [her] maidenhood, and she performed it well; and after her many thousands, through her good example, kept their purity and suffered therefore many kinds of martyrdom. Neither God nor the apostle bade [anyone] to keep this maidenhood, except those who would vow it with their good will. But when it is vowed, it must be kept, if they will be saved. It is angelic life of Heaven whoso humbly keeps maidenhood on earth. *Qui potest capere, capiat*, 'Whosoever can have it, let him receive and keep it!' He is certainly blessed.

Of chastity.

Castitas is also [a] very holy virtue, that is, chastity. Without maidenhood man can be saved, but without chastity or right spouse no man can be saved. Of this said the apostle: *Pacem et sanctimoniam diligite, sine qua nemo videbit Deum*, 'Love peace and holiness, that is, this chastity; without it man never shall see God.'

mann him maiȝ don, wiðuten senne one, he wile þolieȝen for
godes luue. Ðat sade Salemun: Melior est paciens uiro
forti, 'Bettre his,' he sade, ' ðe þolemode mann þanne þe stronge
þe nimð casteles.' For þan euel to done nis non strencþe, ac 4
is unmihte, fo(r)¹ þi he is ihealden strengere ðe ouor-cumþ his
auȝen mod, þanne he ðe slecð *and* casteles nemð. Lieue² saule,
al ðe (h)wile³ ðe þu wunest on ðe smec-huse of ðine likame,
hwanene cumeð⁴ manies kennes smekes of unþolemodnesse, ðe is 8
swiðe michel nied ðat ðu þese mihte mid þe habbe; *and* full-
ȝewis hie þe bringð to ðare riche ðar ðu naurema ne scalt finden
(no)ne⁵ (þinge) þe ðe misliki.

Of maiden-had. 12

VIRGINITAS is an swiðe derwurðe mihte, ðat is, maiden-
had⁶, ðe folȝið ðe hali lombe, *and* him his neȝest. For
þare michele clannesse ðies ilke hali mihte is ȝehalȝed on Criste,
seinte Marie sune, þe was *and* is aurema maiden. Hie behet 16
maidenhad to healden, *and* hie wel it ȝelaste; *and* after hire
maniȝe þusend, for hire gode forbisne, here clannesse ihelden *and*
manieskennes martirdom ðar fore ðolede. Naðer ne godd ne þe
apostel ne hieten þis maidenhad to healden, buten ðo þe wolden 20
mid here gode wille hit behaten. Ac seððen hit is behaten,
siðþen hit is to healden, alswa hie willen ben iborȝen. Hit is
angelich lif of heuene, se ðe eadmodliche halt maidenhad on ierðe.
Qvi potest capere, capiat, ' Se ðe hit mai habben, he hit neme 24
and healde!' He is iwiss isali.

Of clannesse.

CASTITAS is ech swiðe hali mihte, þat is, clannesse. Wið-
uten maidenhad mann mai bien ȝeborȝen, ac wið-uten 28
clannesse oððer rihte spuse nan mann (ne)⁷ mai ben ȝeborȝen.
Hier of sade ðe apostel: Pacem et sanctimoniam diligite,
sine qua nemo uidebit deum, ' Luuieð sibsumnesse *and* hali-

---

¹ r *added, red.* ² *Before* l *another one by another hand.* ³ h *inserted red.*
⁴ ð *corr. from* t. ⁵ nan ðare *underdotted.* ⁶ *page* 80. ⁷ *red above the line.*

This holy virtue has three gifts from the Holy Ghost, that is, that the devil never can overcome it, where it reigns, by any kind of lechery, [neither] working with limbs, nor speaking with ill-mannered speeches, nor thinking with foul thoughts; but anon if they come they are driven out of the heart with sorry mood and with running tears. So one shall do with them who will not [keep] peace.

Pudicitia is her sister, [a] maiden holy in thoughts, and pure from all filth. That says St. Austin: 'If a maiden has this holy virtue in her thoughts, though she became deflowered against her will, she is before God nevertheless maiden;' and afterwards: 'She who is a pure maiden in body, and has not this holy virtue in her thoughts, but willed what she may not, she is no maiden before God.' *Pudicitia* is the pure maidenhood of the thoughts, as *castitas* is the purity of the body.

Of continence.

Continentia is continence concerning fornication. It is very much loved by all those who hope in God's mercy. Because the apostle has well promised them that, if they keep and love these three holy virtues together: *castitatem, pudicitiam, continentiam*, though they have lost their bodily maidenhood, he has espoused them to Christ, and says thus: *Despondi enim vos uni viro, virginem castam exhibere Christo*, 'I have wedded you to one husband [as a] chaste maiden, that is, to Christ,' that is [a] right spouse to every good soul. For all Christ's chosen are Christ's limbs, and He is the head of all of us, and with right belief we are all one with His flesh and with His blood, so that nothing can divide us. *Quis nos* dom, þat is, þes clannesse ; wið-uten hire ne scal naure mann isien godd.' Þies hali mihte haueð of ðe hali gaste þrie (ʒiues)¹, þat is, þat naure deuel ne mai hes ouercumen, þar hie rixið, mid naneskennes galnesse, mid lemes werchinde, ne mid unðeaufulle ⁴ spaches specinde, ne mid fule þowtes þenkinde ; ac anon ʒif hie cumeð hie bieð idriuen ut of þare hierte mid sari mode and mid ierniende teares. Swa me scal don of hem ðe grið ne willeð ².

P VDICICIA is hire suster, hali maiden of þanke, *and* clane 8 of alle felðes. Ðat seið *sanctus* Augustin*us*: 'Gif maiden hafð þese hali mihte on hire þanke, þeih hie wurðe hire unðankes forleiʒen, hie is to-foren gode naþelas maiden' ; *and* eft : 'H[i]e ðe is clane maiden on likame, *and* ðese mihte ne hafð on hire 12 ʒeþanke, ac wolde þat hie ne mai, hie nis naht maiden to-foren gode.' Pudicicia is ðe hlutter maïden(h)ad of þe þanke, alswa castitas is þe clannesse of ðe likame.

Of wið(h)ealdnesse³. 16

C ONTINENCIA is wið[h]ealdnesse³ after þe forleire. Hie is swiðe ʒeluued of alle ðe hopieð to godes mildsce. For þan þe apostel hem hafð⁴ wel hehaten þat, ʒif hie healdeð *and* luuieð þese þrie halie mihtes to-gedere : castitatem, pudiciciam, 20 continenciam, þeih hie here likamliche maiden-had habbe forloren, he [h]is haueð ʒespused to Criste, *and* þus seið : Despondi enim uos uni uiro, uirgine*m* castam exibere *Christo*⁵, 'Ich ʒew habbe bewedded ane were clane maiden, þat 24 is, to Criste,' *þat* is riht spus ta alchere gode saule. For þan alle Cristes ʒecorene bieð Cristes lemen⁶, *and* he is ure alre heaued, *and* mid rihte ʒeleuen mid his flesce *and* mid his blode we bieð all an, swa ðat nan þing ne mai us twammen⁷. Qvis nos separa- 28

¹ *Written above* þinges, *which is underlined.* ² *page* 81.
³ wid- *MS.* ⁴ hafd *MS.* ⁵ xp̄o *MS.*
⁶ m *partly on erasure.* ⁷ *The first* m *on erasure.*

separabit a caritate Christi ? Full certainly these holy virtues bind us also together.

Of harmlessness.

Innocentia is another holy virtue, that is, harmlessness. He is certainly *innocens*, that is, harmless, who never yet did harm to himself or to any other. Such was none except Christ. The holy children who were martyred for Christ are rightly called *innocentes*, because they never yet did harm either to God or to man, either in thoughts or in words. Therefore they are blessed. Follow this holy virtue in thoughts, in words, in works, and think that first thou doest harm to thyself, if thou thinkest amiss, or speakest or doest anything in another way to thy fellow-Christian, than as thou wouldst wish that he did to thee. Think hereof! Again, says the holy Writ about this : *Manus in manus non erit innocens malus*, '[Though] hand [join] in hand, the evil man is not guiltless.' That is said about the man who has done evil against God and against his neighbour, and thinks and deceives himself that he does no more evil, than the man who sits idle and holds his one hand in his other, and does evil to nobody. Yet, though this man do so, he is not *innocens*, except he atones for what he has broken before. Ever too few men think about to have this holy virtue, and [yet] without it no man can please God well.

Honestas is called another virtue, which is needful to every good man. That is, that he looks decent with all the limbs of his body. It (honesty) withholds his eyes, lest they be too much looking hither and thither; the ears, lest they blithely listen to vanities, and therewith prevent the soul hearing good thoughts of good words; the tongue, lest he become the unworthier for it, and when it shall speak with God in its prayers, the more disagreeable. It makes the man look decent who loves it, both with his hands and his feet. It does not let the hands play with [a] stick or with bit a karitate *Christi*? Fulȝewis ðese haliȝe mihtes us bindeð ec to-gedere.

Of vneilindnesse.

INNOCENCIA is an oðður hali mihte, þat is, uneilind[ness]e. He is iwis innocens, þat is, uneilinde, þe nauerȝete him seluen ne eilede ne nan oðður. Þat nas nan wiðuten Criste. Ða hali children ðe waren ȝemartired for Criste, hie bieð mid rihte icleped innocentes, for ðan hie ne eileden nauerȝiete ne gode[1] ne manne, ne a þoutes ne a wordes. For þi hie bieð eadi. Folȝe ðese hali mihte on þouhtes, on wordes, on workes, *and* þenc þat arst þu eilest ðe seluen, ȝif ðu misþencst, oðður spekest oðður dest auht oðerliker onȝeanes þin emcristen, þanne ðu woldest þat he dede ðe. Þench hier of ! Ȝiet[2] seið þat hali writ herof: Man*us* in manus non erit innocens malus[3], 'Hande on hande nis naht ðe euele man gylt-leas.' Ðat is iseid[4] bi ðo manne ðe euele haueð ȝedon aȝean godd *and* aȝean [h]is nexte, *and* beþeincð him *and* beswicð þat he namare euel ne dieð, þanne ðe ma*n* ðe sitt idel *and* halt [h]is on hand in oðer, *and* none manne euel ne deð. Ȝiet[2], þeih ðis mann swa do, nis he nauht innocens, bute ȝif he biete[5] ðat he harrer hafde tobroken. Aure to feawe men bien abuten to habben ðese hali mihte, *and* wið-uten hire ne mai non ma*n*n godd wel ȝecweme*n*.

HONESTAS is cleped an oðer mihte, ðe is niedfull alche gode manne. Þat is, ðat he worðliche him loki mid alle hise lemes of his likame. Hise eiȝene, þat hie ne bien to swiðe gawrinde hider *and* ȝeond; þo earen, ðat hie bliðeliche ne hlesten ydelnesses, *and* ðare mide benime ðare saule gode þohtes of gode wordes to ȝe(he)ren[7]; þe tunge hie wiðhalt, þat he ne wurðe for hire ðunworðere, *and* þanne hie wið gode scall speken on hire benes, þe uncwemer. Wurðliche hie deð lokin ðe manne ðe hes luuieð, baðe his handen *and* hise fett. Ne lat hie nawht ðe hande

---

[1] page 82. [2] G *is altered into* ȝ *by inserting a* j *above.*
[3] In libro sapiencie red, *at side.* [4] d *corr. from* ð.
[5] beȝiete *MS., the* ȝ *underdotted.* [6] wid *MS.* [7] he *written above* a, *red.*

[a] straw—that is no good token of a mature man, the heart is not yet steadfast—nor [a man] sit tottering with [his] foot, nor throw the one over the other. Blessed is that man who takes good heed of himself, and thinks that nobody lives for his own behoof alone, but is an example either of good or of evil to all who see him or hear of him. If thou takest heed hereof, thou wilt be honoured before God and before man.

Of abstinence.

Another holy virtue is called *abstinentia*, that is, abstinence. Concerning the man who withholds himself not only from eating and drinking, but from all the things which God forbids to do, said the apostle: *Abstinete vos a carnalibus desideriis, quae militant adversus animam,* 'Abstain,' said he, 'from the lusts of the flesh, which war against the soul.' That is that wholesome abstinence. Again, he said for it: *Haec est enim voluntas Dei, sanctificatio vestra,* 'This is verily the will of God,' said he, 'that ye be holy,' *ut abstineatis vos a fornicatione,* 'and that ye should abstain from fornication,' *ut sciat unusquisque vas suum possidere,* 'and that ye should know how to hold the vessel of your body with great worthiness and with great purity, as the same vessel wherein ye bear the precious treasure, that is, the Holy Ghost.' When a great lust comes to thee after a thing, do not yield to it anon, but bethink thyself well eagerly and abstain firmly. If it comes often smiting to thy heart, know thou forsooth that it is of the devil. If thou yieldest to it, thou makest thyself [a] slave, and not [a] man's, but the devil's. If thou doest something else, and refrainest this lust, and overcomest it with prayer, thou shalt have great reward from God, and make thyself free.

pleiȝende mid stikke, ne mid strawe—nis þat non god tocne of
ripe manne¹, nis ðe hierte nauht ȝiet stedefast—ne mid fote sitten²
toterinde, ne ðen eune worpen ouer ðan oðre. ȝesali³ is ðe ilke
mann ðe gode ȝeme nimð (of him seluen), *and* þencð þat no mann 4
ne leueð to [h]is aȝene be[h]ofte ane, ac is forbisne oðre of gode
oððer of euele to alle ðe hine ȝeseð oððer of him hiereð. ȝif³ ðu
herof ȝieme nemest, þu best ȝewurðed to-foren gode *and* to-foren
manne. 8

Of wiðheldnesse⁴.

ABSTINENCIA hatte an oðer hali mihte, *þat* is, wið[h]eald-
nesse. Ðe mann þe him wiðhalt naht one of ates *and* of
drenches, ac fram alle ðo þinges ðe godd forbett to donne, herof 12
sade ðe apostel : Abstinete uos a carnalib*us* desideriis, que
militant aduersus⁵ animam⁶, 'Wiðhealdeþ,' he saide, 'ȝew wið
þa flesches (h)lustes⁷, ðe winneð aȝean ðare sawle.' Þat is ðat
halsume wið[h]ealdnesse. ȝiet⁸ he sade for ðare : Hec est enim 16
uoluntas dei, san[c]tificat*io* u*es*tra⁶, 'Ðis is iwis godes
wille,' he sade, 'þat hie ben hali,' vt abstineatis uos a forni-
cacione, '*and* þat ȝie wið[h]ealden ȝew fram galnesse,' vt sciat
unusquisq*ue* uas suum possidere⁶, '*and* ðat ȝie healden 20
cunnen ȝewer fatt of ȝewer likame mid michele wurscipe *and* mid
michele clannesse, alswa ðat ilke fatt ðe⁸ ȝie bereð inne þat der-
worðe tresor, þat is, ðe hali gast.' Danne ðe cumð a michel lust
after ane þinge, ne teiþe þu him naht anoan, ac beðenc ðu ðe wel 24
ȝerne *and* fastliche wið[h]eald⁹ þe. ȝif³ hitt cumð ofte smitende
to ðin hierte, wite þu to soðe ðat hit is of dieule. ȝif ðu him tei-
þest, þu makest ðe seluen þrall, *and* noht mannes, ac deules. ȝif³
ðu dest sumþing elles, *and* dwellest þisne lust, *and* mid ibede hine 28
ouercumst, þu scalt habben michel lean of godd¹⁰, *and* ðe seluen
makest frie.

¹ *page* 83.   ² *an erasure between* s *and* i.   ³ *a* j *inserted above in* G.
⁴ wiðhelðnesse *MS*.   ⁵ deum *underdotted*.   ⁶ apostolus, *red on the margin*.
⁷ (h)lustess *MS*., *the last* s *underdotted*.   ⁸ de *MS*.   ⁹ wid eald *MS*.
¹⁰ *page* 84.

Of fasting.

Jejunium is another virtue which has often cooled God's wrath, that is, holy fasting. Through fasting God's wrath became assuaged against Nineveh, the great city which took three days to go [round it]. All the people that dwelt therein were to be destroyed through God's right doom, if they had not fasted. Then this holy virtue helps much in all the needs which man has to do. It gets forgiveness for the sinful, rest for the toilful, gladness for the sorry. Christ Himself hallowed this fasting when He fasted forty days in the wilderness, [away] from all men. There He gave to anchorites and hermits who love loneliness [a] good example to flee the world and to love loneliness, since He, whom nobody could hinder, nevertheless flew from men when He would fast. So did Moses. He fasted forty days when he took the law from God Himself, upon the Mount of Sinai. So did Elijah, the prophet, in the wilderness; forty days he fasted. All these three fasts were as wonderful as no others, viz. without all kinds of meats. God is ever fasting. Therefore ought all who think to dwell with Him to love fasting much, just as one can suffer it. In great trouble we are while we shall strive and care about meats. But there are some who think too much of them, and give their heart ever too much to them. So strongly they are deceived, and so sweet it seems to them and pleases them so [much], that they have no other bliss, nor care to have, but of eating and of drinking and of their body's lusts. When they shall fast at all, they fast scarcely all the noon; then after noon they drink all the day, and some still by night. They do not understand that it is as great a sin to break fasts by drinking after noon without great need, as it is before noon by eating without just as much need. Such unhappy men bemoans the apostle weeping sorely, who says: *Quorum Deus venter est,* 'Of their belly they make their God.' For the good man is thinking night and day how he may please God, and obey Him best. So is this deceived man thinking night and day how he may fill his unhappy belly with sweet meats and drinks. *Quorum finis interitus,* 'They are certainly lost who end in this.' *Quoniam*

Of fasten.

IEIVNIUM is an oðer mihte ðe godes wraðþe hafð ofte ikeled, þat is, hali fasten. Đurh fasten warð godes wraðþe ʒeleid of Niniue, ðare muchele burʒh ðe ʒelaste ðrie daiʒes fare. All ðat folk ðe þerinne was scolde ben forfaren þurh godes rihte dome, ʒif here fasten nare. To alle ðo nedes ðe mann hafð[1] to donne þanne is (þes)e[2] hali mihte swiðe helpinde. Hie beʒiet ðe senfulle forʒifnesse, ðe swinkfulle reste, ðe sari gladnesse. Crist self halʒede ðis fasten þo þe he faste fowerti daiʒes on ða wilderne, fram alle mannen. Đar he ʒaif ancres *and* hermites ðe luuieð onnesse gode forbisne ðe world to flene *and* onnesse to luuien, seððen he, ðe no mann ne mihte letten, fleih naðelas menn, ða ðe he fasten wolde. Swa dede Moyses. He fastede fowerti daʒes þar (ðe) he þe laʒhe nam of godd self, uppe ðe munte of Synay. Swa dede Helyas, ðe prophete, on þe wilderne; fowerti daiʒes he faste. Alle þese þrie fasten waren swa selcuðliche swa non oðre, wið-uten alles kennes metes. Godd is haure fastinde. For ði aʒen alle ðe mid him þenken to wunien, michel to luuien fasten, swa swa me hit þolien mai. On michele ʒeswinke we bieð ðar [h]wile ðe we abuten metes sculen striuen[3] *and* hoʒiʒen. Ac hit bieð sume ðe to michel þar of þenceð, *and* aure to michel her hierte þar to doð. Swa swiðe hie bieð beswiken, *and* swa swete hit hem þincð *and* swa him likeð, þat hie nan oðer blisse ne habbeð, ne[4] ne reccheð to habben, buten of ates *and* of drenches *and* of here likames hlustes. Þanne hie alles fasten sculen, ðane fasteð hie all þat none uneaðe; ðanne after non drinkeð all daiʒ, *and* sume ʒiet benihte. Ne understandeð hie naht þat alswa michel senne hit is to breken fasten mid drinke after none wið-uten michele nede, a(l)swa hit is to-foren non of aten wið-uten alswa michele niede. Of ðelliche unsali menn bemaneð ðe apostel sore wepinde, *and* seið: Qvorum deus uenter est, 'Of here wombe hie makieð here godd.' For ðau ðe gode mann is niht *and* daiʒ þeinkinde hu he muʒe gode icwemen, *and* him betst hersumen; alswa is ðies beswikene mann niht *and* daiʒ þeinkinde hwu he muʒe fellen [h]is unʒesali beli mid swete metes *and* drenches. Quorum finis interitus, 'Hie bieð

---
[1] h *corr. from* i.   [2] þes *written above* ðe.   [3] steruin *MS.*   [4] *page* 85.

ebriosi regnum Dei non possidebunt, 'Great drinkers shall never, never forsooth, enjoy the kingdom of Heaven.' Thou who committest this and wilt not be deceived, go to the burying-place of him who committed this with thee or before thee, and think how lonely he lies from all his fellows with whom he was wont to drink and to play, and how dark he lies there who was accustomed to the fair fire and to the bright candles, and think that the foul belly is crawling full of worms, which he was wont to fill with good meats and sweet drinks, and try; if thou doest not shudder hereof, thou art not in the life which thou shouldst live. Woe be to the same man who sees and hears this and never is the better!

Of sobriety.

Sobrietas is another virtue, that is, sobriety. This makes the man sober who was too greedy. Of this said the apostle: *Sobrii estote et vigilate, etc.,* 'Be sober and watch with thoughts, because your adversary goeth about every man whom he might swallow with some cardinal sin. As the lion who goes about the animals to swallow them, so does the devil about you.' Beware whoso will! *Sobrietas est nimii cibi et potus repressio.* This virtue makes the man who will follow it sinless and free from shame before God and before man as for eating and drinking. There are some who know no moderation in feeding themselves, as there are ever too many other men who give without distinction as well the things which they should not give, as those which they should give. That this virtue wills that thou givest those things gladly which shall be given rightly. *Quia hilarem datorem diligit Deus,* 'God loveth a cheerful giver.' And those things which shall not be given, are to be withheld with great discretion. One ought to give [neither] church-things, nor tithes, nor offerings, nor alms anywhere but where great need is and where he nevermore in this life seeks to have reward or meed. Think hereof ye who love the world's love!

iwis forlorene ðe hier on andieð.' Quoniam ebriosi regnum
dei non possidebunt, 'Ðe michele drinkeres soðliche naure,
naure heuene riche ne sculen bruken.' Ðu ðe þis befelst *and* ne
wilt [bien] beswiken, ga to his berieles ðe ðis beuall mid þe oðer 4
beforen ðe, *and* þenk hu anliche he lið fram alle hise felawȝes ðe
he was bewune mide to drinken *and* to pleiȝen, *and* hu ðiester he
lið ðar þe was bewune to ðe faire fiere *and* to ðe brihte kan-
deles, *and* þench ðat ðe fule wombe is crewlinde full of weormes, 8
þe he was bewune[1] to fellen mid gode metes *and* swete drenches,
and fonde ; ȝif þe herof noht nagrist, nart þu naht liues þar ðe ðu[2]
libben scoldest. Wa mai bien ðe ilke mann ðe þis ȝesikþ *and*
ȝehiereð *and* na ðe bettre ne bieð! 12

Of ȝe-meðe.

SOBRIETAS is an oðer mihte, þat is, maðe. Ðies makeð
þanne mann maðfull ðe was to grady. Her of sade ðe
apostel: Sobrii estote *et* uigilate, *et cet.*, 'Bieð imeðfull *and* 16
wakieð mid þoutes, for ðan ȝewer wiðerwine gað abuten alche
manne (w)ham he mihte forswoleȝen mid sume [h]eaued-senne.
Alswa ðe lyon ðe gað abuten þe dier hem to forswoleȝen, swa deð
deuel abuten ȝew.' Bie war se ðe wile! Sobrietas est nimii[3] 20
cibi *et* potus repressio. Ðies mihte, hie makeð þanne mann
ðe hire wile folȝin senne-leas *and* scameleas to-foren godd *and* to-
foren manne of ates *and* of drenches. Hit bieð sume þat non
imeðe ne cunnen of hem seluen to feden, alswa bieð aure to fele 24
oðre menn ðe ȝiueð wið-uten schele alswa ða þinges ðe hie naht ne
scolden ȝiuen, alswa ða ðe hie scolden ȝiuen. Ðat wile þies mihte
þat þu ȝiue ða ðinges þe sculen bien mid rihte iȝiuen, gladliche.
Qvia hillarem datorem diligit deus, 'Gladne ȝiuere luueð 28
godd.' And ða þinges ðe ne sculen ben iȝiuen, þa bieð to wið-
[h]ealden mid michele skele. Chierche-þinges, tiȝeþes, ne offrendes,
ne almesses ne awh me nauhwer to ȝiuene buten ðar þe michel
nied is *and* ðar he naure ma on ðese liue lean ne mede ne secð to 32
habben. Þeinkeð hier of ȝie þe luuieð worldes luue!

---

page 86. [2] bewunen *MS*. [3] *The second* i *is half erased*.

Of conscience.

Again, there is another virtue—very happy [he] who may get it!—which is called *pura conscientia*, that is, pure conscience. It dwells so concealed in the heart that nobody can see or know it but God alone. It bears good witness of all kinds of good deeds, because it is glad and blithe of them, [and] of all kinds of evil works, words, or thoughts which come before it—so they must all, evil and good. All these it receives blithely or sorrily. All which are agreeable to God are very welcome to it. Of those which are not so and come before it, it is very sorry, and reprehends the heart strongly and accuses [it] before God. Concerning this said the blessed apostle St. John: *Si cor nostrum non reprehenderit nos*, 'If our heart,' he said, 'does not reprehend nor accuse us of any sin which God hates and thou lovest: whatsoever we beseech God for, He will soon grant us.'

Of prayer.

Now we have quite come to this blessed virtue which one calls *oratio sancta*, that is, holy prayer. It is not right that we leave it, without saying something of it. When we read in the book, God speaks with us; when we say our prayer, we speak with God. If thou wouldst beseech the king for any thing, and thou camest into his hall where he sat among his rich men, and thou shouldst speak alone before all his men, thou wouldst speak with great dread and with great consideration. With much more fear and love thou oughtst to come before God, who is King of all kings, and beseech Him very humbly for thy need, so that thou shouldst say at the end of each petition what Christ said Himself as an example for us, because we do not know whether we beg what is agreeable to God and useful for us, or is not so: *Non sicut ego volo, sed sicut tu vis*, 'Lord,' He said, 'do not as I will, but as Thou wilt.' Christ

Of inȝehied.

GIET is an oðer mihte—swiðe eadi ðe hes beȝeten mai!—þe[1] is icleped pura consciencia, þat is, hlutter inȝehied. Hie wuneð swa derneliche on þare hierte, ðat[2] no mann hes ne mai isien ne witen bute godd one. Hie berð gode ȝewitnesse of alleskennes gode dades, for ðan hie is ðer of glad *and* bliðe; of alles kennes euele workes, wordes oðer þoutes ðe cumeð toforen hire, swa hie moten alle, euele *and* gode. Alle hie his underfongð[3] bliðeliche oððer sariliche. Alle ðe gode beð icweme, hie bieð hire swiðe welcume. Đa ðe swa ne bieð *and* cumeð toforen hire, hie is ðarof swiðe sari, *and* swiðe ða hierte undernimð *and* wreiȝeð toforen gode. Herof sade ðe eadi apostel sanctus Iohannes: Si cor nostrum non reprehenderit nos, ' ȝif[4] ure hierte,' he sade, 'us ne undernemeð naht ne ne wreihð of nane senne ðe godd hateð *and* ðe luuieð: hwat so we beseceð at gode, he us wile sone teiþin.'

Of biene.

NU we alles bieð ȝecumen to ðessere eadi mihte ðe me clepeð oratio sancta, þat is, hali bede. Nis hit naht riht þat we hie forlaten, þat we of hire sum ðing ne seggen. Danne we on boke radeð, ðanne speked godd wið us; ðanne we ure bede seggeð, þanne speke (we) wið gode. Gif þu woldest at te (k)inge[5] ani þing beseken, *and* ðu come into his [h]alle, ðar he sate mang (his) riche mannen, *and* ðu scoldest ane speken to-foren alle hise mannen, mid michele dradnesse *and* mid michele embeþanke ðu scoldest speken. Mid muchel mare eiȝe *and* luue þu auȝhst to cumen to-foren gode, ðe is alre kinge king, *and* him swiðe eadmodliche besechen of ðiere niede, swa þat[6] þu hat alchere bede ænde [scoldest] seggen þat Crist sade himself us to forbisne, forðan we ne witen hweðer we bidden ðat godd be ȝecweme *and* us biheue, oððer hit ne bie: Non sicut ego uolo, set sicut tu uis, 'Hlauerd,' he sade, 'naht alswa ich wille ne do ðu, ac alswa ðu wilt.' Crist self us tahte hu we scolden don, *and* sade: Tu

---

[1] *page* 87.   [2] ðar *MS.*   [3] fonȝð *MS.*   [4] G *with* j *inserted.*
[5] k *corr. above* þ.   [6] *page* 88.

Himself taught us how we should do, and said : *Tu autem, cum oraveris, intra in cubiculum tuum, etc.*, 'When thou wilt pray,' He said, ' go into thy bed-room and shut the door upon thee, and pray so to thy Father, God Almighty. And He who knoweth and seeth all things will hear thee.' Go into thy bed-room, that is, into thy heart—there ought to be thy rest—and shut the door, so that thou lettest no other thoughts into thee but of God and of thy need. Thus He taught with word and showed with works that we should seek loneliness and a private place for such a need. The Gospel says of Him : *Ascendit Jesus in montem solus orare.* It says that ' He went up into a mountain apart to pray.' All the men of the world were about Him; they could not prevent Him to think one thought but as He would. But [He did so] in order to give an example to hermits and anchorites, who ought to love and to keep loneliness more than all other men. And those who cannot dwell in loneliness, however, when they will pray their prayer to God, may do it as secretly as they can. For all the needs which ever come to man he always ought to beseech God first of all things, and then it will speed him always the better. This holy prayer is very agreeable to God, if it is sent forth with tears, with clean heart, and with burning love. Of this said the prophet : *Dirigatur, Domine, oratio mea, etc.*, ' Lord,' said he, ' so may go upwards my prayer before Thee, as the incense doeth out of the censer!' All the goods which one ought to have, must all be got through holy prayer and through good works. *Multum valet deprecatio justi assidua.* This said St. James, the holy apostle: ' The prayer of a righteous man availeth much,' and he gives such an example of it : ' There was a man, mortal as we are, and he besought God that it should not rain, to chasten the people. God heard him—that was Elias—and withheld all the rains three years and six months, so that they were all overcome through hunger and with thirst. And so they turned to God and begged forgiveness; and again, this

OF PRAYER. 143

autem, cum oraueris, intra in cubiculum tuum, et cet.,
'Danne ðu wilt ȝebidden ðe,' he sade, 'ga into þine bedde, and
s(c)ette þe d(ure)[1] uppen ðe, and bidde þe swa to þine fader,
godd almihtin. And he þe wat and isikð alle þing, he ðe 4
wile ȝeheren.' Ga into þine bedde, þat is, in to þine hierte—
ðar ah to bene þine reste—and scete ðe dure[2], swa ðat þu ne lat
none oðre þauhtes[3] in to þe bute of gode and of þine niede. Ðus
he tahte mid worde, and mid workes he sceawede þat we annesse 8
and senderlicne stede scolde scechen to þelliche niede. Ðat
godspell seið of him: Ascendit Iesus in montem solus orare.
Hitt seið þat 'he steih uppen ane dune ane him to bidden.' Alle
ðe menn of ðare world waren abuten him; ne mihten hie him 12
benemen anne þouht to þenken buten alswa he walde. Ac for to
ȝiuene[4] forbisne her(e)mites and ancres, ðe annesse aȝen to luuen
and to healden ouer alle oðre manne. And ðo þe on annesse
wuniȝen ne muȝen, hure and hure, ðanne hie willeð here ibede to 16
godde bidden, swa[5] derneliche swa hie muȝen, swa don hie! To
alle ðo niedes ðe aure cumeð to manne aure hie awh gode to
beseken alre ðing arst, and ðanne scal him aure ðe bettre ȝelimpen. Dies hali ȝebede, hie is gode swiðe ȝecweme, þan hie mid 20
clane hierte and mid barninde luue forð mid teares bieð ȝesant.
Ðar of sade ðe prophete: Dirigatur, domine, oracio mea,
et cet., 'Hlauerd,' he sade, 'swa go upp mine ȝebede to-foren ðe,
swa ðat stor dieth ut of storf(a)te[6]!' Alle ðe gode ðe mann awh 24
to habben, alle hie moten bien beȝeten purȝh hali bede and þurh
gode workes. Multum ualet deprecacio iusti assidua.
Ðis sade sanctus Iacobus, ðe hali apostel: 'Swiðe michel
helpð þas rihtwismannes bede,' and ðar of he seið ðelliche 28
forbisne: 'Hit was (on) mann, dedlich alswa we bieð, and he
besohte at gode þat naht ne scolde reinin, for ðe folke to kastin.
Godd him ihierde—þat was Helyas—and wið[h]eld alle reines
þrie hier and six monepes, swa ðat hie waren ðurh hunger and 32

---

[1] *Two letters have been scratched out*, ure *is written above, and* ur *inserted on the erasure by a later hand.*
[2] *One or two letters erased.*   [3] a *corr. from* o.
[4] ac for to ȝ *is written twice, but the second time underdotted.*
[5] *page* 89.   [6] *Corrected from* storafte.

same Elias besought God for rain, and all joy came to them.' Again, it is written: *Qui avertit aurem suam ne audiat legem, oratio ejus erit execrabilis*, 'From him that turneth away his ears from God's law, will God also turn away, when he beseecheth Him for aught.' Again, God Almighty Himself says: *Antequam vocetis, dicam : ecce assum*, 'Ere thou shalt cry to Me, I shall say: Look, here I am, beg what thou wilt.' When thou wilt beseech God for anything, kneel down before His feet, and think as if He were right there before thee, and say as he did who esteemed himself all guilty and got forgiveness: *Deus, propitius esto mihi peccatori*, 'Lord God, have mercy upon me sinful!' I am well conscious that I am all guilty as he who has lost and despised the happiness of the kingdom of Heaven, and deserved the pain of hell. But I believe that Thou art the Highest God, and graceful and willing to forgive, and that Thou wilt, through Thy great goodness, and that Thou canst, because Thou art almighty, make sinful me righteous, and that Thou canst make me, who am all guilty, one of Thy chosen ones, if I have true repentance, so that I would sin nevermore again. But I cannot have this, except Thou wilt give it me through Thy great goodness and through Thy great mercy. And I believe and know it well that as good and as merciful Thou art to-day, so Thou wast that day when St. Peter forsook Thee. But as soon as Thou lookedst at him he quickly repented that he had done so, and he bewept it with bitter tears, and so Thou forgavest it him. So Thou didst to the guilty thief who hung on Thy right [hand]. So Thou didst to guilty Mary Magdalene. Thou madest her, sinful as she was, [a] thoroughly holy [one]. So Thou hast done to all to whom it was Thy will to give true repentance in their hearts. Now, my dear Lord, I beseech Thee, through Thy great goodness, to look upon me as Thou didst upon St. Peter, and send a drop of Thy sweet mercy to my wretched, dry heart, so that it might soften and melt and send out some tears. Then I may hope that Thou mid ðurst all ouercumen. *And* swa hie wanten to gode *and* forʒifnesse beden; *and* eft ðies ilke Helyas besohte godd of reine, *and* heom cam alle winne.' Eft is ʒewriten: Qvi auertit aurem suam ne audiat legem, oracio eius erit execrabilis, 'Se [4] ðe want his earen fram godes laʒhe, alswa wile godd wanden fram him, þanne he him awht besekeð.' Eft seið goddalmihti[1] him self: Ante-quam* uocetis, dicam: ecce assum, 'Ar ðanne ðu clepiʒe to me, ich segge: loke, hier ich am, bide þat ðu [8] wilt.' Ðanne ðu wilt at gode ani þing beseken, cnyle ðar niðer to-foren hise fet, *and* þinc swilch he bie riht ðar to-foren ðe, *and* seiʒe alswa he dede ðe him [h]eald all forgelt *and* forʒifnesse beʒat: Deus, *pro*picius esto m*ihi* peccatori[2], 'Hlauerd godd, [12] [h]aue are[3] of me senfulle!' Ich am wel becnawe ðat ich am all forgelt alswa se ðe hatð forloren *and* forgaud ðo eadinesse of heuen-riche, *and* of-earned helle-pine. Ac ich ilieue þat þu art heiʒest godd, *and* orefull *and* forʒiuenlich, *and* ðat þu wilt, for [16] þine michele godnesse, *and* ðat þu miht, for ði þat þu art almihti, of me senfulle maken rihtwis, *and* of me allforgelt miht makien on of þine ʒecorene, ʒif ich hadde soðe berewnesse, þat i(c)h nauerma eft seneʒin nolde. Ac ich þis ne mai habben, bute ðu for ðine [20] michele god-nesse *and* for þire michele mildsce[4] hit me ʒiuen wille. And ich ilieue *and* wel hit wot *þat* alswa god[5] *and* alswa milde þu art nu to daiʒ, alswa ðu ware ðas daiʒes ðe seinte Peter þe forsoch. Ac swa raðe so ðu to him lokedest, sone him rewh þat [24] he hadde swa ʒie-don, *and* mid bittere teares hit bewop, *and* swa ðu hit him forʒaue. Swa þu dedest ðe (al)[6]-fo[r]gelte þieue þe he(ng) on þire[7] swiþere. Swa ðu dedest ðe forgilte Marie Magdalene. Ðu makedest of hire senfulle ðat hie was, þurʒhali. [28] Swa ðu hauest ʒedon alle þar þin wille was soðe berewsinge to ʒieuene on here hierte. Nu, min leue hlauerd, ich ðe besieke, for þire michele godnesse, þat þu lokie to me swaswa þu dedest to seinte Petre[8], *and* sand ane drope of þire swete mildsce to mire [32] wrecche, fordruʒede hierte, þat hie mihte nexxin *and* mealten *and* ut-sanden sume tear. (Ðanne mai ic hopien) ðat tu wilt of me

---

[1] almihtin MS. * page 90. [2] Ewangelista red at side.
[3] an erasure before a. [4] an erasure above ld. [5] the second d underdotted.
[6] the second l erased. [7] page 91. [8] corrected above Marie.

wilt have mercy upon me as Thou hadst upon them upon whom Thou lookedst and to whom Thou gavest tears.

Of tears.

Know thou forsooth that these tears which we speak about are certainly God's gift, and very needful to the needy ones who shall be heard by God. Of them said the prophet: *Fuerunt mihi lacrimae meae panes die ac nocte,* 'My tears,' said he, 'were my bread day and night; so good they seemed [to be].' Of other kinds of tears he said: *Lacrimis meis stratum meum rigabo,* 'I shall water my bed with my tears.' This bed betokens the *conscientia,* that is, the conscience within. Where the good soul has its rest, there the evil soul has its pain. Therefore he said that he would wash with tears the conscience from that of which his heart accused him. We find nowhere that God denied anything for which any man besought Him with tears. God sent to Hezekiah, the king, by His prophet, and said: *Dispone domui tuae, quia morieris tu, et non vives,* 'Bequeath thy legacy,' He said, 'for thou shalt be dead, and thou shalt not live.' The King became sorry, as it is loathsome to leave riches, and very dear to live. He then turned to the wall, and did the best. 'Oh Lord God,' said he, 'remember now that I have loved Thee and have done blithely for Thy love, and give me still a little respite through Thy goodness!' This was a good conscience, that he could show forth his good deeds when he had need. Therefore God heard him and said to His prophet, who was homeward: 'Turn again,' quoth He, 'and say to the king: *Vidi lacrimam tuam,* 'I saw,' quoth He, 'thy tears, and I heard thy prayer. Thou shalt still live fifteen years; so much I have increased thy life.' When thou in great need wilt beseech God it is very good for thee that thou canst draw forth some good deeds; thy heart is the gladder, and thou mayst beg the more assuredly. Let us now say with the prophet: *Ciba nos pane lacrimarum,* 'Lord, feed us with the bread of sweet tears,' *et* habben are¹ swa swa ðu hauest ȝe[h](a)fd² of hem ðe ðu to lokedest and teares ȝe(a)ue.

Of teares.

WITE ðu to soðe ðat þese teares ðe we embe spekeð³ hie bieð iwis godes ȝiue, *and* swiðe niedfulle to ðan inede⁴ þat iherd sculen [bien] of gode. Of hem sade ðe prophete: Fuerunt m*ihi* lacrime me panes die ac nocte, 'Mine teares,' he sade, 'me waren bred daiȝ *and* niht; swa gode hie þouhten.' Of oþres kennes teares he sade: Lacrimis meis stratum meum rigabo, 'Ich scal watrien min bedd mid mine teares.' Ðies bedd tacneð þe consciencia, þat is⁵, þat inȝied wið-innen. Þar ðe gode sawle haueð hire reste, þar haueð se eule sawle hire pine. For þi he sade þat he wolde mid teares wascen þat inȝied⁶ þar of ðe his herte him wreiȝede. Ne finde we nawher þat godd wernde ani þing ðe ani mann mid teares him besouhte. God sante to Ezechie, þe kinge, be his prophete, *and* sade: Dispone domui tue, quia morieris tu⁷, *et* non uiues, 'Becweð þine⁸ cwide,' he sade, 'for ðan þu scalt bien dead, *and* naht ne scalt tu libben.' Ðe king warð sari, alswa richeise is lað⁹ to laten, *and* swiðe lef to libben. He wante þo to ðe wauȝe, *and* dede þat¹⁰ betste. '(A) hlauerd godd,' sade he, 'þench nu ðat ich ðe habbe ȝe-luued *and* for þine luue bliðeliche idon, *and* ȝif me ȝiet a litel ferst, for þine godnesse!' Ðies was god inȝied, þat he mihte his gode dade forðsceawin þa þe he niede hadde. For þi him ȝeherde godd *and* sade to [h]is prophete, ðe was ham-ward: 'Wand aȝean,' cwað he, '*and* sai to þe kinge: Vidi lacrimam tuam, 'Ich iseih,' cwað he, 'þine tear, *and* ich iherde þine bene. Þu scalt ȝiet libben fiftene ȝear; swa michel ich habbe ieiht þi lif.' Ðanne ðu on michele niede gode wilt beseken, þanne is ðe wel god þat þu muȝe forðdraȝen sume gode dade; þin hierte bieð ðe gladdere, *and* ðe sikerliker ðu miht bidden. Segge we nu forð mid þe prophete: Ciba nos pane lacrimarum,

---

[1] *a letter erased before* a.
[2] ȝefadd *MS.*; a *is underdotted, and an* a *is put above* e.
[3] speked *MS.*   [4] n *corr. by erasure from* h.   [5] is *corr. from* þ.
[6] d *corr. from another letter.*   [7] *et* tu *MS.*
[8] *page* 92.   [9] ð *corr. from* d *by a later hand.*
[10] at *on erasure.*

potum da nobis in lacrimis in mensura, 'and give us to drink of other kinds of tears, and that in measure.' I will that thou be well warned that, if God gives thee these sweet tears, no wine in the world is so sweet. And as a man may drink too much wine, so a man may weep too much, though they [viz. the tears] are sweet; and therefore it is good for thee that thou beseechest God for one virtue which is called *discretio,* that is, discretion.

It is very useful among all the other virtues. Thus say the holy Fathers: 'She is mother of all the other virtues; where she reigns man can never perish who wills her to reign and will follow her.' It is said in *Vitas patrum* that the holy Fathers were gathered together in some room, and were speaking among themselves in which way one might come to God most rightly and most surely. Some said: through fasting, some: through vigil, some: through prayer, some said: through obedience, some said: through loneliness, some said: through harbouring wretched men and feeding and shrouding [them], some said: through looking after sick men; and in manifold ways they mentioned according to what the holy Gospel says. Then said one of the oldest and one of the wisest: 'Through all these we have seen and heard a great many saved, and many by all these named virtues perished, because *discretio* failed them, that is, discretion and discernment. For some did much more than they could well complete, some did too little, some did evil and fancied to do well, some began well and ended badly. But we never saw that a man who had this holy virtue with him ever fared amiss.' Get it whoso can!

One holy virtue is called *perseverantia.* It is not to be disregarded, because it makes the man to whom God sends it persevere in his goodness. In the old law it was bidden anent all the animals which

'Hlauerd, fed us mid ðo breade of swete teares,' *et potum da nobis in lacrimis in mensura*, '*and* ȝif us drinken of oðreskennes teares, *and* ðat mid imete!' Đat ich wile þat ðu wel be iwarned, ȝif¹ godd ðe ȝifð þese swete teares, þat non win in ðare world nis swa swete. *And* alswa alswa man² to michel mai drinken of ðare wine, alswa mai ðe mann to michel wepen, þeih hie swete bien; *and* for ði þe is god þat þu beseke at gode one mihte ðe hatte discrecio, þat is ³, sckelewisnesse.

HIE is swiðe beheue mang alle ðe oðre mihtes. Đis ðe hali faderes seggeð: 'Hie is moder of alle ðe oðre mihtes; ðar ðe hie rixið ne mai naure⁴ man forfaren þe hire wile rixin *and* folȝin.' Hit seið in Vitas patrum ðat at sume sal waren ðe hali faderes to-gedere igadered, *and* waren spekinde betwen hem on (h)williche wise me mihte rihtist *and* sikerest to gode cumen. Sum sade: þurh fasten, sum: þurh wacchen, sum: ðurh bede, sum sade: þurh hersumnesse, sum sade: ðurh annesse, sum sade: ðurh herborȝin⁵ wrecche menn *and* feden *and* screden, sum sade: ðurh seke menn to lokin; *and* on manieskennes wisen hie namden after ðan þe þat hali goddspell seið. Đa sade on of ða eldest⁶ *and* on of ða wisest: 'Đurh alle ðesen we habbeð iseȝen *and* iherd swiðe maniȝe ȝeborȝen, *and* manie of alle ðesen inamde mihten forfaren, for þi ðat hem trukede discrecio, þat is, scadwisnesse and skele. For ði⁷ sume deden michel mare þan hie mihtin wel andin, sume deden to litel, sume deden euele *and* wenden wel don, sume wel a-gunnen *and* euele andeden. Ac naure ne ȝeseiȝe we manne þat hadde þese hali mihte mid him, þat he aure misferde.' Beȝete se ðe muge!

PERSEUERANCIA hatte an hali mihte. Hie nis naht⁸ to laten, for ðan hie makeð ðanne man ðe godd (h)is to-sant þat he þurwuneð on his godnesse. On ðare ealde laȝe hit was i[h]oten⁹ þat alle dier ðe me gode scolde offrin, þat hie lokeden wel

---

¹ Gif *MS., with a* j *inserted in* G. ² *a letter erased after* n.
³ *page* 93.   ⁴ *two words erased*.   ⁵ 3 *on erasure*.
⁶ t *destroyed by a hole*.   ⁷ ði *on erasure*.   ⁸ *page* 94.
⁹ io *corr. from two other letters by erasure*.

one should offer to God, to care well that the tail were on every animal. That betokens that each man who offers God any service persevere therein. In this new law said Christ: *Qui perseveraverit usque in finem, hic salvus erit,* 'He that endureth in his goodness which he has begun, shall be saved and not otherwise, for no good which he has done, whatsoever it is.'

Ratio dicit animae:

Dear soul, I have made this little writ with sore toil—He knows it who knows all things!—in order to instruct thee, to warn thee, and to help thee and to save thee. If thou wilt understand it well and learn and follow and keep [it] without any doubt, thou mayst save thyself with God's help and surely gain the joy of the kingdom of Heaven with these holy virtues.

Nunc auctor loquitur finaliter:

Let us now thank and praise our Lord, Almighty God, for this knowledge and for this wisdom which we have here gathered from His hoard and from many a holy man's labours, who worked much for the love of God and in order to teach us! It is right that we praise and thank and bless Father and Son and Holy Ghost in the Holy Trinity, which is one true God in unity, who liveth and reigneth evermore world [without end]. Amen. Never forget thou to praise God and to thank [Him] for all good things. Just as we have need to beg Him by day and by night, and often and frequently, so it is need to praise Him. Amen.

ðat ðe¹ tail ware on auriche netene. Þat tocneð ðat ilke mann ðe gode ani seruise offreð, þat he þar on þurȝwunie. On ðessere newe laȝe sade Crist: Qvi perseuerauerit usque in finem, hic saluus erit², 'Se ðurȝ-³wuneð on his godnesse ðe he hafð 4 agunnen, he worð iborȝen and naht elles, for none gode þe he don hafð, hwat (hwat)⁴ it is.'

Ratio dicit anime:

LIEUE (saule)⁵, ðis little writt ic (habbe)⁶ sare beswonken—he it 8 wat þat⁷ wot alle þing!—for⁸ ðe to wissin, for ðe to warnin, and for ðe to helpen and for ðe to berȝin. Ȝif⁹ ðu wilt wel hit understonden and liernin and folȝin and [h]ealden wið-uten alche¹⁰ twene, þu miht mid godes felste ðe berȝen and heuneriches merchþe 12 mid þese halie mihtes sike(r)liche¹¹ iwinnen.

Nunc autor loquitur finaliter:

HVTE we nu þ(a)nkin¹² and herien ure hlauerde, almihtin gode of ðese witte and of ðese wisdome ðe we hier habbeð 16 igadered of (h)is horde and of maniȝes¹³ haliȝes mannes ȝeswinkes, þe michel sw(u)nken¹⁴ for ðe luue of gode and for us to wissin! Hit is riht ðat we heriȝen and þankin and bledscin fader and sune and hali gast on ða hali þrinnesse, se ðe is on soð godd in onnesse, 20 se ðe l(i)ueð¹⁵ and rixeð aure ma a woreld. Amen. Ðat ne forȝeit¹⁶ ðu naure, þat ðu godd ne heriȝe and þanke of alle gode. Alswa swa we habbeð niede him to bidden be daiȝ and be nihte, and ofte and ȝelome, alswa hit is niede him to heriȝen. Amen. 24

Veni, creator spiritus, mentes tuorum uisita; implet superna gracia que tu creasti pectora¹⁷.

---

¹ ðe *was written twice, the first erased.*
² *Ewangelista, red on the margin.*   ³ durȝ *MS.*
⁴ *written above on erasure.*
⁵ *red, corr. above* ratio, *which is red underlined.*
⁶ *corr. above* write.   ⁷ þa *MS., with underdotted* a.
⁸ f *is later inserted.*   ⁹ G *with inserted* j.   ¹⁰ c *corr. from* l.
¹¹ r *corr. above* l.   ¹² a *corr. above* e.   ¹³ *page 95.*
¹⁴ u *correction above* i.   ¹⁵ i *written above an underdotted* e.
¹⁶ i *over erasure.*   ¹⁷ *the Latin verses are written in a much larger type.*

The manufacturer's authorised representative in the EU for product safety is Oxford University Press España S.A. of El Parque Empresarial San Fernando de Henares, Avenida de Castilla, 2 - 28830 Madrid (www.oup.es/en or product.safety@oup.com). OUP España S.A. also acts as importer into Spain of products made by the manufacturer.
Printed and bound by CPI Group (UK) Ltd, Croydon, CR0 4YY

20/03/2026

02075329-0004